MW00325821

Medellín v. Texas

LANDMARK LAW CASES &AMERICAN SOCIETY

Peter Charles Hoffer
N. E. H. Hull
Williamjames Hull Hoffer
Series Editors

For a complete list of titles in the series, go to www.kansaspress.ku.edu.

ALAN MYGATT-TAUBER

Medellín v. Texas

International Justice, Federalism, and the Execution of José Medellín

UNIVERSITY PRESS OF KANSAS

© 2022 by the University Press of Kansas
All rights reserved

Published by the University Press of Kansas (Lawrence, Kansas 66045), which was
organized by the Kansas Board of Regents and is operated and funded by Emporia State
University, Fort Hays State University, Kansas State University, Pittsburg State University,
the University of Kansas, and Wichita State University.

Library of Congress Cataloging-in-Publication Data

Names: Mygatt-Tauber, Alan, author.
Title: Medellín v. Texas : international justice, federalism, and the
execution of José Medellín / Alan Mygatt-Tauber.
Description: Lawrence, Kansas : University Press of Kansas, 2022. | Series:
Landmark law cases and American society | Includes bibliographical
references and index.
Identifiers: LCCN 2021061606
ISBN 9780700633616 (paperback)
ISBN 9780700633623 (ebook)
Subjects: LCSH: Medellín, José, 1975-2008—Trials, litigation, etc. |
Trials (Murder)—Texas. | Trials (Rape)—Texas. | Vienna Convention on
Consular Relations (1963 April 24). | International and municipal
law—United States—Cases. | Federal government—United States—Cases. |
Capital punishment—Law and legislation—United States—Cases. |
Mexicans—Legal status, laws, etc.—United States—Cases.
Classification: LCC KF224.M43 M94 2022 | DDC
345.764/02523—dc23/eng/20220622
LC record available at https://lccn.loc.gov/2021061606.

British Library Cataloguing-in-Publication Data is available.

Printed in the United States of America

10 9 8 7 6 5 4 3 2 1

The paper used in this publication is acid free and meets the minimum requirements of
the American National Standard for Permanence of Paper for Printed Library Materials
Z39.48-1992.

To Heather and Alexander

CONTENTS

EDITORS' PREFACE

In his book-length essay *The Court and the World*, US Supreme Court Justice Stephen Breyer reminds readers that "the Court must increasingly consider the world beyond our national frontiers." That consideration began with the founding of the nation and continues to this day. In *Medellín v. Texas* (2008), the Court had the chance to show the world that the United States respected its treaty obligations, shared international justice conventions, and a neighboring government (Mexico)—in short, that we were committed to a regime of international law.

Alan Mygatt-Tauber's splendid book tracks this episode in the history of the Court, from the single act, a homicide, through the Texas state courts, to the federal courts, the desk of the president of the United States, back to the Texas courts, and then to the US Supreme Court. The issue was the right of a foreign national indicted for a crime to have the chance to consult with their own country's consul. This right was part of the Vienna Convention on Consular Relations and was reaffirmed by the International Court of Justice in *Case Concerning Avena and Other Mexican Nationals* (2004). Texas saw the issue as one of state sovereignty and declined to retry Medellín. He appealed to the Supreme Court on the basis of our treaty obligations. The Court's decision and its impact on our reputation in the world conclude the book.

Mygatt-Tauber leads the reader step by step through a maze of domestic and international law. Familiar players like Senator Ted Cruz and President George W. Bush are joined by judges less familiar to us—until now. By putting human to the law, Mygatt-Tauber demonstrates how landmark cases like *Medellín* can change the world.

ACKNOWLEDGMENTS

The desire to write a book about the story of *Medellín v. Texas* arose when I was in graduate school, studying the effects of position-taking by the executive branch in Supreme Court and lower court cases involving international law. However, the impetus to sit down and actually write it did not come until several years later, when I was approached by a law school classmate, Eric Koester, to take part in a writing program he had developed at Georgetown University. It was thanks to this program that the book exists. I would also be remiss if I did not thank my initial editor in that program, Robert Keiser, for helping to make the book accessible to a lay audience.

Professor Julie Novkov of the University of Albany provided invaluable help in preparing my book proposal and providing an introduction to David Congdon at the University Press of Kansas. Without her, this book would likely never have seen print. I am also in debt to the staff at the University Press of Kansas, including my editor, David Congdon, who helped shepherd this book through the sometimes labyrinthine acquisition process. Kelly Chrisman Jacques skillfully guided me through the production process, and Susan Ecklund did a fantastic job copyediting.

I also wish to thank Professors Paul B. Stephan, Margaret E. (Peggy) McGuinness, and John Quigley and two anonymous reviewers for their comments on both the book proposal and the final manuscript. Their contributions are reflected here, and any errors that may remain are solely mine.

I am indebted to those who worked on the issues discussed in this book and who generously gave their time to speak with me, both on the record and on background. While a fuller discussion of their contributions is listed in the bibliographic essay at the end of the book, it would not be nearly so rich or detailed without the invaluable contributions of Professor Sandra Babcock, John Bellinger, Councilman Rodney Ellis, Daniel Geyser, Ambassador Juan Manuel Gómez Robledo, Professor Harold Hongju Koh, Judge Kristopher Monson, Ambassador Santiago Oñate, and Mark Warren, as well as those who contributed but wish to remain anonymous. Each of these individuals provided important insight and gave life to what would otherwise be a fairly dry piece of reporting, as well as providing information that is not available in the documentary record.

Finally, I am eternally grateful to my wife and son, who gave me the time and space to pursue this project. I appreciate their patience and understanding more than words can say.

CHAPTER I

Introduction

The story of José Medellín begins with a murder and ends with an execution. But like most subjects in law, the totality of the story begins long before Medellín took part in a brutal gang rape and murder of two teenage girls in Houston, Texas, and continues long after his death on August 5, 2008, at the hands of the state. In the course of his short life, Medellín would find his case before the International Court of Justice, the Inter-American Commission on Human Rights, and the US Supreme Court, twice. It pitted the federal government against the State of Texas and Texas against the world. President George W. Bush, Texas's former governor—and no critic of the death penalty—would eventually find himself arrayed against his home state, asking it to reconsider that penalty.

Medellín v. Texas is a case at the intersection of three areas of law that have seen heightened interest in the twenty-first century: the death penalty, federalism, and international law. At the core of the case were questions about the United States' ability to honor its international obligations and to require compliance with those obligations from the fifty US states; the power of the president to act as the "sole organ of foreign policy" for the United States; the meaning of treaties; the proper body to interpret their meaning; the duty to strictly adhere to treaty requirements when death is on the line; and the power of states to run their own criminal justice systems.

At the time Medellín committed his crime, the application of the death penalty in the United States was at its modern height. In 1972, the Supreme Court established a de facto moratorium on its use when it decided the case of *Furman v. Georgia*, striking down the process states used to sentence criminal defendants to death. The victory of death penalty opponents was short-lived. Within two years, states had amended their statutes and restarted the machinery of death. Challenges to these new procedures followed and quickly wound their way through the federal court system. In 1976, the Supreme Court issued a new decision in five companion cases from various states, under the heading of the lead case, *Gregg v. Georgia*. There, the Court approved the new system of capital punishment propounded by the states, and those states that wished to utilize the death penalty wasted no time. By 1981, more than 200 people per year were being sentenced to death, a trend that would continue for the next two decades. In most years, the number of death sentences topped 250. In all, more than 8,500 people have been sentenced to death since the 1970s, with more than 1,500 sentences carried out. One state, Texas, has led the charge and is responsible for over a third of those executions. Even as all states have lessened their use of the penalty, Texas has continued to forge ahead, routinely executing three times as many inmates per year as any other state.

Since 1976, the Supreme Court has continued to police state imposition of the death penalty to ensure its application conforms to constitutional requirements. But since that time, it has only categorically limited its use in three instances: in 1977, in *Coker v. Georgia*, the Court held that it was unconstitutional to apply the death penalty solely for the crime of rape. In 2002, the Court struck down application of the death penalty to those who possessed an IQ of less than 70 in *Atkins v. Virginia*. Finally, in 2005, in *Roper v. Simmons*, the Court ruled that the Eighth Amendment prohibited executing individuals who were under the age of eighteen at the time they committed their crime. Aside from these three rulings, the Court has satisfied itself with, in the words of Justice Harry Blackmun, "tinkering with the machinery of death" but never addressing it wholesale.

Traditionally, when determining the reach of the Eighth Amendment and its application to the death penalty, the Court looks to the practices of the states and the federal government to identify the "standards of decency which mark the progress of a maturing society." Interestingly, in the latter categorial cases, *Atkins* and *Roper*, the Court looked beyond these typical sources in determining that sentencing those individuals to death was cruel and unusual; it looked to the practices of the international community as well. This was quite concerning to death penalty supporters, as the United States is largely out of step with the rest of the international community, particularly our closest allies, when it comes to capital punishment. According to the Death Penalty Information

Center, more than 70 percent of countries have abolished capital punishment, through either laws or practice. Furthermore, while there is no international norm against the death penalty per se, many countries consider its use a human rights violation. Every member of the European Union has abolished the death penalty for all crimes, in accordance with Protocol No. 6 to the European Convention on Human Rights. Of the G-20 countries, only five others (Japan, Indonesia, China, Brazil, and Saudi Arabia) still practice the death penalty for any crimes, though in Brazil it is reserved only for military offenses.

While this reliance on international trends elicited a great deal of anxious agitation among a certain branch of lawyers, it was a recognition of a truth the Court spelled out in the 1900 case *The Paquete Habana*: that "international law is a part of our law." The Constitution in several areas recognizes that international law is within the purview of the federal government's powers and responsibilities. Article I, Section 8 provides Congress the power to regulate commerce with foreign nations and the power to define and punish piracies and felonies committed on the high seas, as well as offenses against the law of nations. Article II provides that the president may make treaties with foreign nations, with the advice and consent of the Senate. Article III grants jurisdiction to the federal courts to hear cases arising under treaties, as well as cases between states and their citizens and citizens of foreign states, their citizens, or subjects. Finally, Article VI states that treaties shall be the supreme law of the land, on the same level as the Constitution and federal statutes, and that judges in the states are bound by them, state laws and constitutions notwithstanding.

This tells us several things. First, at least as far as treaties are concerned, they are to be applied by our courts; this includes both federal and state courts. Second, if there is a conflict between state laws or constitutions and duly ratified treaties, state law must give way in the same way that a federal statute would preempt state law. Third, treaties are on a par with federal statutes. Courts have thus applied rules of statutory construction and reconciliation with regard to treaties. If there are two plausible readings of a treaty or potentially conflicting statute, one of which avoids the conflict, that is the interpretation to be preferred. If such a conflict is unavoidable, then the later in time controls. Thus, a statute passed after treaty ratification can undercut the commitment of the United States to the treaty, including putting the United States in violation of its obligations under international law.

One statute that plays a critical role in review of state death sentences is the Antiterrorism and Effective Death Penalty Act (AEDPA) of 1996. This statute, which would play a critical role in Medellín's case, limits the ability of criminal defendants to file successive petitions for a writ of habeas corpus. Following a criminal conviction, all criminal defendants have a right to appeal their conviction and sentence, challenging any errors that took place during the trial. This is known as a "direct appeal." Once that appeal process is finished, those who were unsuccessful may still have other avenues of attack on their convictions and sentences. Such appeals, which are not direct, are known as "collateral appeals." Unlike direct appeals, which are available as of right, courts have discretion in entertaining collateral appeals that rely on the writ of habeas corpus.

The writ is used by prisoners to challenge aspects of their detention and is often seen as a backstop against procedural and substantive errors made in criminal prosecutions that escape review on direct appeal. Direct review occurs in state courts, while defendants will file their writs seeking collateral review in federal court. The AEDPA serves to limit the discretion of federal courts hearing these collateral appeals. It limits both the procedural and the substantive scope of the writ. Perhaps the biggest change the AEDPA made is that it limits the circumstances under which a criminal defendant can file a second or successive writ, forcing defendants to put all their claims into one appeal. If a defendant fails to include a claim in their first writ, subject to certain highly circumscribed exceptions, they have waived it, regardless of merit. Additionally, AEDPA limits the substantive relief that can be provided. While the habeas statute allows a prisoner to claim that they are being held in violation of the Constitution, laws, or treaties of the United States, AEDPA provides that where a state court has ruled on the merits of the prisoner's claim, a federal court can only intervene where the prisoner shows that the state court decision was contrary to clearly established federal law, as determined by the Supreme Court of the United States, or was based on an unreasonable interpretation of the facts presented in state court.

Furthermore, AEDPA requires that before a prisoner can appeal to the federal circuit courts of appeals from an order in a habeas corpus proceeding arising out of process provided by a state court, he or she has to receive a certificate of appealability from a circuit justice or circuit judge. In order to receive such a certificate, the prisoner has to make a substantial showing of the denial of a constitutional right. Thus, unlike the basic habeas statute, which specifically allows a claim based on a treaty violation, under AEDPA, only the violation of the Constitution matters. Because AEDPA was enacted in 1996, under the rules of treaty interpretation outlined in this chapter, it would supersede any treaty ratified before that time, to the extent there is an irreconcilable conflict between the two.

There is one other tool courts have used, unique to treaties, to avoid these conflicts. Since at least 1829, the Supreme Court has noted a difference between a treaty that "operates of itself, without the aid of any legislative provision," known as a "self-executing" treaty, and those that are "addressed to the political, not the judicial department" and that require Congress to act before they become a rule for the courts to apply, known as "non-self-executing" treaties. Such treaties do not create judicially enforceable rights unless Congress passes implementing legislation. While no clear test or "magic words" clearly divide the two classes of treaties, in general, where the treaty provisions define the rights and obligations of private individuals, they are typically treated as self-executing. On the other hand, treaties that are addressed to public authorities, or that require the payment of money, the cession of territory, or participation in international organizations, are typically treated as non-self-executing. Courts have a particularly hard time determining how to enforce a treaty when it addresses both in the same document.

Interpreting treaties can be a tricky business for courts because doing so implicates not just the rights of individuals who seek to enforce treaty provisions but often also the foreign policy of the nation as a whole. Treaties are solemn agreements between nations, evidencing commitments to certain ideas or actions. There is a presumption in international law, and an expectation, that countries will keep to their word and honor the treaties they enter. Thus, judicial decisions that hamper the ability of the United States to honor its commitments can have far-reaching negative effects on the United States' international standing. After all, we can safely presume the president does not enter treaties that are against the interests of the United States, and by signing, the president has indicated his judgment that such a treaty would be beneficial. A supermajority of the Senate has concurred through the act of consenting to ratification. This is not a judgment to be set aside lightly. Additionally, the enforcement of treaties depends on reciprocity. We can only expect our treaty partners to live up to their agreements if we do the same. Indeed, some treaties provide specific escape clauses, which relieve one party from complying with its dictates if other parties fail to uphold their end. Thus, a court's decision that refuses to give effect to a treaty can have impacts not just domestically but also abroad.

Furthermore, when determining what the impact of a court ruling on the meaning of a treaty is, the president is often given great deference. In fact, in the 1936 case *United States v. Curtis-Wright Export Corporation*, the Court described the president as the "sole organ of foreign policy." The president is empowered to speak to the world with one voice on behalf of the United States, and courts are loath to second-guess or undercut those statements.

But treaties bring up a conflict with a third area of the law that the Supreme Court, since at least 1995, has seemed very interested in: federalism. The United States is a system of divided sovereignty, wherein the states retain all powers not voluntarily surrendered to the national government. Observing our international obligations can be difficult because of the divided nature of sovereignty within the United States. While compliance with many treaties can be accomplished by action at the federal level, that is not the case with every treaty. Some require actions by state and even local officials to carry out. In such circumstances, there can be a great deal of tension between the federal government, which is responsible to the nation as a whole and which must defend the nation's interests and honor, and the state and local officials who are answerable to only one small part of the nation's population. In those circumstances, the opportunity for mischief is rife. It would seem that federalism concerns are answered by the supremacy clause in Article VI. But, in practice, this has not been the case. One treaty that illustrates these tensions, and which is at the heart of *Medellín v. Texas*, is the Vienna Convention on Consular Relations.

———

The Vienna Convention on Consular Relations (VCCR) is a treaty signed by forty-eight countries (referred to as "States" throughout the document), with 180 parties, representing nearly every country on Earth. The treaty was opened for signature in 1963 and came into effect in 1967, following its ratification by twenty-two countries. Like many treaties, the VCCR merely codified consular practices that had been governed by customary international law and bilateral treaties between States. The treaty, consisting of seventy-nine articles, covers a variety of subjects related to consular protections and duties.

Article 36 of the VCCR governs communications between consulates and nationals of their States. It provides that when a State or one of its subunits detains a foreign national, consular officials shall have the right to communicate with their nationals and that those nationals have the right to speak with their consulates. Subparagraph 1(b) of Article 36 requires that, if a foreign national so requests, the "competent authorities" inform his or her consulate that he or she has been "arrested or committed to prison or to custody pending trial or is detained in any manner" and shall do so without delay. Furthermore, the article requires those competent authorities to inform the arrested or detained individual of those rights, also without delay.

Subparagraph 2 of Article 36 provides that the rights in subparagraph 1 shall be "exercised in conformity with the laws and regulations" of the State in which the foreign national is detained, so long as the laws and regulations enable "full effect" to be given to the purposes of the rights protected under Article 36. In other words, the treaty is not intended to overrule local laws but instead is to be interpreted consistent with those laws. However, those local laws must not be used as an excuse to avoid providing notification of the rights to consular notification, nor enforcement of those rights when requested.

In codifying the preexisting international norms surrounding consular assistance, the nations that signed the VCCR recognized the importance of early intervention by consular officials of the detained person's home State. When traveling abroad, individuals are often unfamiliar with local laws and may not speak the language or do so less than fluently. Consular intervention can help a detained person avoid a criminal conviction by inadvertently confessing, waiving rights, or signing something they do not understand. Oftentimes, the legal rules and norms practiced in different countries are completely alien. In the United States, for example, most criminal cases end in a plea bargain, but this practice is virtually unknown in Mexico. Consular officials are also important in securing qualified representation for their detained nationals, which can be the difference between a conviction and an acquittal. Finally, and of particular importance in capital cases, in jurisdictions such as the United States, where the decision to seek the death penalty is discretionary, consular officials have had a great deal of success in convincing prosecutors to forgo seeking the death penalty in the first instance.

The United States is an original signatory to the VCCR, having ratified it on November 24, 1969. Since then, the United States has been an active participant in the convention. At the time the Senate offered its advice and consent, the legal adviser to the State Department told the Senate that Congress was not required to enact legislation implementing the VCCR. The Senate Foreign Relations Committee apparently agreed. It was believed that implementing the convention would not conflict with federal law, at least in part because two years earlier the Department of Justice had implemented regulations requiring federal officers to provide consular notification of the arrest of a foreign national when made by them, unless the foreign national expressly requested that notification not occur. These regulations were implemented to satisfy earlier bilateral treaties regarding consular notification, but they also satisfied the requirements of the VCCR.

However, detention by federal officials is not the only concern for treaty compliance. The convention does not distinguish between detention by federal, state, or local officials; under its plain terms, any arrest or detention is covered by the VCCR. Thus, it is possible for state and local officials to place the United States in violation of its international obligations. Despite this, Congress has not passed any laws requiring states or localities to comply with the VCCR. This could be due to the fact that, under the supremacy clause of the US Constitution, treaties, like federal statutes and the Constitution itself, are the "supreme law of the land," and thus states are bound to comply with them even without specific direction from Congress.

Nevertheless, the State Department has taken steps to ensure compliance by states and localities via the regular distribution of manuals, pocket cards, and other training resources to state and local officials. In 1998 the State Department first issued a seventy-two-page manual, *Consular Notification and Access: Instructions for Federal, State, and Local Law*

Enforcement and Other Officials Regarding Foreign Nationals in the United States and the Rights of Consular Officials to Assist Them. It also created pocket-size reference cards for individual officers to carry, which list the consular notification requirements. As of 2003, over one hundred thousand copies of the manual and over six hundred thousand pocket cards had been placed in circulation. Today, the fifth edition of the manual, clocking in at 130 pages, is available for download on the State Department website, as is the pocket card.

Following specific complaints from Mexico, which was also an original signatory of the convention, about the failure to inform detained Mexican nationals of their rights, the US government made special efforts to ensure states and localities were complying with Article 36 when arresting Mexican nationals. Unfortunately for José Medellín, the bulk of these efforts began in the late 1990s, after he was arrested, tried, and convicted.

Additionally, the State Department has given consular notification trainings at various law enforcement conferences throughout the United States. Beginning in 1997, the department has provided forty-three separate trainings on consular notification in Texas alone. Six of them have targeted the Houston Police Department, which arrested Medellín, the first in 2000 and the latest in 2017.

At the same time the VCCR was drafted, two optional protocols were also written. The second of these is titled the Optional Protocol concerning the Compulsory Settlement of Disputes. It provides that parties to the convention, which also ratify or accede to the Optional Protocol, agree that disputes about the interpretation or application of the treaty are within the compulsory jurisdiction of the International Court of Justice (ICJ) in The Hague. Thus, parties may seek relief there. Neither the VCCR nor the Optional Protocol discusses enforcement of ICJ decisions. Instead, enforcement is discussed in the United Nations Charter. According to Article 94 of the charter, all member nations undertake to comply with decisions of the ICJ in any case to which they are parties.

The United States also joined the Optional Protocol when it signed the convention in 1963. The Optional Protocol was signed by thirty-eight parties, ratified by twenty-one, and, as of 2020, joined by a total of fifty-two, including Mexico in 2002. Thus, after 2002, disputes between the United States and Mexico about the meaning of the VCCR were within the exclusive jurisdiction of the ICJ. The United States was one of the first countries to invoke the mandatory dispute resolution procedure following the seizure of the US embassy in Tehran, Iran, following the revolution in 1979.

However, the United States would soon find the shoe on the other foot as three countries—Paraguay, Germany, and Mexico—would bring suits of their own, alleging that the United States' failure to comply with Article 36 denied rights to their citizens and resulted in death sentences. Mexico's case focused on fifty-two of its nationals, including José Ernesto Medellín. Mexico would eventually win the day, with the ICJ finding that the United States breached its international obligations when the Houston police officers who arrested Medellín failed to inform him of his Article 36 rights. The resulting battle to enforce the ICJ's judgment would place Medellín at the center of a dispute between the State of Texas, the executive branch, the ICJ, and the judicial branch over who had the right to interpret the Vienna Convention and whether or not the president could ensure that Texas remedied breaches of the United States' international obligations for which it was responsible.

CHAPTER 2

A Heinous Crime

Jennifer Ertman was fourteen years old and had just completed her freshman year at Waltrip High School in Houston, Texas. By all accounts, she was a rule follower and a loyal friend. On the night of June 24, 1993, those traits would lead her to a set of horrible circumstances that would result in her death and the death of her friend Elizabeth Peña. Elizabeth was slightly older than Jennifer. But the sixteen-year-old, who had suffered some setbacks, had recently turned over a new leaf and, according to her parents, Jennifer was an important part of that.

The two girls were enjoying the early summer evening. Jennifer's dad, Randy, had dropped her off at Elizabeth's house around 4:15 in the afternoon. It was a beautiful sunny day in Houston, with the temperature peaking at eighty-nine degrees. At 8:00, Elizabeth's mother, Melissa, dropped the girls off at the Silver Creek Apartments on Magnum Road, just a short distance from the Peña residence, so they could spend some time with their friend Gina Escamilla. After a couple hours of chitchat, the girls met up with Gina's ex-boyfriend, Chris, and two of his buddies. After chatting and having fun, Chris suggested they head over to hang out at the pool at the Spring Hill apartment complex, where he lived. The girls agreed and met up with another friend, Roseanne Mendoza. They arrived at the pool by 10:05 p.m.

There is some disagreement regarding the exact details, but all accounts agree the girls had a curfew for returning to Elizabeth's house, about a thirty-minute walk from the Spring Hill complex. Due to the vagaries of teenage goodbyes, and an ill-timed page from Elizabeth's friend Vanessa, the girls didn't start walking back until around 10:40 p.m. Jennifer, ever the rule follower, was concerned about arriving home after curfew. She didn't want to get in trouble, so she and Elizabeth made the first of two fateful decisions that evening. Arriving at the Clearbrook Apartments, Jennifer and Elizabeth separated from Gina and Roseanne

in order to take a shortcut through T. C. Jester Park, using a train trestle bridge to cross the White Oak Bayou. The shortcut would save the
girls ten minutes of walking and ensure they got home before curfew. At
approximately 10:45 p.m. the girls crossed the Clearbrook Apartments
parking lot. The chain-link fence there had been unbound from its post,
allowing the girls to scoot under and take the trail to the train bridge.

Just north of the tracks, eight young men had been having a different kind of fun evening. The eight were Peter Cantu; José "Joe" Ernesto
Medellín; José's younger brother Venancio, known as "Yuni"; Derrick
Sean O'Brien; Efrain Perez Jr.; Raul Villareal; and twin brothers Roman and Frank Sandoval. Police would describe them as members of the
Black and White gang conducting an initiation of a new member, though
the ringleader, Cantu, thought it was hilarious when Villareal asked to
join their "gang." He viewed the guys as just a bunch of friends who hung
out, but he was happy to play the part of gang leader this evening. The
young men, mostly seventeen to nineteen, had spent the evening drinking beer and hanging out. But when Villareal asked to join, things turned
violent. Cantu, responding to boasts about Villareal's fighting prowess,
decided that in order to join the Black and Whites, he had to go toe to
toe with each existing member for five minutes and remain standing.

The first to fight Villareal was Roman Sandoval, one of the twins.
The two stood toe to toe and began to punch each other, grappling and
wrestling. At the end of five minutes, Villareal was still standing. José
Medellín, just five feet five and weighing around 130 pounds, with dark
hair and eyes, was up next and jumped in immediately, punching and
fighting with great intensity. Villareal had three inches and 45 pounds
on Medellín, but the two young men went the full five minutes. Villareal remained standing. Cantu motioned to Frank Sandoval next, but
the nineteen-year-old demurred. So Derrick Sean O'Brien stepped up
and started pummeling the bigger man. After ten minutes of punishment, Villareal was slower but still managed to get in a few good licks.
However, O'Brien, the best fighter of the bunch, punched Villareal in the
stomach, causing him to double over, followed by an uppercut to the jaw
that sent him sprawling. Villareal was unable to rise for several minutes,
during which time the rest of the guys went back to drinking. Despite
Villareal's failure to complete the challenge, Cantu announced he was in.

Villareal joined the others in drinking and celebrating, with the teenagers trading insults for the next half hour.

At around 10:45 p.m., the party began to break up. First, the Sandovals decided to call it a night, heading back down the railroad tracks toward the Clearbrook Apartments, where the guys had parked their cars. They were followed shortly by José and Yuni Medellín, who were slower to make their way down the tracks. As the Sandoval twins reached the gravel embankment leading down to the apartments, they passed Jennifer and Elizabeth, who were making their way up to the tracks. Yuni Medellín also passed the girls, but José took a different approach. He reached out and grabbed Elizabeth's left breast. She swatted his hand away, and he then grabbed her and said, "You ain't going nowhere, bitch!" and threw her to the ground. Elizabeth screamed for help.

Frank Sandoval, having reached the bottom of the gravel embankment, looked back up at the tracks, but he did nothing. He just turned and walked back into the woods toward the apartment complex parking lot. He would later note that it appeared Jennifer had passed the group of guys and could have fled to safety if she had taken off running. Instead, she made the second fateful decision of the night—she turned back to help her friend. She was grabbed by Cantu and O'Brien and was thrown to the ground as well.

What followed was later described by police as "a sadistic frenzy." At the end of the assault, Peter Cantu approached Yuni Medellín, just fourteen years old, and whispered that they were going to have to kill the girls. "They've seen our faces," he said. "We can't leave behind any witnesses. We've got to kill them."

Jennifer Ertman and Elizabeth Peña were the 250th and 251st murder victims in Houston in 1993. But their murders were undoubtedly two of the most disturbing and vicious. A police spokesman noted that the crime was truly random. The girls didn't know their assailants. "They just happened to cross each other's paths. It was convenient. This event wasn't planned. They weren't stalked." Investigators called the crimes "an almost unfathomably mindless act of violence."

At 12:30 a.m. on Friday, June 25, 1993, José Medellín, Raul Villareal, and Efrain Perez arrived at the home of Peter Cantu and knocked on the door. Cantu lived with his brother Joe and Joe's sixteen-year-old wife,

Christina. Christina answered the door, expecting to see her brother-in-law, Peter. Instead, she saw three men, only two of whom she knew, all looking the worse for wear. Christina asked what happened to them. The young men began to smile and laugh, and Medellín told her that they had "had fun." Joe Cantu entered the room and noticed that the young men seemed to be worked up about something. He also asked what happened. "Let's just say we had a lot of fun," Medellín told Joe. As the others laughed, he continued, "You'll hear about it on the news."

But the Cantus wouldn't have to wait to hear about the guys' exploits on the news. Over the next several minutes, José Medellín related the events of the evening, continuing to boast about his exploits. During the course of this retelling, Peter Cantu arrived back at the house and joined in. He also reached into his pockets and pulled out around forty dollars in rolled-up currency and various small pieces of jewelry, which he had taken from the girls' bodies. He divvied up the loot, giving some money to Perez for gas and a ring with the letter *E* on it to Medellín, to give as a gift to his girlfriend, Esther.

Throughout the telling, Christina Cantu had been walking in and out of the room, unable to deal with what she had been hearing. She would head to her bedroom and collect herself, before returning to the living room, where the boasting went on and on. Trying to mask her disquiet, Christina asked what happened to the girls. Medellín informed her that they had been killed so they could not identify their attackers. He then expressed his only regret of the evening: "It would have been a hell of a lot easier if we had a gun." Joe Cantu asked where the bodies were. Perez stated, "We just left. They're out in the woods, man." Overall, the conversation lasted nearly two hours, as the young men went into gory detail about both the assaults and the murders.

Christina stewed over the story for a day and a half. On the morning of June 26, she convinced her husband to go for a walk to a nearby park. There, she explained to Joe that the knowledge of what her brother-in-law and his friends had done was eating her up inside. She urged Joe to contact the police. At first, he was hesitant. He did not like the idea of ratting out his brother. But Christina kept pressing him. At last, she convinced Joe to call Crime Stoppers to report the location of the bodies, so their parents could put the girls to rest.

Despite his promise, Joe waited another twenty-four hours before calling in the tip. Christina continued to have nightmares about what she had been told by Medellín and the others. Joe Cantu picked up the phone and dialed Crime Stoppers. When someone answered, he gave a fake name and told the representative that the bodies of Elizabeth Peña and Jennifer Ertman could be found by the White Oak Bayou near T. C. Jester Park.

Police conducted a search of the area but stayed on the west side of the bayou, searching the wooded areas on both sides of the track but failing to cross the railroad bridge. That night, Joe and Christina watched the news, looking for reports that the bodies had been found. But nothing was mentioned. Christina was upset. She felt it was important for the families to be able to put their daughters to rest. She urged Joe to do more. He pledged to call back in the morning, to try and give a better description of the location.

Houston police officer Mike Cromwell was on patrol around noon on Monday, June 28, 1993, when he got a call to search for the bodies of two missing girls in the vicinity of T. C. Jester Park. He started searching the woods near the train trestle and was joined by other officers, one of whom directed Cromwell across the railroad bridge and to the other side of the tracks. As he searched the trees beyond the bridge, something caught his eye. Searching through the brush, he spotted what he thought was a body. Eventually he entered the copse of trees.

Approximately twenty feet from the entrance, he found two bodies. Two detectives, Ramon Zaragoza and Bob Parrish, responded to a dispatch call. Zaragoza helped the crime scene unit collect evidence, while Parrish interviewed members of the crowd that had begun to form when Cromwell and his fellow officers showed up. Although he was not interviewed, one of the onlookers was Derrick Sean O'Brien, one of the perpetrators, who lived in the nearby apartments.

Detective Larry Hoffmaster was a twenty-three-year veteran of the Houston Police Department and an officer in the Homicide Division. Hoffmaster, along with his partner, had been dispatched to the scene of the murder on June 28, 1993. He helped interview friends of the girls. Around five o'clock that evening, Officer Hoffmaster received a call from Officer Weiner in the Crime Stoppers Division. Based on that call, Hoffmaster dispatched two officers to try to locate two witnesses—Joe and Christina Cantu.

Hoffmaster took Joe Cantu's statement, in which Cantu relayed the conversation he had had with Medellín, Perez, Villareal, and his brother, Peter. At the time, it was the only evidence tying the young men to the murders. Following his interview with Cantu, and after speaking with the detectives who interviewed Christina, Hoffmaster spoke with Assistant District Attorney Ted Wilson. Wilson prepared arrest warrants for five men, the individuals known to Joe Cantu, and a sixth man, who would turn out to be Raul Villareal. At 1:45 a.m., Hoffmaster took the warrants to the home of Judge Ruben Guerrero, who reviewed and signed them. Hoffmaster then returned to the station, where a plan for six simultaneous arrests was formulated.

At 4:00 a.m. on Tuesday, June 29, Hoffmaster and his partner were stationed outside the home of José and Yuni Medellín. After getting the go-ahead from their lieutenant, they approached the single-story home on Brackley Street, in a section of Houston known as the Heights. Hoffmaster knocked on the door, which was answered by Venancio Medellín Sr., José and Yuni's father. When detective Hoffmaster told the elder Medellín that he needed to talk to José, Mr. Medellín pointed down the hall toward a back bedroom.

Hoffmaster drew his sidearm and took out his flashlight. He headed down the darkened hall. There, in a small bedroom, Hoffmaster found José and Yuni asleep in their beds, sharing a room. José was wearing nothing but a pair of boxer shorts. They were arrested without incident. After he arrested Medellín and placed him the back of his patrol car, Hoffmaster read to him from a small blue card, containing what is known as a magistrate warning or a 38.22 warning, named after the section of the Texas Code of Criminal Procedure, but more commonly known as a *Miranda* warning, after the famous 1966 Supreme Court case that created the requirement.

Detective Hoffmaster read each of the four rights on the blue card and, after each one, confirmed that José understood the rights provided to him. In each case, José indicated he did. He was informed he had the right to remain silent and not make a statement, and that any statement he did make could be and probably would be used against him at any trial. He was informed he had the right to have a lawyer present to advise him both before and during any questioning. He was told that if he was unable to employ a lawyer, he was entitled to have one appointed to advise him prior to and during any questioning. Finally, he was informed he had the right to terminate the interview at any time. José indicated that he understood all four rights and that he was willing to waive them and speak with Detective Hoffmaster.

Before heading to the station, Hoffmaster asked José if he knew the sixth man they were looking for. José told Hoffmaster that he only knew the man's first name but could point out his address, which he subsequently did. To prevent the teens from collaborating on a statement, José, Yuni, and Raul were all transported to the police station in separate automobiles and were placed in separate interview rooms.

Hoffmaster again read José the magistrate warning and confirmed that he was willing to talk about the case. He offered José food, which José turned down, as well as cigarettes. Hoffmaster also offered José some clothing, but he declined.

At that point, Hoffmaster attempted to activate the video recording equipment to record José's confession, but it was not working. They moved to an office, and Hoffmaster used a computer in that room to take down José's written statement. During the move, José was uncuffed and walked beside Detective Hoffmaster.

The office they moved to was quite small. Hoffmaster sat at the desk so he could access the computer, and José sat to Hoffmaster's right. Hoffmaster typed out the magistrate's warnings and read them to José a third time, typing out his response of "yes sir" to each. The two were so close that José could read the computer screen over Hoffmaster's shoulder and would offer corrections to the spelling.

And so Hoffmaster asked José about what happened with Elizabeth Peña and Jennifer Ertman and transcribed the responses as best he could. José read along and would suggest changes when he didn't like what Hoffmaster had typed. In all, the interrogation lasted just over an hour, beginning at 5:54 a.m. and concluding at 7:15 a.m. At the end, they had produced a statement that was three pages long. José read over the statement and initialed next to each of the magistrate warnings as well as his waiver of his rights. He then signed the bottom of each page, which was witnessed by two other officers, Sergeants Novak and Doyle.

After completing the statement, Detective Hoffmaster went home, having worked for twenty-four hours straight. Perhaps this explains why, despite the opening paragraph of the confession indicating that

José Medellín was born in Laredo, Mexico, Detective Hoffmaster, who had been so careful to notify José of his rights under *Miranda*, failed to notify him of his rights under the Vienna Convention on Consular Relations. More likely, this occurred because neither the Texas Code of Criminal Procedure nor Houston Police Department policy required that detained foreign nationals be informed of their rights under the Vienna Convention. This lapse set off a fifteen-year legal battle.

———

If he wished to avoid the death penalty, José Medellín could not have picked a worse place to commit his crime. Houston, Texas, in Harris County, is rightfully known as the "Capital City of Capital Punishment." While twenty-eight states have the death penalty on their books, only twenty-five actively practice it (the governors of Oregon, California, and Pennsylvania have all declared a moratorium on executions). Of those twenty-five states, Texas is far and away the biggest practitioner, having put 570 people to death between 1976, when the Supreme Court allowed states to once again impose the penalty in *Gregg v. Georgia*, and 2020. The next most active states, Virginia and Oklahoma, together have executed fewer than half that number. Between 1976 and 2010, Texas alone accounted for 37 percent of all executions conducted nationwide.

Even within Texas, the application of the death penalty is not uniform. There are 254 counties in Texas, and Harris County is the most active death penalty jurisdiction. In fact, as of 2008, if Harris County were a state, it would rank second, behind the rest of Texas and ahead of Virginia and Oklahoma, in number of death sentences handed down, with over 280 defendants sentenced to death. Harris and the 4 major urban counties (Dallas, Tarrant, Bexar, and Travis) account for the state's reputation. Indeed, between 2004 and 2009, 88 percent of Texas's 254 counties sentenced no one to death. Of the 32 counties that did pursue the death penalty in that period, more than half (17) sentenced just one person to death during the entire five-year span. Harris County again led the pack with twenty-one death sentences during this period. To put this in perspective, Harris County accounted for approximately 16 percent of Texas's population in 2012 but accounted for 28 percent of its death sentences.

Of course, not every person sentenced to death is eventually executed. Here again, Harris County leads the way. As of September 2020, 129 of the defendants who were sentenced to death in Harris County since 1976 had actually been executed. In that same period, the states of Virginia and Oklahoma executed 113 and 112 people, respectively. Again, things are not uniform within the state. Harris County remains the standout, executing almost as many people by 2020 (129) as the other major urban counties combined (159).

But location is not the only factor to consider. The fact that one of Medellín's victims was a white female also made the crime especially likely to result in a death sentence. Numerous studies have shown that the death penalty is more likely to be applied when the victim is white. One Florida study found that, all else being equal, a criminal defendant was 3.4 times more likely to receive the death penalty if the victim was white than if the victim was African American. This racial disparity is repeated nationwide. A study conducted in 1995 by Professor Steven Bright, director of the Southern Center for Human Rights in Atlanta, found that although African Americans made up approximately 50 percent of homicide victims across the United States, in 82 percent of cases where the execution was carried out, the defendant was sentenced for the murder of a white victim. This number increases when the victim is a white female. A study conducted of all death penalty cases in Texas between 1976 and 2016 found that "an execution was 2.8 times more likely in cases with a white female victim than one would expect in a system that was blind to race and gender."

Things are even more pronounced in Harris County. Since 2001, white females were the victims in only 5 percent of death-eligible crimes, while 27 percent of those sentenced to death had murdered white female victims. Thus, the death penalty was imposed at a rate more than 5 times greater than one would expect, all things being equal. And this was in an era when the number of death sentences being sought was decreasing. At the time Medellín committed his crime, juries were 1.5 times more likely to sentence a defendant to death if his victim was white. When rape is involved, the likelihood of a death sentence increases further.

José Medellín's race likely played a role in his sentence, although in a less obvious way. While studies have consistently shown that the race of the victim matters in capital sentencing, the role of the defendant's race is less clear-cut. Indeed, multiple studies of Harris County's death penalty found that while Black defendants were more likely than whites to receive the death penalty, there was no difference between white and Hispanic defendants. Still, as one law professor who studies the death penalty noted: "Often, the only member of a racial minority who participates in the process is the accused."

Timing also played a role in Medellín's case. At the time he was put on trial, Harris County was experiencing its peak period of death sentences, which ran from 1992 to 1996. During those years, an average of forty-two defendants were sentenced to death. In 2005–2009, that number had dropped to only fourteen death sentences per year, a 70 percent decline. According to the Death Penalty Information Center, in 2019, only thirty-four death sentences were imposed nationwide. In short, if Medellín was looking to avoid a sentence of death, he picked the worst possible crime to commit, in the worst possible place to commit it, during the worst possible time frame.

———

Following the arrests, all eyes turned to John B. Holmes Jr., the Harris County district attorney. Holmes had held this position since 1979, when, after spending ten years rising through the ranks, he was appointed to complete the unfinished term of his predecessor. In the fourteen years since taking over, the Houston Law grad with the white handlebar mustache had developed a reputation as a no-nonsense, tough-on-crime district attorney who was more than willing to seek the death penalty. Indeed, during Holmes's tenure, Harris County imposed more death sentences than in any other period before or since.

He liked to say that he never wanted to be a lawyer, instead telling people, "I wanted to be a prosecutor." And in that role, he was famous for outworking anybody on his staff. Traditionally, the district attorney position is managerial, involving setting policy and overseeing the work of the line attorneys working under him. District attorneys themselves typically do not handle the day-to-day work of prosecuting. Holmes, in contrast, took pride in personally handling capital cases.

Given Holmes's reputation, the general consensus in Harris County was that he would be seeking the death penalty for all five of the young men involved in the Ertman and Peña murders. But five death penalty charges for one case, even in Texas, was unprecedented. Texas had restored the death penalty in 1974 and had executed a total of fifty-four people in the two decades since. By the end of the 1990s, that number would be just shy of two hundred. But at the time of these murders, Texas's reputation regarding its use of the death penalty was still in the future, and Holmes had to debate the myriad permutations in prosecuting the perpetrators. Yuni Medellín was not considered, as his young age took the death penalty off the table.

Holmes pondered the problem, at one point telling the media, "I don't have the foggiest idea what call I'll make on this one." There was a great deal of publicity surrounding the murders, which would have translated into a great deal of pressure to secure convictions. He could offer a deal to one of the individuals charged, in exchange for testifying against the others—this lucky person would likely get life in prison, while the others faced lethal injection. But who to choose? Without a clear picture of what happened that night, Holmes could inadvertently grant a reprieve to the ringleader. And any deal that spared the life of one of the perpetrators was going to upset the families and likely the public. But it was possible that the young men would end up pointing the finger at each other, as they largely did in their confessions, and it might be impossible for a jury to determine who was specifically responsible for the girls' deaths. In that case, they could all avoid the needle.

In the end, Holmes didn't have to offer anyone a deal—Yuni Medellín ended up as the state's key witness. As a result, Holmes ordered his office to pursue death penalty charges against all five young men.

A grand jury was convened, and on Monday, August 30, 1993, it returned five indictments against the older teenagers for murder and rape. With the exception of Villareal, they were also indicted for robbery.

The next question that had to be dealt with was a logistical one: How do you try five separate trials for the same murders? Nothing like it had ever been attempted before in Harris County. One official suggested holding one giant trial with five separate juries at once, one for each defendant. The argument in favor was largely to spare the families from the need to testify multiple times. Instead, they could give their testimony before all five juries at once. The same would be true of other common witnesses. But for this scenario to work, the defendants and their attorneys would have to agree. Such agreement was not forthcoming. One of the defense attorneys, Don Davis, who had been appointed to represent Peter Cantu, had been party to a similar case involving seven gang members accused of a single rape. In his view, the trial was a failure. In this case, the defendants all confessed to taking part in the rapes, but when it came to the question of who was responsible for murdering Jennifer and Elizabeth, they tended to minimize their own involvement, while placing the blame on their codefendants. In such a case, logistical problems regarding introducing the confessions would arise.

The reason for separate juries is that some evidence is only admissible against certain defendants and not against others. For example, if one defendant's confession implicates a codefendant, that codefendant cannot cross-examine the one giving the confession, because the confessing defendant has a Fifth Amendment right not to answer. So, when introducing José's confession, the juries for the others would have to be excluded from hearing it. But that means that juries would be constantly moving in and out of the courtroom. Additionally, with five defendants, it would be necessary to have a total of seventy jurors—twelve for each defendant, plus two alternates for each jury. The logistics could quickly become problematic. So that left the idea of five trials, happening simultaneously in five courtrooms.

The families objected to this approach. There was a belief that five simultaneous trials would make things easier on the families, but the girls' parents insisted they wanted to attend each trial, which would not be possible if they occurred simultaneously. The district attorney was pushing for simultaneous trials because he was concerned if the trials were conducted sequentially, the later-tried defendants would blame earlier convicted defendants of committing the murders and thereby escape the death penalty.

Despite the families' objections, Judge Doug Shaver, who oversaw the administration of the twenty-two felony courts in Harris County, convinced the other judges that five simultaneous trials, although objectionable to the family and the defense, could be accomplished, at least in the same building, if not the same courtroom. Thus, he suggested that five individual trials, in five separate courtrooms before five separate juries, all be scheduled for the same time. Judge Shaver wanted to move things along quickly and planned to start jury selection for all five defendants at the end of February 1994, with testimony beginning at the start of April.

But things are never easy in Harris County. On Monday, September 27, Judge Bill Harmon, who was overseeing the trial of Peter Cantu, the ringleader of the group, announced that due to concerns about pre-trial publicity, which could lead to a change of venue outside of Houston, he was going to set the trial for January, at least six weeks before the date set by Judge Shaver. Neither the other judges nor the DAs were happy with Harmon's move. They were concerned that the publicity surrounding his trial would potentially taint the jury pool for the other four defendants, leading to further delays by the defense. Because of the notoriety of the Ertman and Peña murders, Cantu's trial was sure to be heavily covered by the press and followed by the public—the same public that would have to serve on juries for Medellín, O'Brien, Villareal, and Perez. To ensure a fair trial, jurors who had been exposed to news about the crimes would have to be excluded from serving. Holding the Cantu trial before the others would make it that much harder to find fourteen citizens (twelve jurors and two alternates) who hadn't been exposed to some media about the murders and the trial, let alone the fifty-six necessary for four trials.

But these concerns fell on deaf ears. And so it was that on Friday, January 7, 1994, jury selection began in the trial of Peter Cantu. His trial began at the end of the month. After four days of testimony, the prosecution rested. The defense offered no witnesses. After hearing closing statements, the jury took less than half an hour to convict.

The sentencing phase of the hearing began immediately the following day. After two additional days of testimony, the jury deliberated for four hours, then pronounced a sentence of death for Peter Cantu.

Then, in one of the first of several instances involving these cases, Judge Harmon made Texas history. The state legislature had passed a law, the Crime Victims' Bill of Rights, which allowed the victims of crime to make a statement. At the time, it had never been used. Judge Harmon decided the time for the law had come. He invited Randy Ertman, Jennifer's father, to address Peter Cantu.

So it was that Randy Ertman, more than six feet tall and weighing in at 245 pounds, who had sat through six days of testimony about the death of his daughter and the key man responsible, stood up and unloaded on the eighteen-year-old. Cantu refused to look back, until Randy Ertman yelled at him, "Look at me! Look!" When Cantu craned his head back, a sneer on his face, Randy told him:

You're not even an animal. I have cats that kill animals. They kill an animal, they eat it. You're worse than that. You're a piece of shit!...

You destroyed a life. You destroyed my life. You destroyed my wife's life.... I haven't seen any remorse from you. You're worse than anything I've seen in my life and I hope that ... I hope that you rot in hell!

It would not be the last time Randy Ertman confronted one of his daughter's killers.

Derrick Sean O'Brien was the next defendant to face a jury. His trial started on April 5, 1994. After two days of testimony, the case was handed to the jury. On the morning of April 7, the jury was sent out to deliberate. It took only ninety minutes to return a verdict of guilty.

Later that afternoon, at 2:00 p.m., the penalty phase began. For two days, the jury heard testimony from several witnesses. After both sides made their pleas, the jury was asked to determine if O'Brien deserved the death penalty. When it returned less than half an hour later, its answer was a resounding yes. Andy Kahan, a well-known figure in Houston who worked as a victims' rights advocate, stated, "The thing I remember most about that trial was how quick that jury came back with a death sentence. I think they were out fifteen minutes. They went in to deliberate his sentence, and within fifteen to twenty minutes, they came back with death. I had never seen anything that fast in my life." While statistics on the typical length of time for jury deliberations are hard to find, comparisons to other famous murder cases are instructive. It took Timothy McVeigh's jury twenty-three hours over four days to reach a verdict. Charles Manson's jury took eleven days to determine his guilt.

Three judges overseeing the trials of José Medellín, Efrain Perez, and Raul Villareal held to the simultaneous prosecution deal, although they started a good deal later than planned. On Monday, September 12, 1994, at 9:00 a.m., trial began for the three young men, in three separate courtrooms, before three separate juries. It was another history-making move, in order to accommodate the families of the victims and the witnesses who would have to shuttle from one courtroom to another in order to testify.

José Medellín found himself in the courtroom of Judge Caprice Cosper at the 339th District Court. Medellín was represented by Jack Millin, a former prosecutor in the Harris County District Attorney's Office, and Linda Mazzagatti, both of whom had been appointed by the court and had a wealth of experience defending capital cases. At the time, Millin was fighting cancer and was in the last year of his life. Additionally, according to appellate counsel, he had been suspended from the practice of law for ethics violations during the pretrial proceedings. The state was represented by two attorneys, Mark Vinson, a tall African American Vietnam veteran, and Terry Wilson, whom a colleague described as a lawyer who wished he was a Texas Ranger. Known for being gruff, Wilson enjoyed investigating as much as litigating. He appeared in the courtroom with his arm in a sling, having recently injured himself in an accident. As a result, he took a backseat for most of the trial.

Medellín was charged with killing Elizabeth by strangling her with a shoelace and his hands, by stepping on her neck, and by using an unknown object. But murder, by itself, is not a capital crime in Texas. Instead, under Texas law, there must be certain aggravating circumstances. In this case, the state charged Medellín with killing Elizabeth Peña during the course of three additional felonies. First, Medellín was charged with killing Elizabeth during the commission of her kidnapping; second, he was charged with killing Elizabeth while in the course of robbing her or attempting to rob her; finally, he was charged with killing Elizabeth while in the course of committing and attempting to commit aggravated sexual assault against her.

Things ran in Medellín's trial in much the same way as in the trials of Peter Cantu and Derrick Sean O'Brien—until, that is, Yuni Medellín took the stand. Despite already having pled guilty to the crimes involved, and despite testifying before the grand jury, Yuni staunchly refused to say a word against his older brother. When the district attorney, Mark Vinson, asked Yuni to describe José's part in the murders of Jennifer Ertman and Elizabeth Peña, he pled the Fifth. Vinson asked Judge Cosper to order Yuni to answer the questions. After the judge informed Yuni that he had no Fifth Amendment rights, because he had already been convicted, Yuni still refused to answer the DA's questions. As a result, Judge Cosper held Yuni in contempt, fined him $500, and sentenced him to an additional six months in jail, on top of his forty-year sentence. But Yuni held firm and refused to speak.

In the end, Yuni's gesture of brotherly love proved futile. It took the jury only thirteen minutes to convict. José Medellín was the last of the five to be convicted, the trials of Perez and Villareal having concluded with guilty verdicts the previous day. All three would go through a quick penalty phase, and all three would be sentenced to death. At the sentencing, which the judges delayed a few weeks to let tempers cool, Randy Ertman spoke again, although unlike in Peter Cantu's trial, he remained calm. Adolph Peña, Elizabeth's father, did not. He stated, "I wish these guys would get executed the way my daughter did. And just be left there on the ground to die."

Medellín filed an appeal, although he challenged only the sentence of death, not the conviction itself. The Texas Court of Criminal Appeals quickly disposed of the matter, issuing a judgment upholding the death sentence on March 19, 1997. Less than two years after their daughters were murdered, it seemed the Ertmans and Peñas would finally see the killers put to death.

A Failure to Act

The process of reviewing the state's decision to execute José Medellín would take more than a decade. Along the way, his case would wind up before the International Court of Justice (ICJ) and twice before the US Supreme Court, all because when he was arrested, the detectives neglected to inform him of his right to contact the Mexican consulate in accordance with Article 36 of the Vienna Convention on Consular Relations (VCCR). Unfortunately, this was a common problem in the United States, and one that had gotten it into trouble on the international stage more than once.

The United States was heavily involved in the creation and drafting of the Vienna Convention in 1963 and was one of the original signatories. In ratified the convention in 1969, six years after it opened and two years after it went into effect. Despite the United States' involvement in the convention's creation, its compliance with Article 36 has left a lot to be desired. According to the State Department, efforts to improve consular notification, particularly regarding Mexican nationals, intensified from 1976 to 1981, after back-and-forth discussions between the US and Mexican governments about Article 36 compliance. It was not until 1992 that the State Department became aware that Mexican nationals were being sentenced to death by various state courts, despite the failure to provide the required notice about consular access, and it was not until 1996, after Medellín's arrest, trial, conviction, and sentence, that it intensified its compliance efforts by urging states to notify Mexico of all cases in which Mexican nationals were arrested and might face capital punishment. This failure to comply with the Vienna Convention is particularly disappointing given that the United States was the very first nation to seek relief for violations of Article 36, among others, before the ICJ when it sued Iran following the taking of hostages at the US embassy in Tehran in 1979.

Statistics on compliance are hard to come by given that, as of 2003, the responsibility lay with eighteen thousand individual state and local police departments employing over seven hundred thousand officers. However, some snapshots are available. In 1997, a Dutch woman named Annette Sorensen who was arrested by the New York Police Department (NYPD) for child endangerment was not provided with information about her right to contact her consulate. She filed a civil suit against the NYPD and sought discovery on the department's compliance numbers. Official records disclosed by the NYPD indicated that in 1997 alone, fifty-three thousand foreign nationals were arrested, but the NYPD Alien Notification Log indicated that notification to consulates was made in only four cases. These difficulties in enforcement are not entirely surprising, given the sheer number of officers in various jurisdictions who are responsible for ensuring that Article 36 rights are given. In the early 2000s, there were eight million Mexican nationals living in the United States, and thousands interacted with law enforcement on a weekly basis. Given the large number of immigrants who make the United States their home, it is not always clear to law enforcement when someone they have arrested is a foreign national.

Unfortunately, US courts did little to enforce the United States' responsibility under international law. In fact, US courts are split on whether a judicial remedy exists for an Article 36 violation. This may not come as a great surprise, as the VCCR itself does not specify a remedy for consular notification violations. As of 2004, federal courts had fractured on the question, with courts in the First, Fifth, Sixth, Seventh, and Tenth Circuits, along with a handful of state courts, holding that no such remedy exists, while several federal district courts in New York, Massachusetts, Illinois, and the US Virgin Islands have held that Article 36 creates individually enforceable rights and defendants have standing to assert them. The Ninth Circuit has split with itself, finding such a right in 1999 and 2000 but denying habeas relief based on an Article 36 violation in 2004.

Despite this confusion in lower federal courts, prior to José Medellín's case, the Supreme Court had weighed in only once, in a per curiam opinion issued in 1998 in a case called *Breard v. Greene*. Angel Breard was a national of Paraguay convicted and sentenced to death by the State of

Virginia for the attempted rape and capital murder of a woman named Ruth Dickie in 1992. Breard was never informed of his right to contact the consulate to seek assistance. Both Breard and Paraguay filed suit in federal court, seeking to enforce Article 36. The lower courts held that because Breard had not raised the Article 36 claim until his habeas corpus proceeding, he "procedurally defaulted" the claim by failing to raise it at trial or in his direct appeal from his conviction and sentence. Procedural default is a doctrine in American law that supports the view that criminal trials are largely state affairs, and thus states should have the first opportunity to correct any errors that may have been made during the course of a criminal trial. Thus, under this doctrine, before a defendant may raise an issue on collateral appeal in a federal court, he or she must first have raised it in state court. A failure to do so will, absent certain exceptions, preclude a defendant from raising the issue in federal court. Because Breard had failed to raise the Article 36 claim before Virginia's state courts, the federal court refused to hear it. As for Paraguay's separate claims that its rights under Article 36 were violated, the lower courts held that such a suit was barred by the Eleventh Amendment's grant of sovereign immunity.

The Supreme Court consolidated the cases and issued an unsigned 6–3 decision assuming without deciding that the VCCR created individual rights. The Court acknowledged that "while we should give respectful consideration to the interpretation of an international treaty rendered by an international court with jurisdiction to interpret such," no such interpretation was present here. Absent a "clear and express statement to the contrary," the procedural rules of a nation governed. In Breard's case, that meant that the procedural default rule could operate to foreclose an Article 36 claim. Furthermore, even if Breard were granted an evidentiary hearing as to the effect of the Article 36 breach, the Court found that it was unlikely that he could show that the violation had any effect on his trial. Without this showing, he could not demonstrate that he was prejudiced by the violation and would not be entitled to relief.

As for Paraguay's claim, the Court held that neither the text nor the history of the Vienna Convention provided a private right of action in domestic courts to overturn convictions or sentences, even when they were obtained in violation of Article 36. Additionally, the Court agreed that the Eleventh Amendment would bar any suit against the State of Virginia, absent its consent.

Justices John Paul Stevens, Ruth Bader Ginsburg, and Stephen Breyer all dissented, lamenting the lack of time and full consideration. Breard's petition was brought as a last-minute challenge to the imposition of the death penalty on April 14, 1998, the date of his scheduled execution. As a result, the Court decided the issue without the benefit of full briefing, the input of amicus briefs, or oral argument. Instead, the Court issued a last-minute decision based solely on the filings.

Due to Paraguay's failure to receive relief from US courts, it sought other avenues of redress. As a result, Medellín's trip to the ICJ was not the first time the United States had been sued for violating the rights of foreign nationals under the Vienna Convention where the foreign national ended up on death row. In fact, it was the third. Both Paraguay, in 1998, and Germany, in 1999, sued the United States on behalf of nationals held on death row.

Not content with the interpretation of Article 36 given by US courts, Paraguay sought an authoritative decision from a court empowered to give it. As a signatory to the VCCR's Optional Protocol, Paraguay filed a petition against the United States in the ICJ on April 3, 1998. Given the pending execution date, Paraguay asked the ICJ to issue "provisional measures"—the equivalent of a temporary injunction in US courts—ordering that the United States not allow Virginia to carry out the execution until after the ICJ had a chance to rule on the merits. The ICJ issued its order six days later, unanimously granting the request and ordering the United States to take all measures at its disposal to prevent Breard's execution. In its per curiam decision in *Breard v. Greene,* the US Supreme Court acknowledged the ICJ's provisional measures order but stated that any decision by the governor of Virginia to stay the execution to allow the ICJ to rule would have to be a matter of his discretion. According to the Court, "Nothing in our existing case law allows us to make that choice for him." Even though Secretary of State Madeleine Albright sent a request to the governor asking him to delay Breard's execution, Virginia carried out the sentence on April 15.

Despite the failure of the United States to comply with the provisional measures, Paraguay pressed ahead with its suit. It filed its opening brief, called a memorial, with the ICJ on October 9, 1998. In addition to the claims that both its own and its national's rights were violated by the United States when it failed to comply with Article 36, Paraguay also argued that the United States violated a binding order of the Court when it executed Breard. Paraguay sought four remedies. First, it asked for a declaration that the United States had violated its rights under the Convention. Second, it requested an order of nonrepetition. Third, it argued it had been entitled to restitutio ad integrum, a return to the situation that existed prior to the breach of Article 36. Finally, it argued that because the United States had rendered restitutio impossible when it executed Breard, it was entitled to alternative forms of reparation.

The ICJ would never get a chance to rule on the merits of Paraguay's contentions. Less than a month after filing its memorial, on November 2, 1998, Paraguay abruptly dropped the case with no explanation. Law professor John Quigley, in his book *Foreigners on America's Death Row*, notes that at around the same time Paraguay filed its memorial, the Office of the US Trade Representative had entered a finding that Paraguay was not taking action preventing its citizens from pirating material protected under US copyright law, a determination that opened Paraguay to sanctions by the United States. Just two weeks after Paraguay dropped its suit at the ICJ, on November 17, the two nations announced that they had reached an agreement in which Paraguay agreed to take a number of short-term and long-term steps to combat piracy, and in exchange the United States would terminate its investigation. While both countries denied the existence of a quid pro quo, the timing is interesting.

However, if Paraguay's withdrawal of its suit could be deemed a victory for the United States, it was a short-lived one. Just four months later, on March 2, 1999, Germany filed suit against the United States on behalf of two brothers, Karl and Walter LaGrand, two German nationals on death row in Arizona, who had not been notified of their rights to contact the German consulate. Unlike Paraguay, Germany would see the case through to its conclusion.

By the time Germany filed suit in the ICJ, Arizona had already executed Karl LaGrand. Walter LaGrand's execution was scheduled for March 3, 1999. The United States admitted breaching Germany's rights under Article 36, so the ICJ was faced merely with the question of what constituted an appropriate remedy. Given the short time frame before

Walter LaGrand's execution, Germany sought provisional measures from the ICJ, which were quickly granted. Notice of the provisional measures order was filed in the US Supreme Court by Germany, in an attempt to forestall Walter LaGrand's death. The Court, in a 7–2 per curiam decision, rejected Germany's application. Walter LaGrand was executed the next day.

This setback did not deter Germany, which filed its memorial, laying out its case against the United States, on September 16, 1999. The United States filed its response on March 27, 2000. Arguments occurred over five days the following November, and the ICJ issued its ruling on June 27, 2001. The court noted that the United States did not deny it violated its obligation under Article 36(1)(b) of the Vienna Convention on Consular Relations to notify the LaGrands of their right to contact their consulate. This violation led directly to violations of Article 36(1)(a) and (1)(c), relating to the rights of consular officers to communicate with their nationals and to visit with them and aid in providing legal assistance. For the first time, and contrary to holdings by numerous US courts, the ICJ held that Article 36 conferred an individual right on the LaGrands, in addition to the rights afforded to Germany.

The ICJ also agreed with Germany that the domestic rules of the United States, particularly the "procedural default" doctrine, which held that a criminal defendant must raise a procedural defect in his arrest, trial, or conviction at the earliest possible date or forever waive it, violated Article 36(2), which required all signatory states to give full effect to the rights protected by Article 36(1). The ICJ was careful to note that the procedural default doctrine itself did not inherently violate the Vienna Convention. But when the failure to raise the Vienna Convention claim was the direct result of US authorities' failure to comply with Article 36, reliance on the doctrine violated Article 36. Such was the case with the LaGrands; therefore, the ICJ found that the United States was also in breach of Article 36(2).

Finally, the ICJ found for the first time that its provisional measures orders were not merely exhortations to the recipient but themselves constituted binding legal obligations. Because the United States had not prevented the execution of Walter LaGrand, the United States was in violation of its obligations under international law.

{ *Chapter Three* }

The case was not a complete win for Germany. First, the ICJ held that the efforts taken by the United States to increase its compliance with its obligations under the VCCR were sufficient to satisfy Germany's demand for an assurance of nonrepetition. But the big win for the United States came in terms of the remedy ordered by the ICJ. Like Paraguay, Germany had sought the remedy of restitutio in integrum, at least as far as any future cases of noncompliance were concerned. But the ICJ would not go that far. Instead, it ordered that should any future cases of Article 36 noncompliance occur regarding German citizens, "it would be incumbent on the United States to allow the review and reconsideration of the conviction and sentence by taking account of the violation of the rights set forth in the Convention." The choice of means as to how to provide such "review and reconsideration" was left up to the United States. Because the LaGrands had already been executed, the meaning of this remedy was not further dealt with in the decision.

But the ICJ was not the only venue where the United States' failure to comply with Article 36 of the Vienna Convention was being raised. Prior to filing at the ICJ, Mexico brought suit before the Inter-American Court of Human Rights, a body of the Organization of American States (OAS). While the United States has not joined any human rights treaties that the Inter-American Court has authority to interpret, because the United States is an OAS member, the Inter-American Court has jurisdiction to issue advisory opinions about the interpretation of any human rights treaty applicable to OAS members.

Mexico argued to the court that the imposition of the death penalty following a failure to honor Article 36 constituted a human rights violation under the American Convention on Human Rights (to which the United States was not a party) and a violation of the due process rights protected by the International Covenant on Civil and Political Rights (ICCPR) (to which it was).

The United States participated in the proceedings, providing comments in May 1999. It argued that the Inter-American Court was an inappropriate body to rule on the meaning of the Vienna Convention, as it was a global treaty and thus not susceptible to regional interpretations. Instead, the ICJ was the appropriate forum. It also noted that it had not accepted the Inter-American Court's jurisdiction in this type of dispute, but Mexico was attempting to subject it to the court's jurisdiction nonetheless. On the merits, the United States argued that the Vienna Convention was not a human rights treaty and it did not guarantee a right to consular assistance. Furthermore, the United States argued there was no connection between consular notification and human rights or due process, because the VCCR does not create individual rights; it is purely concerned with the rights of States.

In October 1999, the court issued its advisory opinion, known as OC-16/99. While it noted that the purpose of the Vienna Convention was addressed to the rights of States and that any concern for the rights of individuals would be the rights of individual consular officers to perform their jobs, it also pointed out that the United States linked the rights of consular notification to the individuals detained when it sued Iran in the ICJ over the taking of hostages in Tehran. Furthermore, the court held that while the Vienna Convention may not be a human rights treaty, Article 36 still concerned human rights, and both the consular official and the foreign national possess the right to communicate with each other. Thus, Article 36 protects the human rights of foreign nationals to contact their consulates and seek assistance.

The court then turned to the question of whether a violation of Article 36 would constitute a violation of the right to due process protected by Article 14 of the ICCPR. Comparing the right to consular notification to the right to have an interpreter, the court concluded that "notification of one's right to contact the consular agent of one's country will considerably enhance one's chances of defending oneself." Therefore, the rights safeguarded by Article 36 "must be recognized and counted among the minimum guarantees essential to providing foreign nationals the opportunity to adequately prepare their defense and receive a fair trial." The rights conferred by Article 36 of the Vienna Convention, the court declared, make the due process right protected by Article 14 of the ICCPR possible.

Turning to remedy, the court announced that the violation of Article 36 is prejudicial to judicial guarantees of due process. Because international instruments, such as the ICCPR, call for the strictest adherence to due process protections when the death penalty is being administered, the imposition of death, when Article 36 has been violated, is a violation of the right not to be arbitrarily deprived of one's life, as protected by Article 6 of the ICCPR. This is particularly important in the United States, where numerous studies have shown that the imposition of the death penalty is unequal and arbitrary.

Only one member of the Inter-American Court dissented on this last point. Judge Oliver Jackman of Barbados, while agreeing in large part with the court's decision, dissented when it came to the effect of failing to abide by Article 36 on due process claims. While he noted the importance of complying with Article 36, Judge Jackman would not go so far as to say that the failure to observe it automatically undercut the validity of any subsequent proceedings.

At the same time the Inter-American Court was deciding the question, the Court of Appeals for the First Circuit was also addressing a case about the denial of consular notification and what impact that had on the trial and sentence of a man arrested for human trafficking. The court of appeals sent a letter to the Department of State, asking whether Article 36 provided individual rights and whether any remedy was available for the violation of the Vienna Convention. The State Department responded on October 15, 1999, just two weeks after the Inter-American Court issued its ruling.

In response to the court's letter, David Andrews, the chief lawyer at the State Department, told the First Circuit the Vienna Convention did not create any rights for individuals, and the violation of Article 36 did not require the reversal of any portion of a criminal proceeding. This did not account for the Inter-American Court's recently issued decision. In February 2000, the First Circuit determined that even if the VCCR provided individual rights, a violation did not require suppression of evidence or dismissal of an indictment, denied any remedy, and affirmed the convictions.

This was hardly a unique outcome. Despite the ICJ's ruling in *LaGrand* and despite the advisory opinion of the Inter-American Court, domestic US courts would continue to deny relief to foreign nationals, even in cases where it was undisputed that they were denied their rights under the Vienna Convention. It did not matter if the claims were phrased as ineffective assistance of counsel claims or due process violations on direct review, or as collateral attacks brought under habeas and framed as domestic constitutional violations. The Ninth Circuit, sitting en banc, overruled a three-judge panel that had ordered suppression of a confession obtained in violation of Article 36. Relying on the Department of State's arguments, it held that no judicial remedy was available because such a remedy could cause conflict with the executive's attempts to resolve violations diplomatically. In a confluence of events, courts in the Fifth, Sixth, Seventh, Tenth, and Eleventh Circuits all issued opinions about Article 36 in the year 2000. None found that a remedy was available. Thus, when an Article 36 violation occurred, it appeared that the courts were unwilling to provide relief to foreign nationals, even in capital cases, where the Supreme Court, due to heightened concerns for due process, requires greater attention to procedural protections.

CHAPTER 4

Mexico Intervenes

As a child, Sandra Babcock, from just north of Baltimore, never imagined she would someday argue before the International Court of Justice (ICJ). The idea of social justice work had always appealed to her, but law was not something she thought about. She graduated from Johns Hopkins University with a degree in international relations in 1986. She earned a Truman Scholarship to pursue work in public service in 1984, and upon graduation received a Thomas J. Watson Fellowship for directed study abroad in Vienna.

"Law was not really on my radar. It was not something I'd ever considered," Babcock said. "I really just didn't have a clue as to what lawyers did." While living in Vienna, she met a law student from the United States who convinced her over coffee that she should apply to law school. She sat for the LSAT on an army base in Munich, Germany, and applied to Harvard Law School. She was accepted, graduated in 1991, and went into criminal defense.

In 1999, Babcock was working in the Hennepin County Public Defender Office in Minneapolis, Minnesota, when she received a call. It was a representative of the Mexican government, and he had a proposition for her. Mexico was interested in founding a US-based public interest organization to provide support to its citizens who were arrested for capital crimes, and it wanted her to run it.

The call was unexpected, but Babcock was no stranger to defending Mexican nationals on death row. Shortly after graduating from Harvard Law School in 1991, she worked for the Texas Capital Resource Center, a federally funded nonprofit group that provided legal representation to people facing the death penalty in Texas. While there, she represented Ricardo Aldape Guerra, a Mexican national who had been wrongly convicted and sentenced to death. During the course of her representation, she worked closely with the Mexican consulate in Texas. Based on her efforts, Guerra was exonerated, which received what Babcock described as an overwhelming amount of press attention.

Guerra was her second client on Texas's death row. Her first client, Joseph Stanley Faulder, was a Canadian citizen who had been on death row for fifteen years. As Babcock recalled, "I contacted the Canadian consulate to let them know he was there. They had no idea he had been on death row for fifteen years. The thing that made his case more dramatic was that his family had no idea he was on death row either. He'd had no contact with anybody from his family since his arrest."

While speaking with the Canadian consulate, Babcock learned about the Vienna Convention on Consular Relations (VCCR), which requires that consulates be notified when a foreign citizen is detained. So she raised the issue in a habeas argument. As she recalled, "I don't think that issue had been raised before, certainly not in a capital case." She contacted several professors of international law and a law firm in Minneapolis for help in drafting an argument that she presented to the courts in 1992. She raised similar arguments in the *Guerra* case.

In the three years following her representation of Faulder and Guerra, Babcock worked on behalf of other foreign nationals accused of capital crimes, including nationals from Vietnam and the Dominican Republic and another Mexican citizen. In each case, she raised Article 36 violations as an issue. Then, in 1996, the Fifth Circuit Court of Appeals issued a decision in the *Faulder* case. The court found that Texas had violated Faulder's rights under the Vienna Convention, but it determined that the failure did not merit a reversal of his conviction because "the evidence that would have been obtained by the Canadian authorities is merely the same as or cumulative of evidence defense counsel had or could have obtained."

Despite the negative outcome, the case made Babcock a national name in legal circles. "People read about it, and other attorneys started to raise the issue, and it mushroomed from there," she said. "I developed this very bizarre expertise on the representation of foreign nationals."

It was this expertise that led the Mexican government to contact Babcock at the Public Defender Office and led her to a new position, running her own firm and as the first director of the Mexican Capital Legal Assistance Program, where she would remain for the next six years. The goal of the program was to track Mexico's efforts on behalf of its nationals arrested in the United States in a centralized manner, co-ordinating all of the Mexican government's efforts to assist its nationals throughout the United States.

The Mexican Capital Legal Assistance Program was the latest in a long history of Mexican assistance for nationals on death row. Since 1829—when Mexico enacted its first law governing the foreign service—consular officials have been required to provide assistance to arrested and detained Mexican nationals. As of 2003, Mexico operated forty-five Mexican consulates across the United States, serving more than ten million Mexican nationals. This consular system has been described as "the most extensive consular presence of any country in the world." Even the United States has recognized that the consular services provided by Mexico are "extraordinary."

Mexico has also taken steps to protect its rights in US courts. It has sought relief on its own behalf for violations of Article 36, but US courts have consistently decided that neither Mexico nor its consular officers have standing to vindicate their rights under the Vienna Convention in federal courts. Additionally, Mexico has filed friend of the court briefs in cases invoking both the convention itself and the *LaGrand* decision. For example, in the 1997 case of Mario Murphy, a Mexican citizen on Virginia's death row for his part in a murder-for-hire plot, Mexico filed a brief urging the US Supreme Court to review the case. It also sent letters to Virginia governor George Allen, offering to transfer Murphy to Mexico to be jailed there if the governor would commute his sentence. Allen declined. Mexico reached out to the State Department, asking it to join in asking Governor Allen for clemency. This request was rebuffed. This pattern was repeated numerous times all across the country. As of 2003, courts had not provided relief. Finally, Mexico has made numerous overtures to the United States through diplomatic channels, attempting to obtain the assistance of the federal executive branch to obtain a remedy, without any meaningful results.

Another example was that of Gerardo Valdez Maltos, a Mexican national on death row in Oklahoma. Valdez was arrested in Oklahoma in 1989 and was provided with his *Miranda* rights and all the other procedural protections provided by the US Constitution, including appointed counsel. He was convicted and sentenced to death. Six different courts reviewed his conviction and sentence. Despite the failure to provide him with his rights under the Vienna Convention, none found any deficiencies in the process. Yet Mexico was able to demonstrate that his sentence was unjust.

Mere weeks before his execution, Valdez, with the assistance of the Mexican government, submitted a clemency petition to then governor Frank Keating. Governor Keating reviewed the clemency petition and met with representatives of the Mexican government who had flown to Oklahoma City to personally plead Valdez's case. Governor Keating sent a letter to Mexican president Vicente Fox, noting that after his review, he concluded that any prejudice to Valdez was small and was outweighed by other factors.

But Governor Keating provided a thirty-day stay of the execution to allow Mexico an opportunity to seek further legal and diplomatic relief. As a result of Mexico's efforts, the Oklahoma Court of Criminal Appeals determined that Valdez was entitled to resentencing. Mexico's participation and the new evidence it uncovered were clearly the basis of the Oklahoma court's decision. But Mexico's involvement did not end there. Mexico recruited a large law firm in Washington, DC, to represent Valdez at the resentencing hearing. This firm, along with Mexico, "vigorously lobbied the prosecutor to waive the death penalty." Thanks to these efforts, the prosecutor did so, and Valdez pled guilty in exchange for a life sentence.

While Mexico recognized that the US criminal justice system provides several procedural safeguards designed to ensure fair trials and equal treatment, Mexican consular officials, supported by numerous studies, have also found that Mexican nationals arrested in the United States face many barriers. Among those barriers are culture, language, and competence, which prevent them from receiving an effective defense. Ethnic stereotypes also have a tendency to affect their cases at every step of the process.

Mexican consular officials have found that those Mexican nationals arrested and charged with capital crimes face many challenges. In addition to living in poverty, they are often illiterate. Despite many having spent years in the United States, they may not speak English with any fluency. It is also not uncommon for them to speak an indigenous Mexican language rather than Spanish. Oftentimes, these nationals have suffered from malnutrition, which has affected their mental capacity; this often goes unrecognized by appointed counsel or police or is attributed to cultural differences.

The first priority of Mexican consular officials is to ensure that their nationals receive effective legal counsel. According to the Mexican government, because they often live in poverty, Mexican nationals residing in the United States usually end up with appointed counsel, and the attorneys assigned to represent them lack the experience and resources necessary to provide an adequate defense. Many of these attorneys do not speak Spanish, which hinders their ability to converse with their clients or their clients' families, which in turn can impede their ability to acquire mitigating evidence. Mexico has noted that, unfortunately, quality legal representation is the exception rather than the rule in capital cases when counsel is court-appointed. Mexico has been successful at petitioning courts to replace inexperienced or incompetent counsel, or has itself recruited quality counsel to represent Mexican nationals on a pro bono basis. It has even gone so far as to retain counsel on their behalf.

Mexican consular officers are instructed to provide funds to capital defense counsel to hire investigators and experts. Mexico has hired bilingual psychologists, neuropsychologists, and investigators in dozens of cases. Consular officers serve as a "cultural bridge" between the defendant and his lawyer, working with defendants' families and friends to uncover information vital to the defense. Mexican nationals are often confused or distrustful when they encounter the US legal system. For example, the concept of plea bargaining, which is common in the United States, is utterly unknown in Mexico. In addition to working with defense counsel and district attorneys to negotiate pleas, consular officials can help explain to a Mexican national the benefit of accepting a deal that takes the death penalty off the table. They can also assist with tracking down records and other documents that may only exist in Mexico.

Another area where consular assistance is vital is in ensuring adequate translation services. Because many Mexican nationals living in the United States speak indigenous languages, a Spanish-speaking translator may be of limited use. Even in cases where the defendant speaks Spanish, the Mexican government has encountered translators who were inadequate. Accurate translation is key to an effective defense. Mexican consular officials can ensure that appropriate translations are provided.

In just one example, the Nevada Supreme Court ordered review in a capital case in 2012 due to poor translation services. In the case of Carlos Pérez Gutiérrez, the Nevada Supreme Court found that a state-provided interpreter misinterpreted key phrases of testimony during the penalty phase of the trial, which resulted in the jury returning a sentence of death. The interpreter misrepresented his qualifications and certifications to the trial court and was eventually prosecuted for perjury for those statements. Because there was only a stenographic transcription of the trial, as opposed to an audio recording, the extent of the mistranslations could not be ascertained. But the Nevada court found that the involvement of the Mexican consulate could have prevented this mistake.

Consular officials can often identify whether a Mexican national is suffering some form of mental impairment, a condition that can be a key mitigating factor, particularly in a capital case. The failure to note or diagnose such a condition can therefore be the difference between life and death.

The need for consular assistance is most vital prior to trial. As Sandra Babcock would one day tell the ICJ, "Perhaps the most critical decision a detained foreign national will ever make is whether to give a statement to the police. Shortly after his arrest, the police will sit him down in a room, and will begin asking him questions." Oftentimes, a *Miranda* warning is read at a speed that makes it difficult to understand if English is not the listener's first language. Additionally, the police have the sole discretion to determine whether an arrestee speaks "enough" English to be interrogated without an interpreter. According to Babcock, "If he speaks, however, the prosecution can and will use his statement as the centerpiece of its case—particularly if he confesses to a crime." Consular assistance before interrogation helps ensure that foreign nationals, including Mexican nationals, do not say things they do not mean, or sign statements they do not understand. Given the importance of the decision to speak with the police, consular assistance is vital at this stage.

Consistent with other death penalty cases that later led to exonerations in the United States, the Mexican government has encountered cases in which Mexican nationals have signed false confessions. One example involved Omar Aguirre, who was falsely accused of murder in Chicago. After three days of interrogation by the Chicago Police Department, Aguirre signed a document that he believed was a release allowing him to go home. Instead, the document, which was written in

English, a language he barely spoke, was a confession. As a result, he was wrongfully convicted and sentenced to fifty-five years in prison. He served five years of that sentence before he was finally released.

In another example, Ignacio Gomez signed a confession that was written in English and contained legal terminology and advanced vocabulary. Yet just two years before his arrest, despite attending school in the United States for nine years, Gomez was unable to speak or write in English. This fact was not disputed by the government when it was brought to its attention. In such cases, consular assistance is vital to ensure that Mexican nationals do not inadvertently sign statements they do not understand.

Early consular assistance is especially important in capital cases because the prosecutor makes the decision whether to seek the death penalty early in the process. This decision is never mandatory—there is always discretion. Mexico has seen great success in convincing prosecutors not to seek the ultimate penalty by meeting personally with district attorneys or even through the simple expedient of sending a letter expressing Mexico's views on the case. Additionally, Mexico is able to procure mitigating evidence, which can influence prosecutors just as easily as judges and juries. For this reason, the ability to develop such evidence as early as possible is vital to persuade prosecutors not to seek the death penalty in the first place.

According to statistics compiled by the Mexican government, between September 2000 and June 2007, in over 140 cases where Mexican consular officials were promptly informed of an arrest in a capital crime, the prosecutors waived the death penalty. As a result, Mexico's consular protection emphasizes early intervention. These experiences demonstrate that, when consular protection is allowed to function as intended by the Vienna Convention, a life sentence, not death, is the likely outcome. When consular protection was delayed or denied, in contrast, the death penalty was far more likely.

There is also a pernicious aspect of the failure of police officials to inform foreign nationals of their rights under Article 36. Because foreign nationals usually are unaware of their rights, they are also unaware of the need to raise the violation of those rights at trial, leading to the application of the procedural default doctrine. Under this doctrine, if a Mexican national—or any foreign national—does not raise a claim at trial relating to the United States' violation of his Vienna Convention rights, he will not be permitted to raise it either on direct appeal or in any subsequent postconviction proceedings, such as habeas corpus. Prior to 2003, every US court to consider the issue had applied the doctrine, denying any relief to Mexican and other foreign nationals whose rights under the convention were violated.

As part of her duties as director of the legal assistance program, Babcock traveled to Texas and met with every Mexican national on death row. One of those Mexican nationals was José Medellín. At the time Babcock met him, his appellate lawyers, Gary Taylor and Mike Charlton, had raised a claim that Medellín's rights under the VCCR had been violated when Texas police failed to inform him that he had a right to speak with someone at the Mexican consulate. At the time, these claims were raised by arguing that an accused's counsel had been ineffective in failing to raise the issue at trial and seeking appropriate relief, including suppression of any confessions or statements. Another aspect of the argument was that trial counsel also failed in not notifying the consulate that one of its nationals was under arrest. In Medellín's case, as in many others, the argument was unsuccessful, largely based on the failure to raise the claim in a timely manner. But that was before Sandra Babcock and the government of Mexico arrived on the scene.

As part of her work at the Mexican Capital Legal Assistance Program, Babcock helped identify over fifty Mexican nationals who were residing on death row in several US states, all of whom had been denied notification of their right to contact the Mexican consulate prior to speaking with the police. "The government of Mexico was a client," Babcock said. "And after a time it was virtually my only client because the program grew over time." By 2002, Babcock and the Mexican government had a plan. They would bring a lawsuit against the United States in the ICJ for numerous violations of the VCCR.

CHAPTER 5

The World Court Weighs In

On January 9, 2003, having acceded to the Optional Protocol concerning the Compulsory Settlement of Disputes to the Vienna Convention on Consular Relations (VCCR) for this purpose, Mexico filed suit against the United States in the International Court of Justice (ICJ) in The Hague. The Optional Protocol, at the time ratified or acceded to by forty-seven member nations, provides that the ICJ has compulsory jurisdiction over disputes arising under the VCCR. Parties agree to consent to the jurisdiction of the ICJ and to abide by its rulings on the meaning of the treaty.

Established in 1945, the International Court of Justice is the principal judicial organ of the United Nations. It was established to be a forum where states could try to resolve disputes, especially those dealing with treaty interpretation. It replaced the Permanent Court of International Justice, which had been in operation since 1920. The ICJ, also known as the World Court, is housed in the Peace Palace. Built in a Neo-Renaissance style in 1913, this building is the heart of The Hague, which has come to symbolize international law and justice. The palace has a large clock tower on the left side and a shorter tower at the back-right corner. The building would not look out of place on a New England college campus.

Mexico's suit argued that the United States had failed to uphold its obligations under Article 36 of the Vienna Convention, by failing to timely notify detained Mexican nationals of their right to contact the Mexican consulate, and for failing to provide such notification to Mexico, resulting in fifty-four Mexican nationals being sentenced to death in numerous US states. Among those specifically mentioned by Mexico was José Ernesto Medellín.

At the same time Mexico filed suit, it filed a request for provisional measures, an order from the court instructing the United States to take all steps necessary to ensure that no Mexican national named in the petition was executed and that no action would be taken that might prejudice the rights of Mexico or its nationals. Essentially, Mexico asked to maintain the status quo until a judgment could be rendered by a competent court. The ICJ held a public hearing on the provisional measures on January 21 and issued an order granting Mexico's request on February 5.

The United States has appeared before the ICJ twenty-five times since 1948 as both complainant and respondent. Perhaps the most famous of these cases was *United States v. Iran*, also known as *United States Diplomatic and Consular Staff in Tehran*, a case arising under Article 36 of the Vienna Convention on Consular Relations, the very provision at issue in Mexico's case. There, the United States sued Iran for invading the US embassy in Tehran and holding the diplomatic and consular staff hostage for more than a year during the Iranian Revolution.

Mexico, on the other hand, had never brought a case before the ICJ. In fact, despite being one of the earliest signatories of the convention, it didn't join the Optional Protocol giving the court jurisdiction until March 2002, less than a year before it filed suit against the United States. To this day, the suit brought on behalf of Avena and other Mexican nationals is the sole case that Mexico has brought in the ICJ. Years of ignored protests and a lack of success in the domestic legal system of the United States had finally come to a head in Mexico.

Mexico filed two documents with the ICJ in January 2003. First, it laid out arguments about the United States' treatment of fifty-four of its nationals in a forty-nine-page application to institute proceedings. These Mexican citizens had been arrested, tried, convicted, and sentenced to death, all without receiving notification of their rights under the convention.

Mexico noted that it had taken numerous steps to try to remedy the violations of the convention before it filed suit in the ICJ. It had intervened in judicial proceedings on behalf of its nationals, started its own original actions in US courts, and lodged repeated diplomatic protests with the government of the United States in an attempt to vindicate its own rights and the rights of its nationals.

Having failed to achieve its goals through legal and diplomatic channels within the United States, Mexico turned to the ICJ, seeking restitutio in integrum (literally restoration to original condition), an international law term meaning reestablishment of the situation as it would have in all probability been, had the violations not been committed. In other words, Mexico sought an order from the ICJ declaring the convictions and sentences of the fifty-four named nationals to be invalid, resetting the cases to the very start. In addition, Mexico wanted any confessions obtained prior to an Article 36 notification to be suppressed. Mexico also requested prospective relief necessary and sufficient to ensure that future violations would not recur.

In its second document, Mexico asked the court to order the United States to delay the executions of any Mexican nationals named in its complaint until the ICJ issued its decision on the merits of the case. The application for provisional measures identified at least four specific individuals who were facing imminent execution. One of them, César Roberto Fierro Reyna, who was on Texas's death row after being convicted of murdering a cab driver in El Paso, faced the possibility of a February 14 execution date, just thirty-six days from when Mexico filed its complaint. On Tuesday, January 21, the court heard oral arguments on Mexico's request for those measures.

Five individuals spoke on behalf of the government of Mexico. Two of the key players, who would continue to represent José Medellín throughout his case, were Sandra Babcock and Donald Francis Donovan, a graduate of the University of Virginia and Stanford Law School, and a partner at the leading New York law firm of Debevoise & Plimpton. Donovan is an internationally recognized expert in international law, a longtime representative of the government of Mexico in the United States, and a former clerk to Supreme Court justice Harry Blackmun.

Donovan argued that the United States could not rely on its federal structure to avoid enforcing its commitments under the VCCR. The United States, including its political subdivisions, is bound by its international obligations, and in any case, the supremacy of federal law over state law includes treaty law. At any rate, the ICJ should not concern itself with internal US law. "This Court is here to vindicate the Vienna Convention and its own Statute, not to enforce United States municipal law."

The United States then spoke in response. The lead representative of the United States was William Howard Taft IV, legal adviser at the Department of State. Taft is the great-grandson of William Howard Taft, the twenty-seventh president and the tenth chief justice of the United States. He graduated from Yale University with a bachelor's degree in English and earned his law degree at Harvard. Although Taft was a veteran of several Republican administrations and several years in private practice, this was his first appearance before the ICJ.

Catherine Brown also argued on behalf of the United States. Brown began her career in the State Department's Office of the Legal Adviser in 1985. She had previously represented the United States at the ICJ in cases brought by Paraguay (*Breard*) and Germany (*LaGrand*). At the time, she was one of the most, if not the most, senior US government attorneys on issues of treaty interpretation and enforcement.

The ICJ issued its decision on provisional measures on February 5, 2003. All fifteen judges voted unanimously to provide Mexico the protections it sought. Given the international community's views on the death penalty and the United States' history with Article 36, this surprised no one. In light of the fact that any execution would cause irreparable prejudice to any rights that Mexico may later be held to possess, the court felt it was appropriate to order the United States to ensure that no executions of named Mexican nationals be carried out until the court issued its final judgment. The ICJ also took the opportunity to clarify that its provisional measures orders were not mere suggestions but also constituted binding legal obligations of the States appearing before it. Following the issuance of provisional measures in *LaGrand*, the United States had taken the position that such measures were nonbinding. The ICJ clarified that that interpretation was incorrect.

Having issued the provisional measures requested by Mexico, the case now turned to the merits of Mexico's case. In the United States, parties typically file briefs laying out their respective sides of the argument. Plaintiffs or petitioners—the ones bringing suit—file first, then the defendant or respondent files a response, and then the plaintiff/petitioner files a reply. In the ICJ, the documents filed by the parties are called a memorial and counter-memorial, respectively. While the parties may file other documents, such as comments, rejoinders, or replies, in this case Mexico and the United States agreed to limit submissions to only the memorial and counter-memorial.

On June 20, 2003, Mexico submitted its memorial. It clocked in at

189 pages and was accompanied by a voluminous appendix consisting of three volumes containing sixty-six annexes and running over 1,400 pages. The United States responded on November 3, 2003, with a 249-page counter-memorial and an even larger set of annexes. The United States submitted two volumes totaling nearly 2,500 pages.

Mexico's memorial proceeded in six parts. After a brief introduction and discussion of the court's jurisdiction to hear the case, Mexico provided a statement of facts. It then turned to the legal arguments. Initially, Mexico argued that the United States violated two provisions of Article 36. First, by failing to notify Mexican nationals of their rights under the convention without delay, it violated Article 36(1). Second, by applying its domestic law, also known as municipal law, in a manner that failed to give full effect to the purpose of Article 36, largely through the use of the "procedural default" doctrine, the United States violated, and continued to violate, Article 36(2). As part of this argument, Mexico strongly argued that clemency was not sufficient to remedy Article 36 violations under *LaGrand*.

Mexico next argued that these dual breaches of Article 36 resulted in fundamentally unfair criminal proceedings. Finally, Mexico turned to the relief to which it believed it was entitled, namely, full reparations. The form of these reparations was threefold: (1) Mexico sought a declaration that its rights and the rights of its nationals were violated; (2) Mexico sought restitutio in integrum, a reestablishment of the status quo ante had the violations not occurred (in Mexico's eyes, this required nothing less than the vacatur of the convictions and sentences, the suppression of evidence, and the prevention of the application of any municipal law bars); and (3) Mexico requested cessation of ongoing violations of the convention and guarantees of nonrepetition from the United States. In the case of Medellín, this would mean reversing his conviction, suppressing the confession he gave to the Houston Police Department, and trying him again without that evidence.

The United States' counter-memorial contained nine sections. After an introduction, the United States offered its own statement of facts. It detailed the guarantees of due process provided by the US criminal justice system, regardless of a defendant's nationality, before concluding with a summary of the United States' good faith efforts to enforce the convention. The next two sections of the United States' counter-memorial made procedural arguments. First, the United States argued that the court lacked jurisdiction to hear many of Mexico's claims. Second, the United States asked the court to find significant aspects of Mexico's application and submission inadmissible.

The counter-memorial then argued that the *LaGrand* judgment set forth the applicable principles governing the dispute between Mexico and the United States. While acknowledging that ICJ judgments are binding only on the parties before the court and do not necessarily have precedential value, the United States had conformed its conduct to the requirements of *LaGrand*, and since the violations alleged here were identical, there was no basis for treating the matters differently.

The United States' counter-memorial then got to the meat of its argument. The United States stated that it complies with all of its obligations under Article 36 of the convention—namely, the United States provides consular notification "without delay," which the United States interpreted to mean within the ordinary course of business and without deliberate delay or inaction. Furthermore, the United States provided "review and reconsideration" both through the criminal justice system and through the clemency process. It argued strongly against Mexico's arguments that Article 36(1) creates rights that are fundamental to due process.

Under Article 36, the Mexican consulate is notified only upon the request of the national. If the national is informed of his rights and declines, there is no need to notify the Mexican authorities. Thus, the mere failure to inform Mexico is not evidence of an Article 36 violation. The counter-memorial concluded its argument with a defense of the clemency process as a means of meaningful "review and reconsideration." The final argument is more defensive. It argued that if the court finds a breach of Article 36, it should only provide the remedy granted in *LaGrand*: "review and reconsideration." The other remedies requested by Mexico were beyond what was necessary or required by the convention.

At the time Mexico filed its initial complaint, it identified a total of fifty-four Mexican nationals who had been sentenced to death after Article 36 violations. However, during the course of its investigations while putting together its memorial, Mexico discovered that one of the identified Mexican nationals held dual US citizenship and thus was outside the reach of Article 36, and another had in fact been informed of his Article 36 rights prior to interrogation. Thus, between the time the United States filed its counter-memorial and the start of oral arguments in the case, Mexico withdrew its complaint relating to those two nationals.

On Monday, December 15, 2003, at 10:00 a.m. in the Peace Palace at The Hague, the chief judge at the ICJ, known as the president, Shi Jiuyong, called the court to order to hear the case of *Avena and Other Mexican Nationals (Mexico v. United States)*. Before welcoming the parties, President Shi took care of some administrative matters. First, he noted that Judge Bruno Simma, the German judge who had joined the court in 2003, had recused himself from the proceedings. Judge Simma had served as a co-agent and counsel to Germany on the *LaGrand* case. Because there was a judge from the United States on the court, Mexico exercised its right under Article 31 of the Statute of the International Court of Justice to choose a Mexican judge to sit ad hoc. Mexico chose Bernardo Sepulveda, a well-respected Mexican jurist and former secretary of foreign relations, as well as the Mexican ambassador to both the United States and the United Kingdom.

Then began four days of oral argument before the ICJ. There are conflicting views on arguing at the World Court. According to Sandra Babcock, it is "the most wonderful experience in the world." Located in the Peace Palace in The Hague, Netherlands, "the place where you argue is called the Great Hall of Justice." Babcock described the experience: "It's one of those magnificent, high-ceilinged rooms that is decorated with art that has been donated by the various member states of the United Nations. And you just . . . you really do feel like you are in the World Court." In describing the atmosphere, she said, "It feels very gospel and at the same time, it feels like a court that really cares about justice. . . . It is really a very special feeling."

It's also quite different than arguing in a US court. "Our arguments went on for an entire week," Babcock said. "Whereas in an appellate court here, you're going to get twenty or thirty minutes max, even in the US Supreme Court, in the ICJ we had a full day to present our side, and the US had a full day to present its arguments, and then we got half a day of rebuttal." These differences provide both benefits and drawbacks. While the parties are given more time to present their case, they aren't able to respond on the fly. "The challenge of arguing in the ICJ is that you have to write it down, you have to write it all out," Babcock recalled.

You have to have a written transcript for the interpreters because it's all being simultaneously interpreted. . . . You can deviate from it slightly. But you can't just go off on something that strikes you at the moment, go off on a tangent. The interpreters won't be able to competently interpret what you're saying. So that makes it really challenging when you actually have to craft every single word before you speak it.

It is this latter aspect that turns off some advocates. One member of the US team, who spoke on condition of anonymity because he wasn't cleared to speak on the record, said that speaking at the ICJ was not challenging or satisfying: "There's nothing spur of the moment. One person gets up and reads a prepared statement, and the next person gets up and reads, and they read the whole day." The judges did not pay much attention either. "There were [fifteen] judges sitting up there and over the course of the week that we were there, there were only two judges that were not asleep, at least a significant part of the time," the US team member said.

Another thing that made the argument challenging was a lack of sleep and, in Babcock's case, a head cold. "We were pulling very, very late nights" preparing for the argument, she said. "Before we actually finished the memorial, we all pulled an all-nighter to finalize it. And the same thing for the argument. I remember, I was very sick, I had a terrible, terrible cold, and was just physically exhausted by the time we got to The Hague. I was completely dosed up on cold medicine."

Both parties were represented by a large group of individuals. While some were the same people who spoke at the hearing on provisional measures, both sides substantially supplemented their rosters. Each side had five representatives at the provisional measures hearing; this time there were eighteen speakers, among whom were international law professors. For the United States, Stephen Mathias was in charge of recruiting these luminaries. One reason for this, according to a member of the US team, is that "there is a received wisdom that at the ICJ you had to have at least one person argue in French or the French judge would automatically vote against you."

Ambassador Juan Manuel Gómez Robledo led off for Mexico, addressing the court in French. He stood at the podium between two long tables occupied by the two parties—his colleagues on one side of him, the representatives of the United States on the other. About twenty feet in front of him, on a raised dais with blue carpet, the fifteen judges of the ICJ sat in a long line behind the slightly curved bench. Mexico was not asking the court to dictate the legal means through which the United States complied with its obligations under Article 36, he told the judges. Instead, Mexico merely sought to ensure that the legal means chosen gave full effect to the Vienna Convention as required by Article 36. The means, he argued, must not be allowed to elevate municipal law over international law. Thus, while the United States was entitled to its choice of means, it had a corresponding obligation to achieve a result founded in law.

He noted that Mexico had supplied ample and abundant evidence that the training programs dealing with Article 36 compliance of which the United States was so proud are at best applied "haphazardly, in random fashion, and have not produced any significant change" in the United States' compliance with the Vienna Convention. Although Ambassador Gómez Robledo did not provide details in his oral presentation, Mexico's memorial provided evidence that Article 36 warnings were provided in just 17.49 percent of cases in which they were warranted, a truly dismal figure.

He concluded his presentation by noting that Mexico was seeking three complementary remedies: the restoration of the rights that Mexico holds on its own behalf; the rights of its nationals as they existed before any violation of the convention; and the effective guarantee that such violations will not be repeated in the future.

Sandra Babcock then stepped up to the podium. In this portion of the argument, Babcock laid out the facts by focusing on the people at the heart of the case. "Fifty-two indigent Mexican nationals are, as we speak, sitting in small, windowless cells on death rows around the United States," she began after introducing herself. She pointed out that nine of these individuals were teenagers at the time of their arrest, and many of the fifty-two had little or no formal education. Consular assistance, she argued, could have meant the difference between life and death.

In contrast to her attempts to humanize the nationals on death row, Babcock minimized the crimes for which they were convicted, noting that the details were entirely irrelevant. The underlying crimes have no bearing on their rights under Article 36. The convention does not draw distinctions; it applies whenever a foreign national is arrested.

Donald Francis Donovan stood up next to discuss the United States' violations of Article 36(1) of the convention. According to Donovan, the Vienna Convention on Consular Relations required the United States to provide notification of the right to consular access immediately upon the arrest or detention of a foreign national and prior to any interrogation. This was in sharp contrast to the United States' position that notification was required "within the ordinary course of business," which usually means twenty-four to seventy-two hours after arrest or detention. Even accepting this interpretation, a complete failure to notify, or to wait until after trial, sentencing, or even initial appeals would be unacceptable. Yet that it was happened in twenty-nine of the fifty-two cases identified by Mexico.

Mexico contended that the requirement that notification happen "without delay" meant prior to any interrogation. To hold otherwise, especially in capital cases, denied the defendant the benefits of consular assistance precisely when that assistance would do the most good. Article 36 is addressed to the criminal process, and thus it must be viewed in that context, Donovan argued. The context indicates that notification must happen upon arrest, before anything else occurs. In order for Article 36 to have any utility, the foreign national must be informed of his or her rights to consular assistance, and have the ability to invoke that right, prior to interrogation, when the foreign national is most vulnerable. The Inter-American Court of Human Rights came to that very conclusion when Mexico requested its judgment in 1999.

Donovan also pointed out that the individual right protected by Article 36(1)(b) was inextricably intertwined with the State's right to provide assistance under Article 36(1)(c). Mexico is not able to provide consular assistance unless it is informed that its nationals request such assistance. And those nationals may not be aware of their right to make such a request unless the authorities inform them. Thus, Article 36 confers rights on foreign nationals and their States, while imposing an obligation on the arresting State.

According to Donovan, Mexico provides an easily applied and objective standard, which all law enforcement officers and courts can understand, as opposed to the US standard, which is subjective and discretionary.

Mexico's standard would also be easy to implement. The United States would have two options to ensure Article 36 compliance. First, it could follow State Department guidance to determine whether someone is a foreign national whenever there are objective indications that such is the case. Or, even easier and more certain, it could provide the same warning to everyone, letting them know that if they are a foreign national, they have the right to contact their consulate. Law enforcement officers could simply add this to the standard *Miranda* warnings they already provide to detained individuals. In fact, several jurisdictions within the United States already did this. While Donovan did not provide specific examples as part of his argument, Mark Warren of the Human Rights Research Center has identified six states with laws that require consular notification: Illinois, California, Oregon, Nevada, North Carolina, and Florida. Interestingly, all six allow the death penalty.

Donovan acknowledged that if the foreign national deliberately misrepresented that he or she possessed US citizenship, there would be no obligation to provide the notification. But if the authorities received objective indications of foreign nationality, then the obligation for immediate notification would arise at that point. According to Donovan, the State Department already provided this guidance to law enforcement authorities in the United States.

In its counter-memorial, the United States complained that Mexico's standard would allow the indefinite delay of interrogation if the consulate tarried in deciding whether to provide assistance. Article 36, after all, does not *require* consular assistance.

Donovan concluded this discussion by looking to the practice of other States. He noted that ten States had adopted rules or practices that delay interrogations until after foreign nationals are given an opportunity to invoke their rights. There is demonstrable evidence that Mexico's interpretation would not hinder law enforcement. Legal systems regularly strike a balance between the interests of public safety and individual rights.

Mexico's morning presentation ended with Katherine Birmingham Wilmore, from Debevoise & Plimpton's London office, arguing that the United States violated Article 36(2). Under the provisions of Article 36(2), the United States is required to accommodate the rights guaranteed by Article 36(1) within its municipal law and to provide an effective remedy in the event of a breach. According to Birmingham Wilmore, the second aspect is arguably more important than the first because "a right without a remedy is no right at all."

But this was how the United States treated consular rights under Article 36—it did not attach *any* legal significance to breaches of the convention and did not allow Mexican nationals to bring effective legal challenges in their criminal proceedings when their rights are violated. Yet the ICJ had already determined that the procedural default doctrine violated Article 36(2) in *LaGrand.*

Birmingham Wilmore noted that the United States admitted that its courts would not grant relief to Mexican nationals solely on the basis of a Vienna Convention claim, at either the trial or the appellate level, and would apply procedural default doctrines at both the state and federal levels to bar such claims if they were not raised in the trial court. She stated, "These are the very facts on which Mexico has based its claim for relief under Article 36(2)."

The judicial noncompliance with the requirements of Article 36(2), Birmingham Wilmore argued, demonstrated that the United States did not accept the importance of that article's requirements. It purported to elevate its municipal law over and above its international obligations to comply with Article 36, which it was not allowed to do. While the Vienna Convention does respect the municipal laws of signatory countries, it does not allow them to use those laws to thwart the convention's ends.

She concluded her argument by noting that the United States is not conducting "review and reconsideration" through the judicial system. Instead, it had made the conscious choice to focus its efforts on the clemency process.

Sandra Babcock returned to the podium in the afternoon to discuss the inadequacy of the clemency process as a means of satisfying the requirements of "review and reconsideration" called for in *LaGrand.* She quoted the US Supreme Court, which in 1998 referred to a clemency petition as "simply a unilateral hope." According to Babcock, the *LaGrand* decision demanded more. *LaGrand* called for "review and reconsideration" of both the sentence *and* the underlying conviction. But in the vast majority of capital cases, the clemency authorities could only look at whether the sentence of death should be commuted to something less severe. They did not review the conviction. More important, no state had *ever* pardoned a death row inmate based on a proven violation of Article 36.

Turning to Texas, where José Medellín was on death row, Babcock told the court that the Clemency Board refused to hold hearings on applications and did not hear testimony from live witnesses. In fact, the board did not meet, even by conference call, to discuss the merits of individual petitions. Instead, its members vote individually by fax, sent to the board's central office.

Moreover, clemency review in death penalty cases is strongly influenced by political considerations. The ultimate arbiter in many states, the governor, is subject to election. Needless to say, Babcock told the ICJ, commutations are not popular with voters.

Carlos Bernal, the chairman of the Commission on International Law at the Mexican Bar Association, spoke next about Article 36 as a guarantor of due process. This question had already been addressed by the Inter-American Court of Human Rights. While not binding on the ICJ, it could consider that opinion, he said, as well as the near-universal recognition and affirmation that it had attracted throughout the world. The United States and six other members of the Organization of American States had participated in the proceedings before the Inter-American Court.

Donovan returned to the podium. He pointed out that in *LaGrand* the ICJ had determined it was "immaterial" whether the LaGrands would have sought consular assistance; whether the German consulate would have provided any assistance; or whether, if so, that assistance would have affected the outcome. All that was required was that the LaGrands had been denied the chance to exercise their rights. Thus, the United States' arguments that Mexico could not demonstrate prejudice were irrelevant.

Donovan then turned the floor over to his colleague at Debevoise & Plimpton in New York, Dietmar Prager, to discuss the prospective remedies Mexico sought—cessation of violations and a guarantee of nonrepetition.

Mexico did not deny that the United States had taken all the steps it listed in its counter-memorial, and that it did so with the best of intentions. But the measures taken are not what counts—results are. And, Prager pointed out, since the ICJ decided *LaGrand*, the program designed and implemented by the United States had failed to prevent the repeated and continued violation of Article 36 by the competent law enforcement authorities in the United States. Of course, Mexico recognized, perfect compliance is impossible. But to find more than one hundred violations in two years, and in the wake of the court's judgment in *LaGrand*, was simply unacceptable and gave rise to a "worrying near-certainty" that such violations would continue into the future.

Of more concern was the United States' interpretation of its obligation under *LaGrand*, which represented a "deliberate decision" to continue to apply doctrines, such as procedural default, which prevented Mexican nationals from obtaining the appropriate "review and reconsideration" in a court of law. "In other words, Mr. President," Prager pointed out, "nothing has changed since the *LaGrand* case."

Oral arguments resumed at 10:00 a.m. Tuesday, December 16. First up for the United States was State Department legal adviser William Howard Taft IV. He began by reminding the court of what it had held in the *LaGrand* case, just two and a half years earlier: that when there was a failure to provide consular information and notification under Article 36 and a foreign national is subsequently convicted and sentenced to a severe penalty, the remedy was for the breaching State to provide "review and reconsideration," through means of its own choosing, and taking account of the violation.

He laid out a powerful argument that no State party to the convention had ever understood the convention to require what Mexico claimed, and that no State party had ever provided the relief Mexico sought. He noted that the United States had taken steps to conform its conduct to the court's interpretation of the convention in *LaGrand*, not just with respect to German nationals but in regard to all foreign nationals detained or arrested in the United States.

Professor Elisabeth Zoller, of the University of Paris, spoke next about the court's jurisdiction and the admissibility of Mexico's claim. A Parisian native, Professor Zoller addressed the court in French. She told the court that even well before *LaGrand*, the United States had a robust program to help all fifty states comply with its obligations under the Vienna Convention. In the wake of that decision, the government had continued to work with police, prosecutors, and judges to explain the importance of consular notification. It also had taken steps to ensure that, in the event a violation occurred, competent state authorities would weigh that violation as a factor during clemency proceedings.

Next to speak was Patrick K. Philbin, associate deputy attorney general from the Department of Justice, who described the due process protections provided to all criminal defendants in the US system. Philbin's argument was that, in the United States, criminal defendants receive due process protections that ensure a fair trial whether they are citizens or foreign nationals and whether they receive consular assistance or not.

In practice, many foreign nationals facing criminal trial in the United States receive no consular assistance even when notification is provided. Neither the convention nor general international law requires a State to provide assistance to its nationals who face prosecution in a foreign land, and limited resources provide restraints on what assistance can be offered. Simply put, the US criminal justice system does not depend on consular assistance as "the guarantor of fairness to non-US nationals."

Philbin then turned to Mexico's proposed rule that interrogations should not occur until after the consular official has had an opportunity to meet with his or her national. He argued that even if prompt notification occurs, there is no basis to assume that the consular officer will respond quickly. Given that there is no requirement to provide assistance in any given time frame, such a rule would require the police and other investigatory authorities to delay for days or even weeks until the consulate was ready to provide assistance. Such a rule would be impossible for any criminal justice system to deal with.

President Shi then recognized John Byron Sandage, attorney-adviser for United Nations affairs at the US Department of State to speak. He argued that where "review and reconsideration" of an Article 36(1) violation had occurred or could occur, Article 36(2) inherently could not be breached. In several of the cases identified by Mexico, "review and reconsideration" had already occurred. Sandage pointed to eleven cases in which the Vienna Convention issues were extensively litigated and where the courts concluded a violation had occurred but determined that no prejudice resulted from the breach. In other cases, defendants made a choice not to raise the issue. Only in some of the cases did notification occur too late in the process to be raised in the courts.

Turning to Mexico's argument that it had identified 102 cases of non-compliance in the wake of *LaGrand*, Sandage pointed out that this is a mere fraction of the number of Mexican nationals, numbering in the thousands, who have cases involving serious crimes moving through the criminal justice system on a daily basis. Furthermore, of those 102 cases, only 6 had even the remote possibility of resulting in a capital sentence. Moreover, in those cases the United States identified individuals claiming to be US citizens or dual nationals, as well as those who had been informed of their rights to seek consular assistance and chose to decline. It also identified several cases where notification was requested and provided the very same day, and in all cases well in advance of trial.

The court called on Catherine Brown to speak about the proper interpretation of Article 36(1). Specifically, Brown addressed Mexico's argument that the phrase "without delay" in Article 36(1) meant "immediately and before interrogation."

She examined the text, object, and purpose of Article 36(1) as well as the subsequent practice of States and determined that Mexico's reading was not supported in any way. In fact, she argued, Article 36 had nothing to do with interrogation of a foreign national and certainly did not require any interrogation to cease while Article 36 procedures were completed.

Mexico's demand that interrogation not occur until after the provision of consular assistance would lead to absurd results, particularly since, as others had mentioned, there was no corresponding obligation to *provide* assistance. This would allow a consulate to hold a criminal justice system hostage based on resource limitations and consular priorities. Finally, it may not be clear a detained individual is a foreign national until an interrogation has begun.

Stephen Mathias concluded the morning's presentation for the United States. He spoke on the appropriate interpretation of Article 36(2). In looking to that provision, he indicated that it had a bifurcated structure—it stated a general rule and then a proviso that limits that rule. Under the general rule, the rights referred to in Article 36(1) are to be exercised in accordance with the municipal laws of the receiving State, which includes laws within the criminal justice system. Parties to the Convention were not required to pass new laws or create new procedures or judicial doctrines in order to comply with their obligations under the Convention. This rule, Mathias argued, is an "insurmountable obstacle" to Mexico's position.

According to Mathias, the import of this general rule is clear:

obligations under the Convention cannot be interpreted in such a way that would lead to the conclusion that existing laws and regulations would generally violate Article 36. The language of the treaty is that the rights contained in paragraph 1 "shall be exercised in conformity with the laws and regulations of the receiving State. . . ." Because States agreed to be bound consistent with their laws, any interpretation of the article must allow for their general application.

The proviso serves as a limitation on the general rule—that the domestic laws of a signatory State must allow full effect to be given to the purposes of the article. What are the purposes of Article 36? The convention states that Article 36 is designed to "facilitate[e] the exercise of consular functions relating to nationals of the sending State."

According to *LaGrand*, the United States has the choice of means to ensure remediation of any Article 36 violations. If the United States chooses a nonjudicial means of remedying any such violation, it is in compliance with its obligations. And, both parties appear to agree, if the United States provides "review and reconsideration" that complies with *LaGrand*, it is not in violation of Article 36(2). According to Mathias, the laws and regulations of the United States *are* structured to provide what the court had previously required.

James H. Thessin, the principal deputy legal adviser at the State Department, a career State Department lawyer, and a veteran of the *LaGrand* case, took the floor. Mathias had concluded the morning by telling the court that the US system provided for "review and reconsideration" as required by *LaGrand*. Thessin opened the afternoon by providing details on how that "review and reconsideration" played out in both the criminal justice system and the clemency process.

Thessin began his presentation by noting that *LaGrand*'s requirement for "review and reconsideration" in each case implied the possibility that such review would result in the same outcome—a conviction and sentence of death. Mexico's requirement for the reversal of convictions would make individualized "review and reconsideration" pointless. What *LaGrand* called for, according to Thessin, was "a specified remedy of process . . . not a particular substantive outcome."

Twenty minutes into his argument, Thessin fainted and fell back from the podium. Quick-thinking members of Mexico's team helped cushion his fall, and medical aid was called in. Sandra Babcock remembered the incident. "The lawyer for the United States, he was the assistant legal adviser, is actually a very nice guy. During his argument, he became dizzy," Babcock recalled. "He lost his balance and fell back and was caught by the legal adviser for the government of Mexico and had to take some moments to recover. It was quite dramatic and worrisome." According to one member of the US team, Thessin suffered from a seizure disorder. He described the scene differently. "He was reading, he was standing there, and his speech just got slower and slower and slower until finally he just stopped and he was standing there at the podium." Thessin was escorted from the courtroom by members of the US delegation to a room set aside for counsel. Paramedics came and checked him out, but he refused to go to a hospital.

The court resumed proceedings, wishing Thessin well and calling on Thomas Weigend, professor of law and director of the Institute of Foreign and International Criminal Law at the University of Cologne, to speak about the remedies Mexico sought as they related to criminal procedure.

He noted that the remedies Mexico called for not only would require far-reaching changes within the United States' criminal justice system but also would be in "open conflict" with the criminal procedure laws of most of the world. Professor Weigend contrasted Article 36 and criminal procedure rules, noting that Article 36 protects not just criminal defendants but all nationals detained for any reason. In contrast, criminal procedure applies to every suspect, regardless of nationality, providing them with certain basic rights. While the two may sometimes overlap and the provision of consular services may, on occasion, enhance a suspect's procedural prospects, that is not the purpose of Article 36. Having consular assistance is not a legal prerequisite to receiving a fair trial, and the availability of such access does not have any direct impact on the correctness of a judgment or sentence. "Put simply," Professor Weigend told the court, "Article 36 of the Vienna Convention does not confer criminal process rights."

Turning to the question of the procedural default rule, Professor Weigend stated that several legal systems, including those of the United States and Mexico, sharply circumscribed the availability of appeals alleging procedural errors. These legal systems all required early protest of procedural defects.

Professor Zoller returned to the podium to discuss what remedy would be appropriate. In the eyes of the United States, "review and reconsideration" was the answer. Both this case and *LaGrand* arose from the same alleged violation of international law. Mexico had failed to demonstrate that *LaGrand*'s remedy did not provide it with the relief to which it was entitled.

So what did "review and reconsideration" look like? According to Professor Zoller, reconsideration applies to the facts of the case. Thus, to comply with *LaGrand*, there must be a procedure that answers the following questions: "Have the facts been properly analyzed? Can we be sure that there has been no manifest error as to the facts? Have all the necessary precautions been taken at the evidence-gathering stage?" Answering these questions does not require vacating convictions.

As to Mexico's claims that the "review and reconsideration" called for by *LaGrand* necessitates judicial review, Professor Zoller opined that if the court had meant that, it would have said it. Administrative review, including through the clemency process, is "an essential part of the tradition of the rule of law and it forms, together with appeal court proceedings, one of the elements of the due process required by the rule of law." Both systems, judicial and executive, are regarded as equally efficient. The system of clemency provided for by all the states of the union meet the requirements of *LaGrand*.

Following Professor Zoller's presentation, the court took a twenty-minute recess. When the judges took the bench again, they were greeted by Thessin, who had returned from his visit with the medics.

"When one gets before the Court," he told them, "one generally has one's blood pressure go up, not down." After reassuring the court that he was recovered, thanking it for its courtesy, and thanking all those in the courtroom for their assistance, he asked the court to allow Taft to substitute in his place. This request was granted, and Taft stepped to the podium to continue Thessin's presentation.

After summarizing the points Thessin made earlier in the day, Taft reassured the court that every foreign national had the chance—during both direct appellate review and the habeas process—to demonstrate how the failure to provide him with consular notification denied him due process or affected the fundamental fairness of his trial. Furthermore, procedural default rules were common around the world, and the court had previously held that they do not, in themselves, violate Article 36(2).

Despite Mexico's focus on the doctrine, in only eight of the fifty-two cases did a US court determine that the Article 36 claim had been defaulted due to a failure to timely raise it. But in most of those cases, the courts either evaluated the harm by determining if the defendant was prejudiced, despite the default, or they reviewed other, related claims on the merits.

Taft concluded by noting that the criminal justice system of the United States allowed for "review and reconsideration" as required by the ICJ. Both the courts and executive officials "unquestionably provide careful, meaningful and fair review and reconsideration of either the consular violations themselves or the effects of any Article 36 violation on the fundamental fairness of the proceedings." Where the United States and Mexico differed was that the United States did not believe the relief required by *LaGrand* could be judged by the result that it reached.

The Mexican team spent Wednesday preparing its rebuttal for Thursday morning. Because of the need for translations into various languages for the judges, the team was required to prepare its talking points, in the form of a written transcript that the members would read from, and the interpreters would provide a simultaneous translation as they spoke. Babcock reflected on the experience. "The night before the rebuttal argument, I pulled an all-nighter. I think most of us did. I think I slept thirty minutes. And I got up and argued on no sleep, which is not something I'd advise anyone to do."

On Thursday, December 18, 2003, Ambassador Gómez Robledo rose for the last time in support of his country's argument that the United States had violated Articles 36(1) and (2) of the Vienna Convention on Consular Relations. He opened his presentation by noting that the United States and Mexico were in agreement on a major point: the *LaGrand* judgment was the standard to rely on in this case. But the United States would only conform its conduct to *LaGrand* as it understood it. Simply put, "It would appear that the United States has adapted the *LaGrand* decision to its conduct rather than adapting its conduct to *LaGrand*."

Babcock spoke next about the facts, causation, and clemency. She asked the court to conclude that the United States had violated both

Article 36(1) and (2) in all fifty-two cases because it failed to notify each defendant, without delay, of his right to contact his consulate. She told the court that it was irrelevant whether the Mexican nationals would have contacted the consulate if they had known of their right to do so. In any event, Mexico provided statements from forty-two nationals in which they confirmed they would have exercised their rights if they had known of them.

Donovan spoke next. He responded to the United States' arguments regarding the interpretation and application of Article 36. He argued that if the ICJ remained true to its judgment in *LaGrand*, this was an easy case. He told the court that *Avena* was "on all fours" with *LaGrand*, a legal term meaning that the two cases were factually and legally identical from the court's view, regardless of any dispute over the meaning of "without delay" or when it comes into play.

But on that point, Donovan believed Mexico had the better argument: that "without delay" was synonymous with "immediately." He looked to the purpose of the communication and contact protected by Article 36 —he asked to what end they were granted. The court answered that in *LaGrand*; Article 36 is "designed to facilitate the implementation of the system of consular protection." Those rights are held not just by the State but by the foreign national as well. And the right to assistance includes the right to help in retaining private counsel and otherwise assisting in the defense of the foreign national.

At 3:00 p.m. the following day, Taft rose on behalf of the United States to begin the last of the oral arguments in the *Avena* case. Like the Mexican team the previous day, the American team had spent the rest of Thursday and through Friday morning preparing its presentations.

Patrick Philbin presented rebuttal about the United States' judicial process and its ability to provide the "review and reconsideration" called for in *LaGrand*. He argued that what *LaGrand* demanded was a *process*—a process through which a criminal defendant could receive an individualized determination whether the breach of Article 36 had any impact on his conviction or sentence and whether that impact could provide a basis for changing the sentence or reconsidering the conviction. That process does not guarantee an outcome. It does not assume that an Article 36 breach will lead inexorably to some negative impact on the conviction or sentence. Instead, it reflects an assumption that such a breach may have had no effect whatsoever. "The whole point," Philbin said, "is simply to examine the conviction and sentence in light of the breach to see whether, in the particular circumstances of the individual case, the Article 36 breach did have some consequence—some impact—that impinged upon fundamental fairness and to assess what action with respect to the conviction and sentence that might require." Absent any prejudice, no further action is necessary.

James Thessin next spoke to the court regarding clemency. Thankfully, he had no further health issues during his presentation. Responding to Sandra Babcock, Thessin told the court that clemency procedures are part of the US criminal justice system, although the United States has never claimed it was part of the judicial process or that it needed to follow judicial rules of procedure. Rather, clemency is designed to supplement the judicial review process. It also has the benefit of being free of any court-created doctrines, such as procedural default, which allows clemency to "fill in any gaps" left by judicial proceedings.

He concluded by telling the court that Mexico's complaints about the clemency process only make sense if the court accepts Mexico's proposition that it is entitled to only one result—the reversal of convictions and death sentences. If *LaGrand* mandates a process, and not a result, as the United States contended, then Mexico will not always receive the result it wishes. But that does not mean that it has not obtained the process that the United States is required to provide.

———

In most US courts, the timing of a decision's release is a complete surprise to the parties, who are not notified in advance on what day a decision will be issued. At the US Supreme Court, the only time one can be sure of a decision's issuance is the last day of the term, when the Court releases any outstanding opinions. The ICJ does not work like that. It informs the parties in advance of the specific date that it will release the decision in their cases. Here, the parties were informed that the decision in *Avena* would be released the last day of March.

On March 31, 2004, representatives of the Mexican government and the United States reconvened in the Great Hall of the Peace Palace to hear the judgment of the ICJ.

The court began by noting that the criminal proceedings about which Mexico complained had taken place in nine different states between

1979 and 2004. Turning to the merits of Mexico's complaint, it began by examining Mexico's arguments that the United States had violated its rights and the rights of its nationals under Article 36(1).

The ICJ stated that the dispute over Article 36(1) between the two parties really came down to two issues: (1) the question of the nationality of the individuals concerned and (2) the question of the precise meaning of the phrase "without delay." As a subdispute of the second, the parties argued over whether the obligation arose upon arrest, or only once the arresting State knew or had reason to know that it had arrested a foreign national.

The court found that Mexico bore the burden of proof to show that the Mexican nationals on whose behalf it brought suit did in fact hold such nationality at the time of their arrest. To meet this burden, the court observed that the Mexican government had produced birth certificates and declarations indicating such nationality and the United States did not challenge the contents of those documents.

It then addressed the question of when, precisely, that duty arose. According to the ICJ, "The duty upon the detaining authorities to give the Article 36, paragraph 1(b), information to the individual arises once it is realized that the person is a foreign national, or once there are grounds to think that the person is probably a foreign national." The court recognized that in those cases in which the arrestee falsely claims US nationality, the recognition of foreign nationality will likely come later in the proceedings.

The court next turned to one of the more contentious disputes between the parties—the meaning of the phrase "without delay." It began its analysis of this question by holding that the United States may not assume to know what any particular arrestee might prefer. The right to deny consular notification lies solely with the detainee, not the arresting officials. Thus, in each case where a warning was never provided, the duty to inform "without delay" was violated. All that remained for the court to decide was whether violations also occurred in those cases where a warning was given.

The ICJ acknowledged that the Vienna Convention itself does not define the term "without delay." It also noted that the convention uses both that term in Article 36 and the term "immediately" in Article 14. The different language versions of the convention use various terms to render these phrases, and dictionary definitions in each language provide diverse meanings for both terms. The object and purpose of the convention is to allow consular officers to communicate with and visit detained nationals of their State. But it does not envision those officers themselves acting as legal representatives for their nationals or directly engaging in the criminal justice process. Thus, contrary to Mexico's arguments, neither the text of the treaty nor its object and purpose would lead to an interpretation of "without delay" to mean "immediately upon arrest and before any interrogation."

Therefore, the court held that it was not a per se violation to conduct an interrogation of the arrested foreign national prior to informing them of their Article 36 rights. Nevertheless, there is a duty upon the arresting officers to provide information about those rights to an arrested person as soon as the authorities realize the person is a foreign national or once there are grounds to think he or she is probably a foreign national.

While the decision did not lay down a bright line as to how long States had to provide such information, it did hold that when an individual's Mexican nationality was apparent from the outset of his detention, the United States violated its obligation to inform him "without delay" of his rights under the Vienna Convention when it waited forty hours. On the other hand, in examining the question of the meaning of "without delay" in the context of notifying the Mexican consulate, the court held that the United States did comply with its obligations when it informed the Mexican consulate of the arrest of a Mexican national five calendar days (corresponding to three working days) after the arrest was made.

The court reiterated its holding from *LaGrand* that the rights protected by Article 36(1) are interrelated and that the legal conclusions drawn from that interrelationship will necessarily depend on the factual circumstances of each case. Here, because of the United States' failure to inform the Mexican nationals of their rights under Article 36(1)(b), Mexico was prevented from exercising its rights under Article 36(1)(a) to communicate with its nationals and have access to them. "It is immaterial," the court stated, "whether Mexico would have offered consular assistance, 'or whether a different verdict would have been rendered.'" It was enough that the rights protected by the convention might have been acted upon. The same is true for the rights protected by Article 36(1)(c), which provides consular officers the right to visit with their nationals being held in custody.

However, when it comes to some rights protected by Article 36(1)(c), particularly the right to arrange for legal representation, the exercise of those rights does not depend on official notification in compliance with the convention. If the consulate becomes aware of the detention of its nationals either in an untimely manner or through some other means, the home State may still be able to vindicate its rights under this sub-paragraph. That was the case for sixteen of the fifty-two nationals.

The court ended its discussion of Article 36(1) by making four conclusions: (1) that the United States committed breaches of its obligations under Article 36(1)(b) to inform detained Mexican nationals of their rights for fifty-one of the fifty-two named nationals, including José Medellín; (2) that the United States breached its obligations under Article 36(1)(b) to notify the Mexican consular post of the detention of forty-nine of the named nationals, including José Medellín; (3) that as a result of these breaches, it also violated its obligations under Article 36(1)(a) to enable Mexican consular officers to communicate with and have access to their nationals, as well as its obligations under Article 36(1)(c) regarding the right of consular officials to visit with their nationals, including in the case of José Medellín; and (4) that the United States, by breaching Article 36(1)(b), also violated Mexico's rights under Article 36(1)(c) to arrange for legal representation for its nationals in thirty-four of the listed cases, including José Medellín's.

It then turned to the parties' contentions surrounding Article 36(2) of the Vienna Convention on Consular Relations, specifically the question of the application of the procedural default rule.

The ICJ began by reiterating its findings in *LaGrand* that the procedural default rule did not, in itself, violate the Vienna Convention. It only becomes a problem when the rule does not allow a detained individual to raise a claim that his rights were violated when the competent authorities of the United States breached their obligations under Article 36. In *LaGrand*, the ICJ found that the procedural default rule, as applied, violated Article 36(2) because it prevented the LaGrands' attorneys from raising claims under the convention. It appeared to the court that the same was true in the present case.

The decision noted the procedural default rule has not been revised in the United States or any of its subjurisdictions and that it could continue to prevent courts from attaching legal significance to the violation of the Article 36 obligations when it has been invoked. This prevents full effect from being given to the purposes of the rights under Article 36(1) as required by Article 36(2). However, because the nationals in forty-nine of the cases at issue had not exhausted their remedies, there was still a chance for courts to provide the "review and reconsideration" called for in *LaGrand*. "It would therefore be premature," the court stated, "for the Court to conclude at this stage that, in those cases, there is already a violation of the obligations under Article 36, paragraph 2, of the Vienna Convention." As to the final three cases, the municipal courts of the United States had utilized the rule to prevent consideration of the Article 36 violations, and they had no further judicial remedies to seek. In those cases, the ICJ concluded the United States violated Article 36(2).

The Court then addressed the final question before it: What remedies were appropriate for the breaches of the Vienna Convention it had found?

The ICJ looked back to a 1927 case from its predecessor, the Permanent Court of International Justice, which held that it was a principle of international law that the breach of an obligation demands reparation in an adequate form. What this constitutes varies depending on the circumstances of the breach, but it must, to the maximum extent practicable, "'wipe out all the consequences of the illegal act and reestablish the situation which would, in all probability, have existed if that act had not been committed.'"

As far as reparation for violations of Article 36, the appropriate remedy was for the United States to permit "review and reconsideration" in its domestic courts, with a view to ascertaining whether any actual prejudice to the defendant resulted from the violation that affected his conviction or sentence. The ICJ recognized that this case did not focus on the correctness of those convictions or sentences. But the question to be addressed was whether the breaches of Article 36, in a causal manner, ultimately led to the convictions and severe penalties. It was up to the municipal courts to determine if this causal connection exists, examining the facts, any prejudice, and whether that prejudice was traceable to the violation.

Contrary to Mexico's request, neither partial nor total annulment of convictions or sentences "provides the necessary and sole remedy." This is because the convictions and sentences themselves are not the violation of international law. It was solely the breaches of the treaty obligations that preceded those convictions and sentences that constituted the violation.

The court refused to decide whether the rights contained in the Vienna Convention constituted human rights because it was unnecessary to reach a decision. It did, however, note that nothing in the text, purpose, or historical materials surrounding the Vienna Convention supported Mexico's arguments to that effect.

It similarly disposed of Mexico's contentions regarding the exclusionary rule. The court felt that it was unnecessary to decide whether such a rule was a general principle of international law. Rather, the court was of the opinion that the question of its application was one that needed to be examined in the "concrete circumstances of each case by the United States courts concerned in the process of their review and reconsideration." Thus, even if those courts were to find prejudice arose from the breaches of Article 36, the ICJ was not prepared to require any specific remedy.

The court took a different tack when it came to the procedural default rule. While recognizing that the *LaGrand* judgment allowed the United States to choose the means of the required "review and reconsideration," in this case it noted that "this freedom in the choice of means . . . is not without qualification." The remedy of "review and reconsideration" must meet four criteria to satisfy international law: it must be effective, it must take account of violation of the rights set forth in the convention, it must guarantee that the violation and possible prejudice caused by it will be fully examined and taken into account during the process, and it must review both the sentence and the conviction. Anything less was unacceptable.

Mexico's claim in this case was not about harm to a right essential to a fair trial. It was a case of violating Article 36. These are rights guaranteed by the Vienna Convention that the United States freely entered into and promised to uphold, irrespective of any due process rights under the US Constitution. "In this regard, the Court would point out that what is crucial in the review and reconsideration process is the existence of a procedure which guarantees that full weight is given to the violation of rights set forth in the Vienna Convention, whatever may be the actual outcome of such review and reconsideration." In this respect, the court agreed with the United States that no specific outcome was required. "Review and reconsideration" very well may result in a finding that the violation did no harm, and the conviction and sentence would be affirmed.

The court then held that whatever means the United States chose to vindicate the required "review and reconsideration," it was the judicial process, rather than clemency, that is best suited to this task. This was an unstated assumption in *LaGrand*, which the court now made explicit. While the ICJ recognized the integral role clemency plays in the US criminal justice system, the question before it was whether that process as actually practiced by the different states "qualif[ies] as an appropriate means for undertaking" the process required by *LaGrand* in an effective manner. The court answered that question in the negative. It determined that the clemency process is "not sufficient in itself to serve as an appropriate means of 'review and reconsideration' as envisaged by the Court in the *LaGrand* case."

The ICJ next determined that Mexico had failed to establish that the United States was continuing to violate Article 36 in respect of the fifty-two individuals listed in the memorial. Therefore, it would not order cessation. Instead, it reminded the United States that those fifty-two defendants were still entitled to pursue remedies in the United States and that those remedies should conform to this judgment.

The court took note of the submissions of the United States regarding its efforts to comply with Article 36. It confessed that continuing violations of these rights in the wake of *LaGrand* was certainly something to be concerned about, but it specifically recognized the "considerable efforts" the United States had undertaken to ensure that its local law enforcement authorities provided consular information to every known or suspected foreign national at the time of their arrest. The ICJ acknowledged that the United States was making good faith efforts to increase its compliance with its international obligations. It suggested, for the second time, that the United States may wish to consider offering conditional Article 36 rights as part of the *Miranda* warnings. The court also stated that it believed that its comments regarding the continuing applicability of *LaGrand* suffices to satisfy Mexico's request for "guarantees and assurances of non-repetition."

The court concluded its discussion by noting that, while the facts of this case focus on the question of Mexican nationals subject to the most severe penalties available in the criminal justice system, its decision addresses broad principles under the Vienna Convention. In other words, no one should imply that the conclusions reached do not apply to other foreign nationals who find themselves in similar situations in the United States. While the court did not directly address the question of less severe penalties, it would appear that the logic would apply regardless of what penalties a defendant faced. The Vienna Convention certainly does not draw distinctions based on the reasons for arrest.

Having completed its analysis of the legal issues, the ICJ issued its judgment. It unanimously ordered that going forward, any Mexican nationals who are sentenced to severe penalties following Article 36 violations must be provided, according to means of its own choosing, "review and reconsideration" as further elaborated on by the court in its judgment.

By a vote of 14 to 1, the court found that the United States violated the rights of fifty-one Mexican nationals under Article 36(1)(b) when it failed to notify them, without delay, of their right to contact the Mexican consulate; that the United States also violated the rights of Mexico in forty-nine cases when it failed to inform the Mexican nationals of their rights under Article 36(1)(b); that the United States violated Mexico's rights under Article 36(1)(a) and (c) to communicate with its nationals in forty-nine cases when it failed to notify the Mexican consulate of the arrest of those nationals in a timely manner; that the United States denied Mexico's rights under Article 36(1)(c) to arrange for legal representation of thirty-four Mexican nationals; that the United States had denied "review and reconsideration" to three Mexican nationals who had completed the appellate process; and that the appropriate reparation in each case was to provide "review and reconsideration," by means of its own choosing, of the convictions and sentences, taking account of both the violation of the rights under Article 36 and as modified by its judgment. In every instance in which José Medellín was listed, the court found that his rights were violated.

In addition to the judgment of the court, six of the fifteen judges wrote separately to note differences with the reasoning of the court's decision. However, most of those differences were minor matters that did not affect the overall outcome. Judge Peter Tomka of Slovakia took issue with the court's holding that the duty to inform a foreign national of his rights under the Vienna Convention only arose once the arresting State knew or suspected foreign nationality. He was concerned that if such a view were to be applied in more areas of international law, it could weaken protection accorded to certain subjects, notably children. According to Tomka, Article 36's obligations arose immediately upon arrest. No knowledge is required. The arrest is an "objective fact sufficient in itself to activate" the State's obligation. Much as in domestic law, ignorance is not a defense to wrongfulness. Only an affirmative claim of US nationality would overcome the presumption that a foreign national is entitled to notification of his or her rights under Article 36.

Ad hoc Judge Sepulveda filed a lengthy separate opinion, running thirty pages, nearly half the length of the court's judgment. He regarded many of the court's conclusions to be unsatisfactory, particularly where the question of remedy was concerned. He believed that the court's judgment in *Avena* retreated from the clarity the court had created when it decided *LaGrand*. He argued that the court provided clear guidance in the earlier case but examined the same questions in a "totally different light" in the present case. The evidence presented showed that domestic courts, even in the wake of *LaGrand*, continued to apply the procedural default rule to deny claims under the Vienna Convention. Here, the invocation of the rule is particularly pernicious because the failure to raise the Article 36 claim can be directly attributed to the breach of Article 36 itself. The post-*LaGrand* practice of the United States demonstrates that it had no interest in providing the "review and reconsideration" required for violations of Article 36.

When it came to Article 36(1)(c), the court gave short shrift to the importance of legal assistance that the consulate is allowed to provide under the convention. Because the role of legal assistance is so important, any action taken prior to receiving the benefit of expert legal advice is "potentially detrimental to [a defendant's] rights." Judge Sepulveda agreed with Mexico that the notification required by the Vienna Convention "should be given immediately and prior to interrogation ... if the exercise of the right is to be useful."

Judge Sepulveda looked to the *Miranda* warnings as a corollary to the Article 36 rights. The US Supreme Court recognized that *Miranda* warnings were vital at the earliest stages to protect due process, and that among those rights was the right to counsel. Thus, consular protection may be an important element to guarantee due process of law, particularly in capital cases. While it is true the rights protected by Article 36 are procedural, Judge Sepulveda argued that violations of those rights may have a profound effect on the due process of law. Thus, these rights should be considered fundamental to due process. Therefore, the denial of these rights subjected these Mexican nationals to fundamentally unfair criminal proceedings.

If the United States is to be left to provide a remedy "by means of its own choosing," the court must provide more concrete guidance and specific measures that the United States must implement. The court's direction must introduce an element of effectiveness that is "mandatory and compulsive" in order to ensure proper enforcement of Article 36. In this case, Judge Sepulveda suggested that the rights protected by the Vienna Convention "should be considered as belonging to the category of fundamental rights that impinge on due process of law." Specifically, he believed that the court needed to be clearer that the procedural default rule was not to be allowed in the process of "review and reconsideration." It may even be necessary to rescind the rule through a legislative enactment. Otherwise, there is "little future" for meaningful judicial "review and reconsideration."

Finally, Judge Gonzalo Parra-Aranguren of Venezuela wrote to explain his dissenting votes on many of the court's holdings. In this case, he noted that Mexico acknowledged it had the burden of demonstrating that violations of Article 36(1)(b) occurred in all fifty-two cases. He did not believe that it met its burden. His decision was based on an important but highly technical point. He believed that Mexico had failed to prove that the fifty-two defendants were Mexican nationals. Mexico had argued that under Article 30 of the Mexican Constitution, all fifty-two individuals were Mexican citizens by virtue of being born in Mexico. The problem, Judge Parra-Aranguren pointed out, is that Mexico never entered any evidence to show what Article 30 of the Mexican Constitution said. Under international law, national law is generally viewed as a fact that must be proved in court. Mexico had failed to meet its burden of proof. Therefore, any claims depending on a showing of Mexican nationality must fail.

At the end of the day, the United States was quite pleased with the outcome. Although the ICJ ruled against it, the court did not order any greater remedy than that required by *LaGrand*. While the court did rule out clemency as a valid means of conducting "review and reconsideration," it still left the nature of a judicial remedy up to the choice of the United States.

According to Sandra Babcock, "The US government was thrilled with the *Avena* judgment when it came down. I talked to the State Department lawyers who were there; they thought this was a great judgment because it didn't give Mexico what it had asked for." She described the judgment as very conservative, calling it the huge irony of the case. Ambassador Gómez Robledo disagreed. He said that, in general, "we were very much satisfied with the ruling.... The ruling went beyond the *LaGrand* judgment on a number of points.... In particular, it gave new hope and legal means for taking back cases to the initial criminal proceedings in domestic jurisdictions." Of course, he recognized that Mexico did not get everything it asked for, and that the real impact of the decision would turn on how the United States decided to implement it. He stated, "Our legal team had foreseen from the very beginning that the battle would need to be continued in the U.S."

It was the reality of implementation that so dismayed Babcock. "My heart sank," she recalled, "because I thought, 'well, that's what they're going to do, they're just going to provide these sham reviews' where they end up denying relief to everyone. I thought it would be an easy thing for them to do to comply with this judgment. And the United States recognized that as well." Despite her initial dismay, however, she was determined to press on and try to wring every positive outcome from the *Avena* judgment that she could. That would result in two trips to the US Supreme Court.

A Ray of Hope

With a win from the International Court of Justice (ICJ) fresh in hand, the Mexican team went looking for one of the fifty-two named nationals whose case was in the right procedural posture to bring before the US Supreme Court. They found José Medellín. "We would never have chosen José to be the person to test these principles of international law," Sandra Babcock said. "But you know, in this world, you cannot pick your plaintiff."

Babcock's choice would have been Osvaldo Torres, a Mexican national convicted and sentenced to death in Oklahoma. Ironically, her advocacy was too effective to allow this to happen. The Oklahoma Court of Criminal Appeals stayed Torres's execution, ordering a new hearing based on the *Avena* decision. Just a few hours later, Brad Henry, the governor or Oklahoma, granted clemency to Torres, commuting his sentence from death to life in prison. Because the *Avena* decision applied only to inmates on death row, Torres was no longer covered by its mandate. So, Babcock went looking for someone else. José Medellín was the next name on the list.

Medellín had filed a petition seeking a writ of habeas corpus in November 2001 and amended it in July 2002. In his amended petition he raised five issues, including the claim that his rights under Article 36 of the Vienna Convention on Consular Relations (VCCR) had been denied, along with claims of ineffective assistance of counsel, lack of an impartial jury, improper use of peremptory strikes by the prosecution, and the withholding of exculpatory evidence. The federal district court denied his requested relief and had also denied him the right to file an appeal, called a certificate of appealability (COA), as required by the Antiterrorism and Effective Death Penalty Act (AEDPA) of 1996. This denial was itself appealable, and Medellín's lawyers, Gary Allen Taylor and Michael B. Charlton, filed an appeal with the Fifth Circuit Court of Appeals. They raised several issues, two of which were related to the denial of Medellín's rights under the Vienna Convention. On May 20, 2004, less than two months after the ICJ issued the *Avena* judgment, the Fifth Circuit issued its opinion denying relief.

Medellín's appeal was almost perfect from a procedural standpoint, for several reasons. First, Texas conceded it had failed to notify him of his rights under Article 36. Second, the court of appeals ruled on two key issues: first, the application of the procedural default doctrine; and second, whether Article 36 created an individual right that was enforceable in domestic courts. It ruled against Medellín on both issues, relying almost entirely on the fact that it was bound by prior precedent. Thus, Medellín's case directly raised the two issues the Court had previously addressed in its 1998 decision *Breard v. Greene*. Because the lower court relied on *Breard* in its ruling, it was the perfect vehicle for asking the Court to overrule its earlier decision in light of *Avena*.

The procedural default doctrine exists to protect the integrity of lower court decisions and to speed the process of review. The basic idea is to try and limit criminal defendants to one bite at the appellate apple. Following conviction, every criminal defendant is entitled to an appeal as a matter of right. Appeals act as a relief valve to correct any errors made by judges and juries. But review takes time and, especially in death penalty cases, causes delays. To minimize those delays, the system incentivizes criminal defendants to raise all their issues at once, so that appellate courts can address them and allow sentences to be carried out. This allows closure for victims' families and preserves state court resources by preventing numerous subsequent appeals.

The procedural default doctrine holds that a criminal defendant's failure to raise an issue in a timely manner waives that issue for all time. Exceptions are few and far between and are typically limited to the creation of new law following the criminal defendant's appeal as of right. If the Supreme Court recognizes a new constitutional protection that did not exist at the time of the appeal, a criminal defendant may, in certain circumstances, file a subsequent appeal, asking a court to apply the new right to the defendant. In Medellín's case, as well as that of the other fifty-one nationals named in *Avena*, states argued that no such exception applied. While *Avena* may have provided a new interpretation of the Vienna Convention, they argued, the right to consular notification itself had existed since the convention was ratified. Therefore, claims under it were susceptible to procedural default. In bringing his subsequent appeal, Medellín's lawyers argued that *Avena* was a new right that did not exist when Medellín filed his initial appeal. They also argued that *Avena* expressly held that the procedural default doctrine, as applied to Vienna Convention claims, was itself a violation of international law. The Fifth Circuit rejected both arguments.

In discussing the application of the procedural default doctrine, the court of appeals recognized the *Avena* decision, as well as *LaGrand*, but held that it was bound by *Breard*. There, the Supreme Court ruled that Vienna Convention claims could be procedurally defaulted, even in cases involving the death penalty. While the panel acknowledged that *Breard* predated the ICJ's decisions, the court determined it was nevertheless bound by Supreme Court precedent. "Only the Supreme Court may overrule a Supreme Court decision."

Even assuming the claim was not procedurally barred, the panel also held that Article 36 of the convention does not create an individual right, something the ICJ had clarified in both *LaGrand* and *Avena*. Here, the court pointed to an earlier Fifth Circuit case in which another three-judge panel, again prior to the ICJ's decision, had determined that no such individual right existed. Under Fifth Circuit precedent, a later panel is bound by an earlier panel's decision on the same legal question either until the whole court overrules the prior panel in an en banc decision or until the Supreme Court says otherwise. Based on these prior rulings, the Fifth Circuit felt it had no choice but to affirm the district court and deny Medellín's appeal.

On August 18, 2004, Donald Francis Donovan filed a petition for writ of certiorari, asking the Supreme Court to hear José Medellín's case. In the petition, Donovan presented two questions Medellín wanted the Court to answer. First, must a domestic court apply the *Avena* judgment in the case of one of the named nationals, notwithstanding the existence of contrary US precedent, without resort to procedural default doctrines? Second, in a case brought by a foreign national of a State that is party to the Vienna Convention, should a court in the United States give effect to the *LaGrand* and *Avena* judgments as a matter of comity?

Comity, in the legal context, occurs when a domestic court gives recognition to the decision of a foreign tribunal. It does this not out of any constitutional requirement but out of a recognition of goodwill toward foreign legal systems. It is a largely reciprocal relationship in which courts recognize each other's judgments in the interests of judicial economy. If two parties have an opportunity to fairly litigate a dispute, the argument goes, they should not have to relitigate it in a second set of courts. Courts in the United States agree to this arrangement so that, were the situation reversed, foreign courts would respect their judgments as well.

In arguing that the Court should take the case, Donovan pointed out that the ICJ expressly adjudicated Medellín's rights in making its decision. In fact, in all four areas where the ICJ found Article 36 violations, it specifically included Medellín in its findings. The ICJ found that the United States breached Article 36 when it failed to inform Medellín and others of their rights under the VCCR; that it denied Mexico the right to provide timely intervention in Medellín's case, as well as others; that it denied Mexico the right to communicate with and have access to Medellín and others; and that it denied Mexico the right to arrange for legal representation of Medellín and others.

Donovan argued that because the United States voluntarily entered into the Vienna Convention and its Optional Protocol, the *Avena* judgment was a "binding adjudication" of Medellín's rights under the convention, which a domestic court could not second-guess. In order to help the United States avoid breaching a commitment it voluntarily undertook, Medellín argued the Court should take the case to overrule *Breard* and any Fifth Circuit decisions holding that Vienna Convention rights were not individually enforceable.

Donovan was concerned about two things. As a representative of the government of Mexico and, in this case, José Medellín, he was arguing that the United States should take seriously its duty to Mexican nationals visiting or residing in the United States. But in a way, he was also arguing on behalf of US nationals who travel, live, and work abroad. Much of international law works only by mutual agreement and reciprocal treatment. If the United States did not respect the rights of foreign nationals under the convention, it could hardly expect other nations to respect the rights of Americans abroad.

In support of the petition, friend of the court briefs, known as amicus briefs, were filed by six groups, including the Mexican government; the

European Union; other foreign nations; Amnesty International; experts in international law; and a group of individuals and organizations, including Ambassador L. Bruce Laingen, who had been held in the US embassy in Tehran following the Iranian Revolution, Bill Hayes, an author who had been held for five years in a Turkish prison, who wrote *Midnight Express*, which became a major motion picture, and lawyers and interest groups involved in consular protection.

The State of Texas, representing Warden Doug Dretke, the named respondent in the case, filed a brief in opposition, filed by Texas Assistant Attorney General Gena Bunn, the chief of the Postconviction Litigation Division. Texas's brief opened with a description of Medellín's crime, a common tactic of state officials defending court decisions in death penalty cases. After laying out the facts as summarized by the Texas Court of Criminal Appeals, Bunn argued that the questions presented were unworthy of the Court's attention. Under the AEDPA, a petitioner seeking a COA must make a "substantial showing of the denial of a constitutional right."

No amici filed briefs supporting Texas's position at the petition for certiorari stage. This may well have been a strategic decision. Studies by political scientists who focus on the Supreme Court's process have found that the more briefs filed by friends of the court, the more likely a petition is to be granted, even if a number of those briefs oppose the grant. The theory is that amicus interest signals the case is salient and thus may be worth the Court's time. Instead, amici that support respondents in Supreme Court cases tend to find they get a better result filing briefs at the merits stage, only after the Court has already decided to hear the case.

———

When the Court is in session, justices meet on Fridays to review petitions and discuss any oral arguments it heard that week. The nine justices go alone into a conference room on the main floor of the Supreme Court building, just outside the chambers of the chief justice. No one else is allowed in the room. Any notes are taken by the justices themselves. The chief justice puts together a list of petitions that he believes may be of interest to the Court, called the "Discuss List." While it takes the vote of five justices to make most decisions at the Supreme Court, the decision to hear a case requires that only four justices agree. The

Court considered Medellín's petition on three successive weeks, on November 24, December 3, and December 10. This is not unusual and has recently become the norm. Finally, on December 10, 2004, the Court issued an order granting the petition and agreeing to hear the case. The case was set for oral argument on Monday, March 28, 2005.

On January 24, 2005, Donovan filed the opening brief of the petitioner. The brief's fact section opened with a description of the Vienna Convention and a brief history of its drafting, a short summary of the United States' ratification history, and an update on the then current status of the treaty. It noted that the United States was the first nation to invoke the Optional Protocol to hale another nation before the International Court of Justice when it sued Iran over its taking of hostages in 1979.

It then turned to a summary of the decisions by the lower courts. While noting that Medellín was arrested "in connection with two murders in Houston, Texas," it did not otherwise go into the underlying crime. Instead, it focused on the fact that Medellín had informed both the arresting officers and Harris County Pretrial Services that he was born in Mexico and was not a US citizen, and yet he did not receive notification of his rights under Article 36. The brief notes that Mexico did not become aware of Medellín's arrest, detention, trial, conviction, and sentence until April 29, 1997, six weeks after the Texas Court of Criminal Appeals had affirmed his conviction and sentence.

Donovan framed the issue before the Court as follows: "This case is about the willingness of the United States to keep its word. This Court must ensure that the courts of the State of Texas and other state and federal courts throughout the land comply with the legally binding international commitments that, by the constitutionally prescribed processes, the United States has made."

The brief made three legal arguments. First, it contended that rights created by treaty are binding and judicially enforceable as a matter of domestic law. Second, the ICJ adjudicated Mexico's claims that Medellín's rights under Article 36 had been violated in the *Avena* judgment and provided a remedy for those wrongs that the court should enforce. Third, it argued that, in the alternative, the court should give effect to the *Avena* judgment as a matter of comity.

The first argument began by noting that when a nation voluntarily undertakes obligations under a treaty, it has a corresponding duty to honor them. This duty binds all of its organs' subjurisdictions. Thus, the courts, both state and federal, are bound to recognize and uphold those obligations. Here, the United States, by consenting to the jurisdiction of the ICJ, undertook an obligation to comply with any judgments that body should issue.

Next, the brief argued that the treaty, the Optional Protocol, and the *Avena* judgment constituted binding federal law. The US Constitution expressly grants the power to make treaties to the federal government. Once a treaty is ratified, it becomes the "supreme law of the land," with the power to displace conflicting state laws. Judges of state courts take an oath to enforce that supreme law. This constitutional design ensures that an inconsistent state policy cannot result in violations of the nation's international commitments.

The brief then argued that the *Avena* judgment was judicially enforceable. The supremacy clause binds state court judges to enforce duly ratified treaties, and Article III of the Constitution grants federal courts jurisdiction to hear cases involving treaties. Donovan argued that judicial enforcement of treaties was "essential to the maintenance of our international commitments." Where those treaties are self-executing, rights conferred by them are directly enforceable in domestic courts, and courts have not hesitated to enforce them. The habeas statute allows individuals to challenge "custody in violation of the . . . treaties of the United States."

Turning to Medellín specifically, the brief maintained that his rights under *Avena* were judicially enforceable. Given the combination of the preceding arguments, there could be no doubt that Medellín was entitled to relief. The remedy ordered by the ICJ was not just susceptible to judicial enforcement—"it can *only* be provided by the judicial process." Because the *Avena* judgment ruled out clemency as a valid means of providing "review and reconsideration," it left only a judicial avenue of redress.

According to Donovan, when the United States agreed to have the case heard by the International Court of Justice it also agreed to be bound by the judgment of that court. The State Department had, on numerous occasions, reiterated the view that when the United States submitted to ICJ adjudication, it regarded itself as obliged to abide by the results. It therefore logically followed that the ICJ's binding interpretation of the convention must be given full effect by the courts of the United States. If the convention itself is enforceable by the courts, the interpretation of the convention by the body duly authorized to definitively interpret it must likewise be enforceable. The appropriate way to enforce *Avena* is to treat it as conclusive of Medellín's rights under Article 36 and bring the state and federal courts in line with the treaty commitments voluntarily entered into by the United States.

With this legal foundation in place, the brief next contended that in order to comply with the United States' international obligations, the Supreme Court should reverse the court of appeals decision. In issuing its decision, the court of appeals expressly acknowledged it was violating *Avena*, but felt itself compelled to do so by the hierarchical nature of the federal judiciary.

The brief then addressed the Court's earlier decision in *Breard* and argued that it does not bar relief in this case. *Breard* was distinguishable because the Court did not have an ICJ decision before it when it made its decision. In fact, in its per curiam opinion, the Court specifically noted that it lacked a "clear and express statement" that the procedural rules of the arresting State did not apply. Here, on the other hand, the Supreme Court had before it the *Avena* decision, which clearly and unambiguously held that the application of the procedural default rule violated Article 36(2) because it prevented the United States from giving full effect to the object and purpose of the rights protected by the Vienna Convention.

Finally, the brief offered a spare five pages to its alternative argument, that the Court should give effect to the *Avena* decision as a matter of international comity. The Court, it argued, had a long history of giving due respect to the judgments of foreign tribunals. And those cases in which the Court *had* respected foreign judgments called for far greater intrusions into the domestic criminal justice system than the "review and reconsideration" called for by *Avena* and *LaGrand*.

Texas was represented by its solicitor general, Ted Cruz. According to the Texas attorney general's website, the Office of the Solicitor General is responsible for appellate litigation in Texas and is to ensure consistency in legal positions taken by the state. It is responsible for handling the appeals with the most significance to Texas's interests. Ted Cruz was given a slightly different mandate.

Greg Abbott, former attorney general of Texas, hired Cruz, whom he had never met before interviewing him. Cruz was just thirty-two at the time. A former Texas Supreme Court justice with conservative views, Abbott was looking for a fellow traveler: "I wanted someone who had the capability to handle appellate arguments in court, but I wanted to do so much more. I wanted Texas to be a national leader on the profound legal issues of the day. I wanted us to be able to have a larger footprint, a larger impact."

Initially, Abbott asked for a two-and-a-half-year commitment. "Ultimately, I ended up staying for five and a half years," Cruz told a reporter, "because the opportunity to fight for conservative principles and lead some of the biggest battles in the country defending the Constitution was just extraordinary."

Abbott's orders for Cruz? To look across the country and identify chances to defend conservative principles. And he did. "He really turned the office into a platform," according to David Bernstein, a law professor at George Mason University. In order to do that, Cruz had a simple philosophy. Always go on the offensive, even when on defense. According to Jim Ho, who became the solicitor general after Cruz, and currently serves as a judge on the Fifth Circuit Court of Appeals, Cruz was constantly looking for opportunities to press a conservative vision of the Constitution.

How did Ted Cruz become such a rock-ribbed conservative? To answer that, you have to look to his childhood. Cruz was the son of a Cuban immigrant father and an Irish and Italian mother. Cruz himself was born in Canada, his parents having moved there for his father's work. Shortly after Ted's birth, the family relocated back to Houston, Texas, where Cruz was raised. When he was a young teen, his parents enrolled him in an after-school program called the Free Enterprise Institute, which was dedicated to instilling the value of a free market in young people. Young Ted, who to this day says his favorite book is *Atlas Shrugged*, was exposed to the works of authors like Milton Friedman and Friedrich Hayek, revered by conservatives. Cruz and his fellow teens would then give speeches at Rotary Clubs and similar venues around the state.

Shortly after Cruz arrived, a spin-off group, the Constitutional Corroborators was formed. Ted was one of five students selected to join and turn his focus from the free market to the Constitution. "We'd meet on

Tuesdays and Thursdays, for a couple of hours each night, and study the Constitution, read the Federalist Papers, read the Anti-Federalist Papers, read the debates on ratification," Cruz said. He also memorized large passages of the Constitution.

In high school, Cruz joined the debate team, a passion he pursued in college at Princeton University. He was quite successful, racking up several national awards. He also continued his study of the Constitution. He wrote his senior thesis on the Ninth and Tenth Amendments, which provide additional limits on federal power. The focus of his thesis? "To elaborate upon a conception of the Ninth and Tenth Amendments which revitalizes the Founders' commitment to limiting government, to restraining the reach of our none-too-angelic leaders." These beliefs would stick with him the rest of his life, shaping his career and the goals he would pursue.

Following Princeton, Cruz attended Harvard Law School, where he continued to sharpen and push his conservative views. He planned to clerk for Michael Luttig, a conservative member of the Fourth Circuit Court of Appeals, and a judge with a reputation for sending his clerks on to work for conservative members of the US Supreme Court. His plans came to fruition. After clerking for Luttig, Cruz landed a spot clerking for Chief Justice William Rehnquist from 1996 to 1997. Rehnquist was still the chief when Cruz appeared to argue *Medellín*.

Even in the rarefied air of the Supreme Court, working with some of the smartest young lawyers in the country, Cruz was impressive. Neal Katyal, a well-known Supreme Court advocate and former acting US solicitor general during the Obama administration, was clerking for Justice Stephen Breyer the same year. "We became friends on the first day of our clerkships," Katyal recalls. "We spent the next year arguing about just about everything, especially the death penalty, which Ted definitely supported. He was conservative, of course, but he was not an ideologue. He knew how to make arguments based on the law. He was obviously already a very good lawyer."

And he remained a committed conservative. Cruz turned down a job offer from a large Washington, DC, law firm (and the attendant large signing bonus for Supreme Court clerks) to work for a newly established boutique firm known as Cooper & Carvin. Former holders of senior roles in the Reagan Justice Department, Charles J. Cooper and Mike

Carvin had opened a firm that combined their passion for high-stakes litigation and conservative politics. Cruz worked on several high-profile matters, including helping Cooper prepare testimony before the House Judiciary Committee in favor of the impeachment of Bill Clinton. But his association with the firm was short-lived. Just two years later, he left to work as a domestic policy adviser on the presidential campaign of George W. Bush. It was on that campaign that Ted met his wife, Heidi.

"Ted has a remarkable talent for strategic thinking," according to Charles Cooper. This assessment has been echoed by others who have spent time with Cruz, and it has been demonstrated by the recognition of his peers. From 2003 to 2007, Cruz appeared as the counsel of record on briefs that won the Best Brief Award from the National Association of Attorneys General.

He was also well respected by his opponents. It was said that he moved easily in the world of the Supreme Court bar, an elite clique of "repeat players" who regularly argue in front of the justices. Those who argued against him or watched him in moot courts preparing for arguments all concurred that Cruz was very, very good.

Cruz, who had grown up in Houston, went to church just a few blocks from T. C. Jester Park, where Jennifer and Elizabeth were murdered. He describes Medellín's confession as one of the most chilling documents he has ever read.

Cruz walked into the case at a significant disadvantage. The Supreme Court has a marked tendency to rule in favor of the president's views in matters of foreign policy. Justice Anthony Kennedy, widely viewed as a swing justice during his time on the Court, was a noted fan of international law, having relied on it to aid in decisions finding the death penalty inapplicable to juveniles as well as his majority opinion in *Lawrence v. Texas*, striking down Texas's criminal sodomy laws, which targeted consenting homosexual adults. Justice Sandra Day O'Connor was also viewed as a swing justice and a potential vote for Medellín. Cruz, ever the strategic thinker, recognized the situation he was in.

Cruz was a fan of Sun Tzu, author of *The Art of War*. Specifically, he relied on Sun Tzu's teachings that every battle is won or lost before it is fought. It is won by choosing the terrain on which the battle occurs. Sun Tzu was speaking literally, but Cruz adapted the philosophy to the realm of legal argument: "I was fortunate to enjoy multiple litigation victories in cases where the outside world deemed the odds all but insurmountable. And I think the way to do so is to focus very pragmatically on how to win the case." In *Medellín*, the way to win the argument was to win the battle for narrative framing.

"The narrative of the other side was straightforward," Cruz said. "It was 'Texas cannot flout the treaty obligations of the United States of America.... And besides, you know how those Texans are about capital punishment anyway.' If that's what the case is about, we lose. If the question is 'Can Texas defy the treaty obligations of the United States?' we lose. And that's why just about every observer said there's no way Texas can win."

Cruz always began by asking, "What's this case about?" "When the judge goes home and speaks to his or her grandchild, who's in kindergarten, and the child says, 'Paw-Paw, what did you do today?' And if you own those two sentences that come out of the judge's mouth, you win the case." Cruz wanted to be sure that Justice Kennedy, the most likely swing justice, would tell his grandchildren he had upheld the Constitution by ensuring that the "World Court" could not tell the Supreme Court how to do its job.

On February 28, 2005, the State of Texas filed its response brief. Unlike the petitioner, Cruz opened his brief with a fairly graphic description of José Medellín's crimes, his recounting of those crimes to Joe and Christina Cantu, and his confession to those crimes to the Houston Police.

While acknowledging that the Houston Police failed to provide Medellín with his rights under Article 36, Texas's brief pointed out that Medellín had lived most of his life in the United States and was provided with his *Miranda* rights. It also noted that Medellín had been appointed counsel who filed numerous motions on Medellín's behalf, extensively questioned the potential jurors, and vigorously challenged the state's case. Medellín's counsel also fought hard during the penalty phase. Despite all these efforts, Medellín's counsel never raised any claims under the Vienna Convention. According to Cruz, it was too late to do so now.

On the legal front, the Texas brief made four points. First, federal law barred Medellín's request for habeas relief because he did not point to a violation of his constitutional rights. Second, the Court should not overrule the *Breard* decision. Third, the *Avena* decision did not alter controlling federal law because the ICJ's decision was not binding on the

United States. And fourth, concerns about comity did not support relief for Medellín.

Cruz opened by attempting to frame the issue in a manner that absolved Texas of any responsibility. The failure to enforce *Avena* was not Texas's doing, Cruz argued. Instead, it was controlled by federal law, namely, the AEDPA. A federal court of appeals lacks jurisdiction to hear a habeas petition unless and until the prisoner successfully obtains a COA.

Under the jurisdictional statute contained in Title 28 governing COAs, they may be issued only when the prisoner can show the denial of a constitutional right. While the habeas statute recognizes violations of federal statutes and treaties as bases for relief, the AEDPA requires a constitutional violation to permit a successive petition. Unfortunately for Medellín, Texas argued, there is no constitutional right to have treaties enforced. While the supremacy clause requires such compliance, it does not transform the failure to comply into a constitutional violation.

Furthermore, under a long-recognized rule of American law, treaties and federal statutes receive the same respect. When there is a conflict between the two, the one that is later in time controls. In this case, the AEDPA was passed well after the Vienna Convention was ratified. Thus, under this "later in time" rule, the statute trumps any inconsistent interpretation of the convention.

Moreover, even assuming Medellín's claim raised a constitutional issue, the statute would still bar relief because it prevents courts from issuing COAs on issues addressed on the merits by state courts unless those decisions are contrary to "clearly established federal law, as determined by the Supreme Court of the United States." But in this case, the state court's decision that the Vienna Convention did not provide Medellín with an individual right flowed directly from the Supreme Court's decision in *Breard.*

The Court had already addressed the question of whether the procedural default rule can apply to Vienna Convention claims in that case, and it held that the doctrine does apply. And here, Medellín procedurally defaulted on his convention claim. State procedural rules, the Court held, can only be displaced by an express statement in the treaty itself. In *Breard*, the Court held that the language of Article 36(2) was not an express statement requiring displacement of state procedural rules.

Medellín could not show that he was prejudiced by the Article 36 violation. The evidence, according to Cruz, was overwhelming, and Medellín confessed long before it would have been practical to inform the consulate of his arrest. There was testimony from other witnesses about how Medellín bragged about his crimes, and the jury was shown physical evidence connecting Medellín to the murders.

Next, Cruz argued that the Court should not overrule *Breard.* Medellín, he wrote, was effectively arguing that the ICJ's decision in *Avena* functionally overruled *Breard.* But, he reminded the Court, only it had the power to do this.

Cruz, in a direct repudiation of *Avena,* told the Court that the Vienna Convention did not create individual rights and that ICJ decisions are not binding on federal courts. Thus, the decision could not displace the AEDPA. While acknowledging that the Vienna Convention is "self-executing," Texas's brief argued that whether a treaty creates individually enforceable rights was an entirely different question. Cruz noted that typically, international agreements, as agreements between States, did not create individually enforceable rights, even when they provide a direct benefit to private parties. When treaties are meant to create individual rights, he argued, they do so explicitly and unambiguously.

The text of the Vienna Convention not only does not clearly create individual rights; according to Texas's brief, it expressly disclaims this intent. The preamble to the convention states that the purpose of the Vienna Convention on Consular Relations is not to benefit individuals but to ensure efficient performance by consular posts. Article 36 notes that its purpose is to facilitate the exercise of consular functions. It is the State whose rights are violated when Article 36 is not observed. Any benefits granted to individuals are collateral at best.

Furthermore, Cruz wrote, this has been the consistent view of the State Department. It has, since ratification, argued that the Vienna Convention does not create rights that individuals may pursue in Court. Contemporary documents from the period of ratification also support this view.

While the ICJ's interpretation may have changed this understanding of the Vienna Convention, the *Avena* decision itself is not directly enforceable in domestic courts without further action. The supremacy clause applies to the Constitution, federal statutes, and treaties. ICJ decisions do not fall under any of these categories. While they may reflect the interpretation of treaties, they are not themselves treaties, which would require the Senate's consent. No foreign nation treats ICJ decisions as enforceable by individuals within their domestic courts.

Medellín could find no refuge in the Optional Protocol. Nothing in the text, history, or implementation of that document demonstrated that it provides such force to ICJ decisions. And if the Court were to accept Medellín's argument that the decision, by itself, provides the rule of decision in his and similar cases, it would create an untenable conflict with federal laws such as the AEDPA, which privilege Supreme Court decisions regarding constitutional rights over all other sources of law.

Texas's brief then turned to the question of remedy and noted that it is the duty of the political branches to enforce the treaty obligations of the United States. The United States always has the political option to disregard treaty obligations when it deems it necessary. The president has the authority to waive treaties, and Congress may enact legislation that is inconsistent with our treaty commitments. The best way in which to fulfill our treaty obligations—or decisions regarding whether to comply with them at all—should be left to the politically accountable branches of government.

A finding that the ICJ's decision was binding over state and federal courts would create its own constitutional issues. Article III of the US Constitution vests the entire judicial power in the courts of the United States. Congress simply lacks the power to delegate that authority to an international tribunal. The argument that ICJ decisions control the actions of domestic courts raises separation of powers concerns. Under long-recognized doctrine, if there are two ways to fairly interpret a treaty, one of which creates constitutional problems and one which avoids them, the Court is compelled to adopt the latter. Thus, the Court should reject any suggestion that it can be overruled by an international tribunal such as the International Court of Justice.

Next, the brief argued that Medellín had other avenues of seeking relief for violations of Article 36. It pointed to four other methods of gaining relief and indicated that this was a nonexclusive list. Among the suggested solutions was that Mexico could prevail upon President Bush to issue an executive order to achieve the same goals. This avenue is "well within" the president's prerogative and duties to see the laws are faithfully executed.

Finally, the brief devotes three pages to answering the argument regarding comity. Cruz noted that comity is not some automatic grant to foreign tribunals but rather is a voluntary observance by courts. But this is not enough to overcome a contradictory federal statute, such as the AEDPA. It is particularly inappropriate in cases where the decision ignores federal and state laws as well as binding Supreme Court precedent.

Twenty parties filed amicus briefs, evenly split between Medellín and Texas. The purpose of amicus briefs is to provide the Court with insight into the views of outside parties that have an interest in the outcome of the case but are not directly involved. They typically attempt to provide information to the Court it might not otherwise have, or provide deeper arguments on a point the parties themselves did not address or addressed only superficially.

Briefs in favor of Medellín's arguments for upholding the ICJ decision were filed by the American Bar Association; Amnesty International; former diplomats; the European Union; a collection of other foreign sovereigns; international law experts; Americans who had previously been held in violation of the Vienna Convention; a group of missionary service organizations, study abroad organizations, and former missionaries; and a collection of bar associations and human rights groups. Briefs in support of Texas fell into two main groups. Those arguing that enforcing the ICJ's judgment would violate the Constitution's provisions were filed by the Alliance Defense Fund, US senator from Texas John Cornyn, and a different set of international law experts. Another group of amici filed briefs arguing that the ICJ decision did not overcome contrary state and federal rules. These amici included the Criminal Justice Legal Foundation; the Liberty Legal Institute; the Mountain States Legal Foundation; the National District Attorneys Association; a group of states; the Washington Legal Foundation and the parents of Jennifer Ertman; and, biggest of all, the solicitor general of the United States.

The Office of the Solicitor General is the federal government's representative in the US Supreme Court. It weighs in on most cases heard by the Supreme Court, and the solicitor general is so widely respected that he or she has often been referred to as the "tenth justice." Empirical research has shown that, in cases involving international law, the solicitor general has an impressive winning streak, winning about 71 percent of all cases in which it participated. Having the solicitor general on your side is incredibly important and is, without a doubt, the single most important amicus a party can have.

Medellín's amici believed that US courts had a duty to enforce the *Avena* judgment and provide the "review and reconsideration" called for by the ICJ, notwithstanding the existence of Texas's procedural default rule. An examination of two briefs provide the basic arguments.

First, and likely of particular interest to the Court, was the brief filed by Sandra Babcock on behalf of the Mexican government. The brief focused on the long history of international cooperation between the United States and Mexico. For two centuries, these countries had settled hundreds of disputes using international tribunals, and in each case, both parties have recognized they are bound by those decisions when they are voluntarily submitted to these tribunals. In only one case did the commitment of the parties waver, "and the results were disastrous."

When the United States refused to abide by an arbitration decision over the border, the so-called Chamizal Dispute, the two countries saw a downturn in relations that colored their discussions for the following half century. Mexico retaliated by refusing to engage in arbitration to resolve disputes with the United States over Mexico's nationalization of the Mexican oil industry, and Mexico also refused to comply with a prior Permanent Court of Arbitration judgment that required payment to the United States. Only after President Kennedy resolved the Chamizal Dispute in 1963 did relations between the two countries fully normalize.

Mexico's brief concluded that there was no dispute that the United States was bound by the ICJ's decision. To the extent the Supreme Court's ruling in *Breard* prevented the Court from providing relief, it should be overruled. Unlike Medellín, Angel Breard "did not have the benefit of a binding adjudication of his rights" at the time he sought review of his Article 36 claim.

A second brief was filed by Yale law professor, former diplomat, and international law expert Harold Hongju Koh and the students of the Allard K. Lowenstein International Human Rights Clinic at Yale Law School. The clinic had a long and impressive history of taking on the executive branch and winning in cases involving international law, having played a key role in a case involving Haitian refugees. So when a brief like theirs appeared in front of the justices, it would have received due respect.

Koh's interest in combating the death penalty was very personal. While a young man, he had not given it much thought, and what little thought he had given it had led him to supporting the death penalty. That all changed in the fall of 1982. A man with a sawed-off shot gun robbed Koh's fiancée. She screamed, and the robber fired. The bullets grazed her head, but she was not seriously injured, although Koh later recounted that even a few millimeters could have made the difference. When he told her that if she had died, he would have supported the death penalty for her killer, she told him he was crazy and that it wouldn't accomplish anything. That conversation changed Koh's thinking. If his fiancée did not want the death penalty for her killer, what right would he have had to seek it on her behalf?

Koh's diplomatic experience also contributed to his change of heart. Whenever he would advocate for stronger protection of human rights, those opposite him would throw the United States' use of the death penalty back in his face. US diplomats of both parties told him that the continued use of the death penalty was "amazingly damaging" to the United States' reputation abroad.

Professor Koh was no stranger to the Supreme Court. He served as a clerk for Justice Harry Blackmun in the 1980s. He was also well experienced in international law, having served as assistant secretary of state for democracy, human rights, and labor in the Clinton administration. He came by his interest in international law honestly, as the son of a diplomat for South Korea. Koh's family had fled to the United States in the 1960s after the South Korean government was overthrown on May 16, 1961. Prior to that, Koh's father had studied at Harvard Law School and is believed to be the first Korean to do so.

Koh first put together a group of diplomats to file an amicus brief about the international implications of the death penalty in two cases involving the application of the death penalty to the mentally disabled and the execution of juveniles. In both of those cases, the Court had sided with the international consensus that applying capital punishment to those two populations was beyond the pale. In neither case had an international tribunal ruled that such punishments were cruel and unusual. One of those two cases, *Roper v. Simmons*, decided on March 1, 2005, the day after Texas filed its brief in Medellín's case, held that it was unconstitutional to execute someone whose crime was committed while they were younger than eighteen, which actually spared two of Medellín's codefendants. And so, when *Medellín* came along, Koh had a familiarity with these arguments and quite a bit of success in helping to convince the Court to rule in favor of international law. The brief was filed on behalf of a bipartisan group of former ambassadors, legal advisers to the State Department, and some of the most senior officials, including former Secretary of State Madeleine Albright, former Undersecretary of State Thomas Pickering, former Legal Adviser Malcolm Wilkey, Special Presidential Envoy James C. O'Brien, and a host of others.

Koh's brief made three points. First, it argued that the treaty power was limited to the federal government following several diplomatic failures under the Articles of Confederation wherein states had violated treaties negotiated by the Continental Congress, including the treaty with Great Britain that secured America's independence. Second, failing to enforce *Avena* would undermine the diplomatic credibility of the United States. The diplomats, with their extensive experience, believed that the failure of the courts to provide the relief required by *Avena* would harm the credibility of the United States with both its allies and adversaries. In 2001, following the execution of the LaGrand brothers, the United States was voted off the UN Commission on Human Rights for the first time in its fifty-four-year history. The United States also failed to win a seat on the Inter-American Commission on Human Rights for the first time since 1959, the year it was created. Finally, the brief argued that our failure to adhere to the *Avena* judgment would affect our foreign policy interest in other treaty regimes. Binding arbitration by international tribunals is a feature of many treaties. If the United States could not be counted on to uphold its obligations as determined by the ICJ, why should other countries expect us to abide by our obligations as determined by other bodies?

The other briefs largely echoed the arguments raised by Donovan in his brief on behalf of Medellín. Although these "me too" briefs are not as useful to the Court as those that provide unique arguments, they go a long way to demonstrating the broad base of support for each party's position. In this case, petitioners managed to arrange for a broad and bipartisan group of supporters to demonstrate to the Court that the United States was required to override Texas's local laws in support of upholding its international obligations.

Texas had an equally long, though arguably less impressive, list of amici, mainly made up of groups interested in what they term victims' rights. Two of the briefs, though not adding much in the way of legal analysis, are worth noting because of who they represented. The first was a brief filed by the attorneys general of twenty death penalty states siding with Texas in arguing that the Vienna Convention is subject to the subsequently enacted AEDPA and that ICJ judgments are not self-executing. Whenever a large group of states pushes a point of view, the Court will take notice.

The final brief worth noting is one written on behalf of a diverse group that included Randy and Sandra Ertman, Jennifer Ertman's parents. Represented by the Washington Legal Foundation, a crime victims' rights group, it was joined by the Allied Educational Foundation and two members of Congress. It largely repeated the arguments of Texas. However, since the parents of one of Medellín's victims were parties, the brief likely garnered extra attention, particularly in the chambers of justices more likely to support implementing the death penalty.

––––––

Unbeknownst to the attorneys on both sides, a debate was raging inside the White House over the proper response to the *Avena* decision. Some inside the Bush White House pushed to ignore the ruling, believing that the United States was already doing everything that was asked of it. Others took a more proactive approach, arguing that the United States should take steps to comply with the ICJ's judgment and provide the "review and reconsideration" ordered.

Chief among those seeking to enforce the *Avena* judgment was John Bellinger, an attorney who worked as the right-hand-man to National Security Adviser Condoleezza Rice serving as legal adviser to the National Security Council. Bellinger was a graduate of Princeton University, the University of Virginia, and Harvard Law School. He was a strong believer in international law and lobbied inside the White House that it would be in the best interests of the United States to robustly enforce Article 36 of the Vienna Convention because of the reciprocal nature of the commitments it contained. Bellinger's main argument was that it was incumbent upon the United States to respect the Vienna Convention because so many of its own citizens depended on the protections of the convention when traveling abroad. He had suggested President Bush issue an executive order, while the Justice Department was more in favor of legislation. Bellinger was concerned that the conservative Republicans in House leadership were unlikely to support such legislation.

While advocating strongly in favor of enforcing *Avena*, following the successful reelection of President Bush, Bellinger was also tasked with overseeing the confirmation of Condoleezza Rice as secretary of state. On January 26, just two days after the petitioners filed their opening brief, Rice was confirmed by the Senate by a vote of 85 to 13. She brought Bellinger with her, where he helped oversee the transition to the State Department.

Bellinger's argument carried the day, which became public knowledge on February 28, 2005, the same day the respondents filed their brief with the Supreme Court. President Bush issued a highly unusual one-page declaration to Attorney General Alberto Gonzales, who had been sworn in less than four weeks prior. The memo was only two paragraphs long. The first paragraph recited the United States' commitment to the Vienna Convention and participation in the Optional Protocol. As a result, the second paragraph said, the president had determined that the United States would comply with the *Avena* judgment by having state courts "give effect to the decision in accordance with general principles of comity in cases filed by the fifty-one Mexican nationals addressed in that decision." The focus on comity was suggested by Vice President Cheney's office.

"I'm not sure who was more surprised," Bellinger said. "Liberals who couldn't believe President Bush was ordering compliance with an ICJ decision, or conservatives who couldn't believe that President Bush was ordering compliance with an ICJ decision." Bellinger noted that this was a tough decision for the president. Most presidents tend to make decisions based on domestic politics, he said. "President Bush made a difficult decision that was flatly not in his domestic political interests to both do the right thing and to uphold our international law obligations."

"We were kind of dumbfounded," Babcock remembers. "It was the kind of thing just nobody expected. . . . We were all caught completely off guard by it." Even the way they found out about it was surprising. The memorandum was attached as an appendix to the brief of the solicitor general. There was no announcement, no press release. "It's a conservative Republican administration. And so they did make for odd bedfellows," Babcock said. But of course they were welcome. As to why the president made his surprise announcement, Babcock can only speculate. "I think that the lawyers sincerely believed that there was, and I really respect them for this, that there was an international legal obligation to comply with the judgment. And they saw that and they convinced the president that this is something he was bound to do and they did the right thing. And I think that took integrity and so I really respected them."

The memorandum also threw a wrench into their preparations, coming as it did after they had already filed their opening brief. "I remember having discussions about 'what does this do to our argument?' Does it completely moot it out? Should we just go back to state court? And ultimately, we decided that we had to go back to state court to litigate it."

And so Medellín's counsel filed a petition in state court, at the Texas Court of Criminal Appeals, the highest court in Texas that deals with criminal matters. While they were waiting for Texas's decision, they still had to appear before the US Supreme Court. Even though Babcock and Donovan thought that a return to state court was inevitable, the Supreme Court still had jurisdiction over the case until it issued a ruling.

But the shocks did not end there. Like most decisions involving the White House, the decision to enforce *Avena* was political, and involved some horse trading. The Justice Department was willing to support the memorandum if the president would take steps to ensure that the United States would not be sued in the ICJ for violations of the VCCR again. In order to make the decision more palatable, President Bush had Secretary Rice deliver a letter to the UN secretary-general just one week later, on March 7, 2005, formally withdrawing the United States from the Optional Protocol concerning the Compulsory Settlement of Disputes to the VCCR, which granted the ICJ jurisdiction over the case. After three cases, and two losses, the view of the United States was that future suits were inevitable and the decisions in those cases preordained. Therefore, to avoid being haled before the ICJ in the future, the United States decided to withdraw its consent to be sued.

The solicitor general played a somewhat unique role in the case. It sided with the State of Texas, arguing that the *Avena* judgment did not, on its own, entitle Medellín to relief in US courts. It argued that Article 36 did not provide Medellín with privately enforceable rights and that the *Avena* decision itself was likewise not privately enforceable. However, the brief concluded with a lengthy argument that, based on the president's determination, the *Avena* judgment should be enforced in state courts as a matter of comity.

It is likely that this split advocacy was the result of the president's late decision to issue his declaration and support the *Avena* decision. It appears the solicitor general was prepared to fully support Texas's arguments that the *Avena* decision did not overcome the AEDPA or provide Medellín with any rights he did not already have. But the president's declaration upended this full-throated support. Coming at the eleventh hour, it was too late for the solicitor general to change his position, and it is not clear that there was any support for a complete reversal.

The arguments raised by the United States largely mirrored those raised by Ted Cruz and the State of Texas. The arguments differed in two respects: first, the United States argued that the *Avena* decision was not, itself, privately enforceable; second, it argued that the president's declaration provided a reason to respect the ICJ's decision as a matter of comity.

Article 36, the government argued, did not mention the effect of an ICJ decision on the rights it protected. Thus, it cannot be the source of private enforcement of *Avena*. The Optional Protocol, on the other hand, is merely a grant of jurisdiction to the ICJ. It does not even compel the United States to enforce any judgment, let alone create a private right of action. It is true that Article 94 of the UN Charter does create an international obligation on the United States to enforce decisions of the ICJ. But neither the text nor the background of that provision creates a private right of action in domestic courts. This is further bolstered by the fact that the enforcement mechanism for violations of Article 94 is resort to the Security Council. Thus, enforcement of ICJ decisions is left to the political branches of a nation. Allowing a private right of action would rob those branches of their discretion. The *Avena* decision itself recognizes this discretion, by leaving it up to the United States, by means of its own choosing, to comply with the judgment.

Nearly a fifth of the brief is taken up with the final argument of the United States, that the president's determination to comply should be enforced in state courts as a matter of comity. *Avena* creates a binding international obligation on the United States to choose a means to provide "review and reconsideration" of the convictions and sentences of the fifty-one individuals named in the decision. This "review and reconsideration" was to examine whether the denial of Article 36 information caused actual prejudice to the defense either at trial or at sentencing.

Because the president is the "sole organ of foreign policy," he enjoys "a degree of independent authority to act" in the field of foreign affairs. The president has the authority to deny enforcement of an ICJ decision and to instruct the US ambassador to the United Nations to veto any Security Council resolution seeking enforcement. Here, by contrast, the president has determined "that the foreign policy interests of the United States justify compliance with the ICJ's decision." Consular assistance is important to US citizens abroad, and the president was concerned that failing to fulfill our international obligations under the *Avena* decision could undermine the United States' ability to secure such assistance for our citizens.

Once the president has made the determination to enforce our international obligations, the brief argued, he also has the power to determine the means of compliance. He can achieve such compliance through unilateral executive branch action, or he may seek implementing legislation from Congress. In this instance, due to the need for prompt compliance with the ICJ's decision, and because both the ICJ and the president determined that judicial review was the best means of enforcement, he determined that he would have state courts perform the "review and reconsideration" "in accordance with general principles of comity." Thus, when any of the fifty-one nationals named in the *Avena* decision sought relief in state courts, those courts should give effect to the decision in accordance with the president's determination.

The president's authority in this area is particularly important in the context of a treaty, such as the Vienna Convention, which not only protects the rights of foreign nationals in the United States but also protects the rights of Americans abroad. The president has the sole authority to protect Americans abroad who are denied liberty. Congress has expressly recognized this authority in statute. Furthermore, the decision to enforce the *Avena* judgment involves "delicate and complex calculations" for which the president is uniquely suited.

State procedural doctrines must give way, the brief stated, in the name of comity because the president's action to enforce *Avena*, taken under his authority under Article II of the Constitution, and authorized by his power to represent the United States in the United Nations, is the supreme law of the land. While state courts were not directed to reach any particular outcome, they were required to evaluate whether the violation of Article 36 caused actual prejudice to any of the fifty-one Mexican nationals, keeping in mind that speculative harms do not warrant relief.

The solicitor general also argued that the president had power to support his declaration arising from his Article II authority to manage foreign affairs. Relying on *United States v. Curtiss-Wright Export Corporation* (1936), the brief argued that the president's power in this area "does not require as a basis for its exercise an act of Congress." Thus, the president had the authority to make executive agreements with other countries that do not require consent by the Senate. Such agreements, the Court has held, preempt conflicting state laws. If that is true, then the president "should be equally free to resolve a dispute with a foreign government by determining how the United States will comply with a decision reached after the completion of formal dispute-resolution procedures with that foreign government." Requiring more would "hamstring" the president in his efforts to settle controversies with other nations and to ensure the United States complies with its treaty obligations. Furthermore, requiring a formal bilateral agreement between the United States and a foreign country would effectively grant that foreign country a veto over the president's exercise of his foreign affairs authority.

Because the president determined that the *Avena* decision should be respected as a matter of comity, state courts were not free to reexamine the merits of that decision. Comity required that foreign judgments be implemented without questioning the legal analysis that underlay them, so long as the court rendering judgment had jurisdiction, it was impartial, its procedures respected due process, and there was no special reason to prevent giving it full effect. The president's declaration indicates that these conditions had been met.

The brief was clear that the president's declaration was limited to just the fifty-one nationals named in the *Avena* judgment. It thus does not prevent domestic courts from reexamining the underlying holding of *Avena* in cases brought by nationals of other countries, or of Mexican nationals not covered by the ICJ decision. It was therefore a limited exercise of the president's power and was consistent with precedent on when judgments against the United States are binding in future litigation.

Finally, the solicitor general argued that states engaging in the "review and reconsideration" called for by *Avena* were prohibited from relying on the procedural default doctrine. This did not conflict with *Breard*, which merely held that the Vienna Convention did not prevent the application of the doctrine. In fact, the solicitor general agreed that *Breard* was controlling on that question. But despite this, the president had determined that the foreign policy interests of the United States in protecting Americans abroad and upholding its international obligations required enforcing this aspect of the *Avena* judgment, without regard to the underlying merits of the ICJ's conclusion. For these fifty-one cases only, the United States would not rely on those doctrines to foreclose relief for violations of Article 36 of the Vienna Convention.

––––––––––

The Supreme Court of the United States sits at 1 First Street NE, in Washington, DC, directly across the street from the US Capitol. Despite being a coequal branch of government, the Court did not move into its own home until 1935, when the Cass Gilbert–designed building was completed at the behest of the chief justice, former president, and great-grandfather of the US representative at the ICJ, William Howard Taft. Prior to that time, it sat in the Capitol, in what is currently known as the Old Senate Chamber.

The marble building is fronted by a huge oval plaza, leading to a large set of stairs that rise to a set of sixteen marble columns, rising up two stories and supporting a pediment on which the words "Equal Justice Under Law" are emblazoned. Two massive bronze doors, weighing six and a half tons each, served as the entrance to the Court at the time, though now they are for exit only. On either side of the stairs are two massive statues, a female figure on the left, known as *Contemplation of Justice*, and a male figure on the right, known as *The Authority of Law*.

Upon entering the doors, a visitor is faced with the Great Hall, with a double line of marble columns rising to the ceiling. At the end of the hall sits the courtroom, fronted by oaken doors. After the majesty of the plaza and the Great Hall, the courtroom is almost intimate by comparison. While the room is tall—the ceiling rises forty-four feet overhead—the room itself feels oddly compact. It seats only about one hundred people. Red is the primary color in evidence.

The back of the courtroom is composed of six or seven rows of pews, which house members of the public during oral argument. In front of the public section, set off by a bronze railing, is the portion reserved for members of the Supreme Court Bar, those advocates allowed to file briefs and offer arguments before the Court. These members sit on individual chairs. To the left and right are rows of red benches, reserved for the press and guests of the justices, respectively. In front of them are a row of black chairs reserved for visiting dignitaries and court officers.

Finally, in front of the bar section are two massive tables reserved for counsel. Between them is a heavy podium with a microphone. And then, far closer than most advocates are comfortable with, is the raised mahogany bench, where the justices sit. In 1972, the bench was altered, going from straight to a winged design, which curves toward the lectern, making it easier for justices to hear. More than one advocate has commented on the sensation of a junior justice asking a question from their peripheral vision.

The justices sit in order of seniority, with the chief justice occupying the center seat and the associate justices flanking him on alternate sides. When facing the bench, the juniormost justice is on the speaker's right side. Behind the justices is a large purple curtain, leading to the robing room, where the justices prepare for argument. By tradition, the justices begin each argument session by shaking hands before taking the bench.

At 11:01 a.m. on March 28, 2005, Chief Justice William H. Rehnquist recognized Donovan to speak on behalf of José Medellín. Donovan opened with an unusual plea, asking the Court to hold the case while Medellín returned to the Texas courts in an attempt to vindicate his rights under the *Avena* decision. Unlike arguments at the ICJ, oral arguments in US courts are far more lively, a much more extemporaneous affair with the judges as active participants. This is even further ramped up in the Supreme Court for two reasons. First, the justices participate in oral argument (Justice Clarence Thomas, while present, almost never asked a question when Medellín's case was being argued; since October Term 2020, he has been much more active). Second, the justices often use oral argument as a conversation between themselves, mediated by the presence of the lawyer. Justice Sandra Day O'Connor got to the heart of Donovan's suggestion, asking if the Court had ever held a case in abeyance pending lower court action, or if it would not be better to dismiss the case as improvidently granted, meaning that the case was not quite ready for Supreme Court review, a path Solicitor General Paul Clement had predicted the Court would take.

Donovan pushed back, arguing that the case was not granted in error. The question it raised was quite important for the Court to decide, but it might be in a better position to do so after Texas acted. He pointed to the import of the president's determination to comply with *Avena*. Staying the decision of the court of appeals would be an acceptable outcome.

Donovan then pivoted to a discussion of the merits of the case, noting that President Bush's declaration removed Texas's objection to enforcing the *Avena* judgment under the supremacy clause. Because it was apparent that many justices were not interested in a stay, Donovan wanted to press his arguments on the underlying question the Court had agreed to address. He noted the "extraordinary amount of agreement" between the parties as to the binding nature of the *Avena* judgment. Texas conceded that it was bound by international law. The only real question for the justices was whether the *Avena* judgment supplied the rule of decision. Rehnquist asked about the creation of a private right of action.

Donovan replied that the treaty lays out an individual right, as determined by the ICJ, but that domestic law provides the means of giving effect to that individual obligation. And here, the supremacy clause provides that treaties are the supreme law of the land. Furthermore, the habeas statute provides for an individual right of action, allowing a person held in custody in violation of a treaty the right to sue. Justice O'Connor asked if that would provide a right of action independent of the ICJ's decision, and Donovan allowed that it could. Texas acknowledged it had violated Article 36 by failing to inform Medellín of his rights. The habeas statute explicitly provided relief when a treaty was violated. Therefore, even without *Avena*, Medellín was entitled to habeas relief. Only the AEDPA stood in the way.

Justice Antonin Scalia posed a hypothetical to Donovan, asking if the president could sign, with Congress's approval, a treaty providing that, in a particular conflict, someone other than the president would be the commander in chief. Donovan answered that the Court's precedents held that the only limits on the treaty power were affirmative limitations within the Constitution itself. But, Donovan acknowledged, a treaty could not amend the Constitution. Scalia then bore down, asking if a treaty could give away the Supreme Court's power to decide all questions of federal law. Scalia was clearly concerned about the implications of Donovan's argument and did not like Donovan's answer.

When Donovan tried arguing that the Vienna Convention did not strip the Court of power, Scalia retorted: "It does if I have to believe that individual rights were created here, without reexamining the question on my own." Donovan countered that Article III had never been read to prevent giving effect to a judgment made by a foreign court or international tribunal.

The next section of the argument turned on the meaning of the president's declaration. Donovan was asking the Court to defer to the president's authority as the voice of America's foreign policy. It also neatly tied into Texas's argument that this was a question for the political branches, not the judiciary. At the time Texas wrote its brief, the president had not weighed in, so this seemed like a safe argument to make. But with the president on his side, Donovan was trying to press his advantage. The justices, on the other hand, were concerned about the effect of such deference on their own power.

Justice O'Connor reentered the debate, asking if the Court was free to apply the Vienna Convention itself, rather than the treaty's interpretation by the ICJ in *Avena*. Donovan conceded that, yes, the Court could reach its own interpretation of the treaty, in accord with the *Avena* judgment. Because the president had weighed in, the Court should respect that determination.

Justice Anthony Kennedy, the other swing justice, asked if the Court would be bound by a president's unilateral interpretation of a treaty. Donovan acknowledged that the Court would be free to ignore the president, but it has traditionally accorded deference to the president in the field of foreign policy.

Donovan told the Court that Medellín was asking it to take account of the president's declaration because Texas's defense was largely based on an argument that the Court should stay out of the case and let the political branches hash it out. The president had stepped in and made a determination and said that not only could the Court give effect to the *Avena* judgment, but it is in the interests of the United States that it do so. Texas had gotten exactly what it asked for. The political branches had weighed in, and they sided with Medellín.

Justice Stephen Breyer, at the time the juniormost justice on the Court, spoke up. He asked Donovan whether his argument was that the president's determination was binding on the Court, such that the justices had no choice but to follow it, or that they should show deference to the president's opinion that the United States should enforce *Avena.* "Well, that's right," Donovan responded. The president endorsed the notion that the United States should comply with the ICJ's judgment. Justices Scalia and Rehnquist then jumped in, noting that prior cases did not deny the Court jurisdiction to decide and that those cases were focused on overseeing arrangements made by the government without involving local authority. Donovan countered that these earlier cases, *Garamendi* and *Dames & Moore*, recognized the president's authority to "give effect to international obligations."

Chief Justice Rehnquist noted that *Dames & Moore*, which he wrote, involved an agreement between the United States and Iran. That was the case here, Donovan replied. The United States and Mexico both signed the Optional Protocol and the UN Charter, which were agreements to allow the ICJ to decide this case and to abide by that decision. And while the Court may have looked at the agreement itself in *Dames & Moore*, it did not reexamine the terms. Instead, it decided that the president had the authority to require American claimants to go to the Iranian–United States Claims Tribunal, instead of to US courts.

Scalia turned to the question under the AEDPA and the need for a COA. What constitutional right of Medellín's was violated? Both Scalia and Kennedy were concerned about limits on the Court's power to hear and decide cases. In an attempt to reduce the number of appeals a criminal defendant on death row could make, AEDPA provided statutory limits on the kinds of cases such a defendant could take to court.

Donovan, Kennedy, and Scalia engaged in a back-and-forth over the need to answer the question until Justice David Souter jumped in to nail down the underlying issue: What was Donovan's answer to the claim that "the COA requires a showing of substantial infringement of constitutional, as distinct from other sources of, rights?" Donovan told Justice Souter that they believed there was a denial of a constitutional right under both the supremacy clause and the due process clause. The denial of a COA, based on the procedural default doctrine, violated the due process clause by arbitrarily denying a forum in which to hear Medellín's claim under *Avena.*

Justice Ruth Bader Ginsburg then moved on to Texas's argument that the AEPDA was a later-in-time statute that would control over the Vienna Convention, ratified earlier. Why, she wanted to know, was this argument incorrect? Donovan argued there was no conflict with respect to the constitutional questions. It would violate due process to deny Medellín relief for failing to raise *Avena* seven years before the case was decided. "You have a constitutional claim based on a denial of a right that did not exist, and you also have a constitutional claim based on the Supremacy Clause itself."

Chief Justice Rehnquist quoted Donovan back to him: "You're talking about denial of a right that didn't exist. That seems perfectly rational, the way you put it.... If the right didn't exist, it should have been denied." Donovan backpedaled a bit, arguing that a more "prudent" way to put it is that the lower courts applied the procedural default doctrine to an argument that Medellín could not have raised, because the *Avena* judgment had not yet been rendered. Simply put, Medellín could not have waived an argument based on *Avena* when he filed his first appeal because *Avena* had not been decided. Donovan then elected to reserve his remaining time for rebuttal.

Chief Justice Rehnquist then recognized Cruz, who began by arguing that the Court had no need to address the "many interesting issues" of international and constitutional law surrounding the case. Scalia drew a laugh from the crowd when he quipped, "They really are interesting, you know." Cruz acknowledged that and somewhat presciently noted that they may launch a thousand law review articles, but that there was an easy out for the Court in the case—that the AEDPA does not allow a COA for nonconstitutional claims.

Cruz seemed a bit more comfortable than Donovan at the podium, which makes sense given his recent experience before the Court. *Medellín* was Cruz's third argument before the justices, with the prior two occurring just the year before. Donovan, by contrast, had appeared only once before, and that was in 1995. Furthermore, Cruz had two other advantages. First, he was arguing in favor of the justices' own power. Second, by going second, he got to see where the justices' concerns lay and could focus his arguments on either magnifying them, if they favored his case, or addressing them, if they did not.

Justice Breyer suggested that since the court of appeals had decided on a jurisdictional ground, the Court could decide if the lower court was right or wrong; if the justices decided it was wrong, they could send it back, and then Texas could argue other reasons the case should be dismissed. Cruz agreed that the Court could address other grounds, but he believed the COA ground was "straightforward" and that Medellín had given the Court no reason to disagree with every other court that had looked at the plain text and determined that "constitutional" meant "constitutional." Cruz wanted a decision saying that Medellín could not raise *Avena*, as that would be the end of the issue. The Court, on the other hand, was potentially looking for a way to avoid a tricky decision involving the foreign affairs of the United States and a potential confrontation with the executive branch.

Justice Souter pointed out that the Court could avoid looking at any of these issues if Texas were willing to comply with the president's directive and provide Medellín with "review and reconsideration" under *Avena*. Cruz attempted to dodge the question, noting that the resolution of any questions pending in Texas courts, as a result of the president's declaration, would not affect the federal law question raised in the present petition—whether the AEDPA provided relief for a nonconstitutional claim. When pressed by Souter, Cruz again said he agreed with Justice O'Connor that the question was not present in this case.

Cruz informed the Court that just that prior weekend, Medellín had filed a state habeas application with the Texas Court of Criminal Appeals, asking it to implement the president's declaration. Justice Souter pressed Cruz on Texas's position in regard to Medellín's claims concerning the president's declaration. Cruz argued that Texas felt there were "significant constitutional problems" with a unilateral directive from the president that attempted to displace generally applicable state criminal laws.

Justice Kennedy asked Cruz to clarify whether there were procedures within the Texas court system that would allow Medellín to litigate these claims. Cruz indicated that there absolutely were procedures in Texas where the validity of the president's determination could be litigated, and that they would be reviewable by the Supreme Court, if necessary.

Justice John Paul Stevens, the seniormost member of the Court, asked Cruz whether it was not possible that the actions in the Texas courts could make the current dispute moot. Cruz acknowledged that was a possibility. He also reassured Justice Kennedy that the question of executive authority could be raised before the Supreme Court on review of the Texas court's decision. For this case, he submitted, the easiest thing to do would be to affirm the Fifth Circuit's decision that this was not a constitutional claim and affirm *Breard*'s holding that the AEDPA superseded the Vienna Convention to the extent the two conflicted. This would be a win for Texas and would likely also ensure that any "review and reconsideration" that occurred would come out in Texas's favor.

Justice Breyer asked Cruz why the president would not have authority to determine the meaning of the Vienna Convention. He noted that Texas was bound by the Constitution. Cruz pivoted to argue that the president's actions underscored the point made by both Texas and the United States that it was up to the political branches to act. But there is no precedent, anywhere in the world, for finding an ICJ judgment is judicially enforceable and forms a binding obligation on domestic courts. In other words, the president was taking an unprecedented step. No country on earth treated ICJ decisions in the way Medellín was asking. The Court should not deviate from this uniform practice.

Justice O'Connor noted that a treaty could become part of federal law if it were ratified, as this one was, and that it was possible the treaty provided individual rights, which the Court could determine, even without looking to the *Avena* judgment.

Cruz agreed the Court could do that but argued that it would conflict with the preamble to the treaty and the consistent position of the executive branch since the Vienna Convention was ratified. Furthermore, it would potentially conflict with *Breard*, which held that the AEDPA barred any claims under the convention. Cruz pointed out that the solicitor general, on behalf of the federal government, agreed in every respect with Texas's position on the questions actually before the Court—that the Vienna Convention did not create individually enforceable rights and that the *Avena* decision did not provide an independent basis for overcoming the AEDPA.

Under questioning from Justice Ginsburg, Cruz fell back on the argument that, under Article 94 of the UN Charter, the proper recourse for noncompliance was the Security Council, which demonstrated this was a political, not judicial, question. The United States always has the option not to comply with an ICJ judgment, and there is precedent where it chose not to do so.

Chief Justice Rehnquist then called upon Michael Dreeben, from the Office of the Solicitor General, to speak on behalf of the United States. For oral advocates at the Court, having the solicitor general on your side is something of a double-edged sword. At the time, in all but the rarest of cases, each side in an argument was granted thirty minutes to speak. If the solicitor general (or someone from the office) also argues, he or she divides time with the advocate on the same side. Thus, in order to secure their all-important support, Cruz had to sacrifice some of his argument time. Considering the last-minute nature of the president's declaration, which put the federal government at least partially at odds with Texas, this must have been an exceptionally difficult sacrifice for Texas.

When it comes to the Office of the Solicitor General, few are better than Michael Dreeben. He is one of only three advocates in the twenty-first century to argue one hundred cases or more before the Supreme Court. This case would mark his fifty-seventh appearance before the justices. He was widely recognized as the solicitor general's expert in the field of criminal law.

Dreeben began by reiterating that the United States and Texas agreed there was no jurisdiction to issue a COA here, and that so holding allowed the Court to avoid many of the other issues raised by Medellín. In response to questions by Justices Kennedy and O'Connor, Dreeben argued that the question of a COA was not waivable because it was jurisdictional in the same sense that a notice of appeal is jurisdictional. All of the procedural niceties must be met or the Court cannot reach the merits.

Dreeben pointed to Medellín's filings in the Texas courts regarding his new application for habeas. Demonstrating his mastery, Dreeben cited the specific page number in Medellín's filing, in which he stated he was relying on the *Avena* judgment and the president's declaration,

{ *Chapter Six* }

two new sources of law that were not previously available. This demonstrated that Medellín had failed to exhaust his available state remedies, which is a prerequisite to receiving a COA.

"The *Avena* decision is not a freestanding source of law that can be administered by this Court wholly apart from the President's determination," Dreeben argued.

> What the President did was to determine not that the treaty has a particular meaning that favors Petitioner's case, but that, as a matter of compliance with the obligation of the United States ... the President would create a new source of law, in effect, that would enable the enforcement of that particular judgment, without respect to the validity of the underlying merits determination that the ICJ made.

Only the president's determination to comply allowed lower courts the authority to provide relief to Medellín and the other individuals named in *Avena.*

It would impinge on executive branch authority to treat the ICJ judgment as an independent source of law because this would prevent the president from determining that a particular decision should not be enforced. The president might, for various reasons, choose not to comply with the decision of an international tribunal, and he must remain free to make that determination.

In response to a question from Justice Scalia, Dreeben noted that the president determined, with respect to the fifty-one individuals named in the *Avena* judgment, that it was in the foreign policy interests of the United States to comply as a matter of foreign policy, not because he agreed with the ICJ's ruling. Dreeben also noted that, because the states could comply with the president's directive, there was no need for the Court to rush to a decision. At the time the Court agreed to hear the case, it did not have the benefit of the president's declaration. It also did not know that Medellín would file a subsequent habeas petition in Texas, based on that declaration, which could provide him with the relief he sought. Therefore, the Court should dismiss the case.

The chief justice then called on Mr. Donovan to present his five minutes of rebuttal. Donovan led off by noting that everyone agreed that America should keep its word; that the treaties are binding; and that the president had decreed that Medellín should get what he has asked for. He noted that Medellín was prepared to go forward in state court, allowing Texas's courts to review the claims he had never before raised. The only question left for the Court was how it would ensure the United States complied with its international obligations that the president had confirmed were in its best interests to enforce. Only a decision on the merits, in favor of Medellín, would achieve this goal. Given the president's determination, ruling for Medellín would not tie the president's hands in any future case.

———

Exactly eight weeks after oral argument, on Monday, May 23, 2005, the Supreme Court issued its opinion. The per curiam opinion, not signed by any specific justice, dismissed the case as improvidently granted, largely because the state court proceeding Medellín filed could provide the relief he requested. However, the decision also noted other threshold issues that could "independently preclude federal habeas relief for Medellín."

Although a majority of the Court agreed with the outcome, it was not a cut-and-dried decision. At least two justices disagreed with portions of the reasoning of the majority. Four justices dissented from the Court's decision.

Justice Ginsburg agreed with the Court's ruling, but not with its reasoning. She wrote a concurring opinion to explain her views. In part I of her opinion, which spoke solely for herself, she noted that the Court was faced with two choices: (1) send the case back to the court of appeals for initial rulings on the difficult issues it noted; or (2) dismiss the writ, with the recognition that the Court would have the ability to directly review any proceedings in Texas's courts. The first course of action would require the Fifth Circuit to stay its proceedings, awaiting action by Texas courts—something the Supreme Court was unwilling to do itself—or to conduct a rival review at the same time. The second option would leave the Fifth Circuit's decision in place; thus the only pending action remaining in Medellín's case would be the Texas court petition.

In part II of her opinion, which was joined by Justice Scalia, Justice Ginsburg explained why she chose the second path. Her argument boiled down to the fact that it was the less messy route and did not call on the court of appeals to address a host of thorny questions that the state courts may well render moot.

Justice O'Connor penned the primary dissent, joined by three of her colleagues. She opened her opinion by stating: "José Ernesto Medellín offered proof to the Court of Appeals that reasonable jurists would find debatable or wrong the District Court's disposition of his claim that Texas violated his rights under the Vienna Convention on Consular Relations and that he is thereby entitled to review and reconsideration of his conviction and sentence."

She then identified three specific issues that deserved further consideration by the court of appeals: (1) whether the ICJ's judgment in *Avena* is binding on American courts; (2) whether the convention itself creates a judicially enforceable individual right; and (3) whether the convention itself requires that state procedural default rules be set aside in certain situations to enable "full effect" to be given to the convention. She would have sent the case back to the Fifth Circuit to address these questions in the first instance. She found the speculation engaged in by the Court, regarding whether Medellín might obtain relief from the courts of Texas or whether he might not secure relief in federal court, to be insufficient reason to avoid the compelling questions on which the Court granted certiorari.

O'Connor's opinion noted the country's troubling history with Vienna Convention compliance and observed that it was particularly concerning given the fact that in 2003, more than 56,000 noncitizens were held in state prisons: "Noncitizens accounted for over 10% of the prison populations in California, New York, and Arizona." This is especially concerning in cases involving the death penalty. As of February 2005, she wrote, 119 noncitizens from thirty-one countries were on state death rows.

She conceded that "at every step" Medellín's claim must be viewed through the framework of the Antiterrorism and Effective Death Penalty Act and that where they conflict, the statute controls over the treaty. Thus, under the terms of the statute, Medellín must show his claim is "constitutional" in nature. On the other hand, Texas had conceded that it first raised this argument before the Supreme Court. Texas's failure to raise this argument below prevented it from raising it in the first instance before the justices.

As to Texas's claim that Medellín did not show that the district court's decision was contrary to established precedent, this is an appropriate consideration for an appellate court. The Texas court's decision is not entitled to deference under the AEDPA. First, it dismissed his claim on procedural default grounds. Thus, it did not reach the merits of his claim, as the AEDPA requires before preclusive effect can be given. Second, the Texas court's holding that individuals can never enforce a treaty in court contradicts Supreme Court precedent. She wrote: "The Texas court neither asked nor answered the right question: whether an individual can bring a claim under *this* particular treaty." Therefore, the district court was free to address these claims in the first instance.

The opinion contained a brief assessment of the merits of Medellín's arguments on the questions presented to explain why the lower court should have been overturned. O'Connor noted that if Medellín is right that domestic courts are bound by the ICJ's decision, then it was not merely debatable, but plainly wrong, for the district court to dismiss his claim. Texas made some compelling arguments about the meaning of Article 94 of the UN Charter, she conceded. In the end, she concluded that "reasonable jurists can vigorously disagree about whether and what legal effect ICJ decisions have in our domestic courts, and about whether Medellín can benefit from such effect in this posture." Because this is the standard for granting a COA, the court of appeals should have done so.

O'Connor recognized that since the time of Chief Justice Marshall, courts have found that self-executing treaties are subject to judicial enforcement to the same extent as a statute. Here, the text of Article 36 specifically instructs States to inform detainees of their "rights" under that article. The government, she acknowledges, also makes plausible arguments for its construction that no such individual rights are created. Given these different plausible readings of the treaty, she would have granted a COA to allow for a fuller discussion by the lower court.

Finally, she noted that the *Avena* decision itself created new international law regarding the question of applying state procedural default rules. Even if *Avena* itself was not binding, it would certainly justify reexamining the Court's decision in *Breard*. All Medellín was required to show in order to be entitled to a COA was that the legal questions in his case were debatable. Because she believed they were, she would have sent the case back to the lower courts to decide in the first instance.

Justice Souter, while joining Justice O'Connor's dissent, wrote separately. He stated that in his opinion, the Court should have stayed the case, pending the outcome of the petition in the Texas state courts. As a fallback position, he believed the next best thing was to address the questions on which the Court granted certiorari, and he would find there was "no room for reasonable debate" that Medellín was entitled to a COA. He would remand without the limits that Justice O'Connor appeared to place on the court of appeals in her dissent. The only limit Souter would support would be a direction to the Fifth Circuit to hold its actions until after the Texas state courts ruled, because that ruling could moot any issues raised in the federal habeas petition.

In Justice Breyer's dissent, joined by Justice Stevens, he agreed the best course of action was to stay the case pending the outcome of Texas's state-level review. However, in the absence of majority support for a stay, he would vacate the Fifth Circuit's decision rather than dismiss the case as improvidently granted, which is why he joined Justice O'Connor's dissent.

The dissents, however, did not carry the day. The Court dismissed Medellín's appeal, leaving in place the Fifth Circuit's decision that the issues he raised in his federal habeas application did not merit review by the federal courts. Therefore, Medellín's only hope was "review and reconsideration" provided by the courts of Texas as ordered by the ICJ and the president's decision to implement it.

Texas Rebels

The Bush White House was elated with the outcome. Solicitor General Paul Clement emailed Daniel Levin, counsel to the National Security Council, and the White House's point man on the case, telling him, "I cannot remember being this excited about a DIG." DIG is an acronym for "dismissed as improvidently granted." Medellín's team was less ecstatic, as they had hoped the Court would at the very least keep jurisdiction over the case. But either way, they lived to fight another day.

After the Supreme Court dismissed his petition for certiorari, and with President Bush's memorandum in hand, Medellín returned to Texas to attempt to get the Texas courts to apply the *Avena* decision. He was preceded by a letter from the US attorney general to Texas Attorney General Greg Abbott, sent April 5, 2005, informing him of the president's declaration and asking him to comply. Before the Texas courts, Medellín relied on two local counsel, Gary Taylor and Michael Charlton. Babcock and Donovan were back to representing the government of Mexico. Texas was represented by attorneys from the Harris County District Attorney's Office and the Office of the Attorney General, as opposed to the Texas Solicitor General's Office.

On June 22, 2005, the Texas Court of Criminal Appeals issued an order noting that with the Supreme Court's decision to dismiss the writ, the Texas court was now free to review the subsequent state petition for habeas corpus filed by Medellín. But, first, the Texas court had to determine if there were any state law bars to hearing Medellín's subsequent habeas petition. The court ordered the parties to brief this question. It specifically invited the United States to present its views. It set oral argument for September 14.

This time, Medellín's legal team felt confident. Unlike the last time, the US Department of Justice was filing amicus briefs in support of Medellín, something nearly unprecedented before and not repeated since.

"We had the president on our side," Babcock says. "Anytime you have the executive on your side in a death penalty case, frankly, I don't even know if there's any other capital case you could find where the executive branch has supported relief for a person condemned to death."

But Texas was not willing to play ball. Instead, the state argued that the president lacked the authority to unilaterally order it to comply. The United States presented its views and even sent an attorney from the Solicitor General's Office, Mr. Michael Dreeben. Kristopher Monson, an attorney in the Texas Solicitor General's Office and one of the authors of Texas's Supreme Court brief, described Dreeben as gracious and recalled that the oral argument went on so long that Dreeben nearly missed his flight back to Washington, DC: "That argument is memorable for being so, so long."

The court took more than a year to decide the case, eventually handing down its decision on November 15, 2006. In the meantime, the Supreme Court had heard and decided another case dealing with an Article 36 violation, *Sanchez-Llamas v. Oregon*. Moises Sanchez-Llamas was a Mexican national, but he was not sentenced to death and thus was not one of the *Avena* defendants. His case, along with a consolidated appeal from a Honduran national named Mario Bustillo, raised three questions before the justices: (1) Did Article 36 create individual, substantive rights? (2) Must evidence obtained following an Article 36 violation be suppressed? And (3) may the state rely on a procedural bar to refuse to consider a claim that a defendant's Article 36 rights were violated?

In a 5–4 decision, the Supreme Court assumed, without deciding, that the Vienna Convention did provide individual rights but determined that it did not require suppression of any evidence and that a state was free to rely on a procedural bar to hearing the claim. Because it found that neither Sanchez-Llamas nor Bustillo was entitled to a remedy, it determined it did not need to answer the antecedent question of whether the Vienna Convention created individual rights. Even if it does, Article 36 does not mandate suppression. Indeed, it does not even guarantee consular assistance. At best, it protects the ability to inform a foreign national's consulate of his or her detention.

As to the question of applying the procedural bar, the Court relied on its earlier decision in *Breard* and held that Article 36 claims could be procedurally defaulted. Addressing *LaGrand* and *Avena*, the Court acknowledged that International Court of Justice (ICJ) decisions were entitled to "respectful consideration," but held that the power to determine the meaning of treaties as a matter of federal law was committed exclusively to US courts. Even according "respectful consideration" to *LaGrand* and *Avena*, Article 36 says it is to be implemented in conformity with domestic law and in the United States that includes procedural default doctrines. Even constitutional protections can be procedurally defaulted, and there is no reason to treat treaty claims any differently. This decision would play a key role in the decision of the Texas Court of Criminal Appeals.

The Texas court produced a unanimous decision, although it was expressed via five opinions. Judge Michael Keasler delivered the main opinion of the court, joined by six other judges in all but one part of the opinion. In that last portion, only three other judges joined. Concurring opinions were filed by Presiding Judge Sharon Keller, the first woman to serve on the court, as well as Judges Thomas Price, Barbara Hervey, and Catherine Cochran.

The court rejected the president's attempts to overcome state law through a unilateral declaration to the attorney general, instructing him to give effect to the *Avena* judgment. It held that the president's action did not constitute binding federal law with which Texas was required to comply under the supremacy clause of the US Constitution. Furthermore, the *Avena* judgment itself was entitled to no more than "respectful consideration," which was somewhat undercut by the decision of the United States to withdraw from the Optional Protocol. Given this, along with a presumption that treaties do not generally displace state law, the Texas court felt that it was appropriate to give effect to the state's procedural default doctrine. Because neither the *Avena* judgment nor the presidential memorandum met the standards for a new legal basis for reconsidering the state court's initial habeas decision, Medellín was precluded from raising it now. This reliance on the procedural default doctrine flew directly in the face of the *Avena* judgment. And this set up another confrontation in the US Supreme Court.

Under the Texas Code of Criminal Procedure, subsequent habeas petitions are disfavored, and a court may not consider the merits or grant relief, except in specific circumstances. One such circumstance, and the one on which Medellín relied, was that the claim or issue could not have been raised previously "because the factual or legal basis for the claim was unavailable on the date the applicant filed the previous application." Here, Medellín made two arguments. First, he argued that the *Avena* judgment and the president's memorandum to the attorney general served to preempt the Texas law that would bar his subsequent habeas application. Second, he argued that they constituted new legal bases that were not available at the time of Medellín's prior application for habeas because they had not yet been issued. The Texas Court of Criminal Appeals disagreed.

The court recognized that treaties were the supreme law of the land and could, in the case of conflict, overcome state laws. But relying on a 1942 Supreme Court opinion, *United States v. Pink*, it recognized a general rule of interpretation that treaties are to be carefully construed "'so as not to derogate from the authority and jurisdiction of the States of this nation unless clearly necessary to effectuate the national policy.'" In other words, if there was a way to read the treaty that did not require overturning Texas's procedural default rule, that reading was to be preferred. Only if there was no other way to fulfill the United States' obligation should Medellín's reading be accepted. The court also noted another presumption that even treaties that provide benefits to private parties are not generally treated as directly enforceable in domestic courts. Thus, even if the ICJ was correct that Medellín had an individual right, that did not open Texas's courthouse doors.

The court rejected Medellín's contention that the *Avena* judgment preempted state law. Here, it relied on *Sanchez-Llamas*, decided that March. The Texas court felt it was bound by the Supreme Court's decision that ICJ decisions were not binding on US courts.

The bulk of the opinion is addressed to the argument made by the United States that the president's memorandum either preempted Texas law or served as a new factual or legal basis on which Medellín could rely, although this portion of the opinion received the votes of only four judges. Medellín and the United States were united in their argument that it did. The State of Texas, on the other hand, argued that the language in the memorandum, while showing the intent of the United States to comply with *Avena*, did not contain any language ordering the states to do anything, let alone ignore state laws, precedents, or judicial doctrines. While the court noted the merits of this argument, it determined that it need not decide it because, in its opinion, Medellín had not demonstrated that the memorandum entitled him to "review and reconsideration."

The court began by recognizing that the federal government has exclusive control of the nation's foreign affairs and that the president's power in this area, while subordinate to the Constitution, is "not necessarily dependent on specific congressional authorization." Thus, the president can make executive agreements that are not approved by the Senate, but which nonetheless may preempt state laws if those laws interfere with the foreign policy goals of the United States.

Here, the president's exercise of power was unprecedented. And, in the opinion of the Texas Court of Criminal Appeals, it exceeded his authority under the Constitution because it impermissibly intruded into the power of the judiciary. Again relying on *Sanchez-Llamas*, the Texas court held that the president may not "dictate to the judiciary what law to apply or how to interpret the applicable law."

Medellín and the United States had relied on a series of cases that recognized the president's power to settle international disputes with foreign nations. As part of those settlements, the Supreme Court had held that conflicting state laws had to give way and were preempted by these settlements. The Texas court ruled that this reliance was misplaced. Unlike in those cases, the president had not entered into any settlement with Mexico regarding the fifty-one nationals whose rights were adjudicated in *Avena*. Instead, the president's memorandum "is a unilateral act executed in an effort to achieve a settlement with Mexico." The Texas court refused to recognize the Optional Protocol as an agreement between the two nations.

It was the absence of a negotiated agreement between the United States and Mexico that convinced the court that the president had exceeded his powers. In response to Medellín's claim that the president was enforcing an obligation that the United States had already agreed to, the court again cited the decision in *Sanchez-Llamas*. The court reasoned the president was not acting to "faithfully execute" the laws of the United States. Rather, he was acting as lawmaker, which the Constitution does not grant him the power to do. Because the president had exceeded his authority in issuing the memorandum, it was not binding federal law and thus did not provide a basis for a new habeas petition.

Judge Cochran filed a concurrence. She agreed that the memorandum did not preempt Texas law, because she did not believe that the president's memo to the attorney general could constitute the enactment of federal law binding on state courts. The memo did not follow the requirements for an executive order or presidential proclamation and was not published in the *Federal Register*. While the president may be "the most powerful man on Earth," even he is constrained by the dictates of the Constitution and federal statutes. Unless he complies with the requirements for issuing a proclamation or executive order, his memo is nothing more than the expression of his personal desires. It takes more to displace the authority of the states to run their own criminal justice systems.

Presiding Judge Keller also concurred in the judgment regarding the president's memorandum. In her opinion, the memorandum impermissibly violated the notions of federalism enshrined in the Constitution, embodied in its structure and in the Tenth Amendment. She noted that state regulation of criminal law has traditionally been recognized as sacrosanct, and the US Supreme Court has not hesitated to strike down actions that unduly interfere in that arena. In terms of treaties, the Supreme Court has gone out of its way to narrowly construe such documents to ensure they do not preempt state laws in areas of traditional state competence.

Criminal justice is a core concern of states and has been since before the founding. Furthermore, "States have an overwhelming interest in the procedures followed in their own courts." According to Judge Keller, the president's memorandum seeks to force states to "conduct proceedings they would not otherwise conduct and to do so in a manner inconsistent with their own procedures." In such circumstances, the balance of interests counsels against preemption of state law.

Judge Price also concurred in the result. He began his opinion by advising law enforcement of the need to comply with Article 36 and inform detained foreign nationals of their right to contact their consulates. He noted that, in his opinion, Article 36 confers individual rights upon detainees. Notification of this right is necessary, he reasoned, because without it, "the vast majority of nationals arrested will almost certainly fail to invoke this right and succumb to our procedural default rules." Because he concurred with the majority's treatment of the procedural default rule, he was concerned that many foreign nationals would not receive the benefit of consular assistance and would be unable to raise it in a timely manner, thus forever foreclosing them from bringing the issue to the attention of courts. While state sovereignty is important, respecting the rights of foreign nationals, as required by international law, is also important and must be recognized.

Finally, Judge Hervey filed a short concurrence. Her opinion is written with more vitriol than the other opinions. She referred to the proceedings as an "international *cause celebre*" centered around a man who did not deny his crimes. She believed that the entire proceedings were "much ado about nothing" because Medellín received "essentially the review mandated by the *Avena* decision during his initial state habeas corpus proceeding." She claimed that Medellín "did not bother telling the police" that he was not a native-born citizen. "Nevertheless, applicant maintains that the lack of intentional, reckless, or negligent wrongdoing by the State (other than, perhaps, lack of clairvoyance) and despite his non-assertion of any privilege or immunity, he is entitled to an immunity heretofore not afforded to any citizen or nonresident under Texas or Federal law—immunity from procedural default."

Judge Hervey's opinion is both factually wrong and unnecessarily acerbic. Medellín did inform the police that he was born in Mexico, and there is no dispute that the police failed to inform him of his rights under Article 36. While there is no evidence this failure was intentional, it was, at the least, reckless. There was simply no reason for writing this opinion, other than to score points with potential voters. Texas is one of twenty-one states with partisan judicial elections, and Judge Hervey was up for reelection in November 2006. Her five-paragraph opinion provides no new legal argumentation, and its tone reads more like a campaign ad than a reasoned judicial opinion. A dispute about the proper role of international law, and the president's power to enforce it, deserved more.

Faced with this loss, Medellín again sought review in the US Supreme Court.

But before the case returned to the Supreme Court, Sandra Babcock's career took a turn. She was interested in teaching and working on broader human rights issues, something that is not easy to do in private practice. As she explained, "You don't make a living doing that. You have

{ *Chapter Seven* }

to be part of an organization or be part of a university." And so she left the Mexican Capital Legal Assistance Program for a job as a clinical professor working with law students in the Center for International Human Rights at the Northwestern University School of Law in Chicago. But despite leaving her role as director, she remained involved in the cases the legal assistance program was working on, including Medellín's.

That continued involvement took the form of a petition before the Inter-American Commission on Human Rights, filed by Babcock and her Northwestern students on behalf of José Medellín and two other Mexican nationals who were also subjects of the *Avena* judgment. There are two essential differences between the ICJ and the Inter-American Commission: first, the ICJ is not a human rights tribunal. "The ICJ, when it decided the case, did not apply principles of human rights law," Babcock said. "If it had, the right outcome would have been to say that [Medellín's] conviction definitely would be vacated. At a minimum that his death sentence should be vacated." The second essential difference is that the right protected by the ICJ belongs to Mexico. It is not an individual right, an argument that Texas had relied heavily on both in the lower courts and before the Supreme Court. But a ruling from the commission would provide Medellín with an individual right. This would provide him with additional ammunition in his claims that he was entitled to relief.

Arguing before the commission is a very different experience from arguing before either US courts or the ICJ. The commission is located in Washington, DC, which is where arguments took place. "You get an hour for the argument," Babcock recalled. "It's less formal. It's a lawmaking commission, but it's not a court. So it doesn't have the same aura of judicial pomp that you see in a courtroom." The hearings are held in a large conference room with simultaneous translation for the judges who don't speak English as a first language. The commission is represented by three individuals from various countries in North and South America. "Each side has an opportunity to present their arguments, and the commission asks questions, and it's a much more streamlined process and a bit less formal," Babcock said. The US government, via the State Department, opposed the petition. "So the Justice Department supported us in the Supreme Court," Babcock said, "but the State Department opposed us in the Inter-American Commission."

The Inter-American Commission took the matter under advisement. While Babcock was waiting for the commission's decision, the US proceedings continued apace.

After the Texas Court of Criminal Appeals denied Medellín's subsequent application for habeas corpus, Medellín's counsel filed a second writ of certiorari with the US Supreme Court on January 16, 2007. The Court granted the petition on April 30, to be argued in the fall. While it is unusual for the same case to make two trips to the high court, it is not unheard of. In fact, people on both sides fully expected the Court to take the case. The Court granted the petition to decide two questions: whether the president had the authority to require states to give effect to the *Avena* judgment in the cases involving the named nationals, and whether state courts are independently bound to honor the "undisputed international obligation of the United States" to give effect to *Avena* in those cases.

Two major changes occurred at the Supreme Court between Medellín's two trips. The first was that Justice Sandra Day O'Connor had announced her retirement shortly after the end of the Supreme Court's term in 2005. DC Circuit judge John Roberts was nominated to replace O'Connor, and things looked like they were heading for a speedy confirmation that would see O'Connor off the Court in time for the first Monday in October 2005. However, before Roberts could be confirmed, Chief Justice William Rehnquist died, leaving a second opening on the Court. President Bush decided to withdraw Roberts's nomination for O'Connor's seat and put him up for the chief justice's position, where he was confirmed. President Bush nominated Samuel Alito of the Third Circuit Court of Appeals to replace O'Connor. Alito was confirmed in January 2006.

While Roberts, who had clerked for then Associate Justice Rehnquist in the 1980–1981 Supreme Court term, was widely viewed as a one-for-one replacement of his predecessor, Alito was viewed as being much more reliably conservative than Justice O'Connor, who had served as the Court's swing vote for years, especially in cases involving criminal defendants. This left Justice Anthony Kennedy as the Court's sole swing vote. While Roberts has sometimes voted with the liberal justices, Kennedy was viewed as a more reliable swing vote, and so most briefs in this era, particularly in politically charged cases, were targeted at him. This case was no different. According to Kristopher Monson, a member of the Texas Solicitor General's Office, and one of the authors of Texas's brief, it was targeted squarely at Justice Kennedy.

Another major change that occurred was that, due to the posture of the case, the solicitor general changed sides. Because they were defending the president's authority to issue his declaration and Texas argued that the president lacked this authority, the full weight of the solicitor general now sided with Medellín.

On June 28, 2007, Medellín filed his merits brief with the Court. In laying out the facts of the case, the brief focused on the United States' agreement to be bound by an ICJ decision and the efforts it took to create and ratify the Vienna Convention on Consular Relations.

The brief opened by arguing that as a matter of both international and US law, the *Avena* judgment was binding on US courts. While recognizing that the United States had since withdrawn from the Optional Protocol, the brief argued that the United States remained a party to the Vienna Convention itself, from which the obligation of consular notification arose, and that such a withdrawal applied only to future cases, not previously decided ones.

The brief attempted to distinguish *Sanchez-Llamas v. Oregon*, which the lower court had relied upon. In that case, the Supreme Court had held that the Vienna Convention did not displace state procedural default rules. But the two petitioners in that case were a national of Honduras and a Mexican national who was not named in the *Avena* judgment. Thus, neither could rely on the binding determination of the ICJ. Medellín argued that the ICJ's decision was a binding judgment as to the fifty-one individuals named therein.

The brief then argued that given the terms of the *Avena* judgment, a court is the only place where the obligation could be fulfilled. The president had, furthermore, made a determination that state courts were the proper venue for vindicating this right, and the Constitution granted him the power.

This power arises from Article II of the Constitution, which provides that the president shall "take Care that the Laws be faithfully executed." According to Medellín, these "Laws" include treaties of the United States. This power includes the authority to bring suit against a political subdivision of the United States as well as other steps the president deems appropriate to enforce federal laws. He does not require congressional authorization to exercise these authorities. If neither a statute nor the treaty provides a means for enforcement, the president has the authority under the clause to choose the appropriate means. In this case, the president had chosen to have state courts act as the means of enforcement.

The president's choice did not require any special actions by state courts. They may utilize the already-existing procedures for postconviction review. This shows the appropriate respect for state functions by allowing state courts the first opportunity to review. But this depends on the state faithfully applying federal law, in the form of treaties, and not disregarding it by relying on procedural default doctrines. Contrary to the views of the Texas courts, the president was not making law. Instead, he directed state courts to apply the existing federal treaty law.

Finally, the brief spent two pages arguing that the procedural default bar is preempted. The *Avena* decision explicitly precluded reliance on the doctrine in the fifty-one cases listed in the judgment. Thus, the Texas court's use of the doctrine, the brief argued, was "flatly inconsistent" with the international obligations of the United States.

Texas's brief was filed on August 23, 2007. On the brief were Ted Cruz, still the solicitor general of Texas; Sean Jordan, the deputy solicitor general and principal author; as well as Kristopher Monson, Daniel Geyser, and Adam Aston. Each of these five played some role in writing the brief, which would win a Best Brief award from the National Association of Attorneys General, part of a long streak by the Texas Solicitor General's Office. The brief acknowledged that Medellín did not receive his rights under the Vienna Convention but noted that at no point during his trial, sentence, or direct appeal did he raise any claims under the treaty.

Every Supreme Court merits brief contains a section called the summary of argument. Here, the parties and amici give a short summary of the fuller argument to come. The best briefs use this as a form of advocacy every bit as important as the main body of the brief. And Texas's brief was no exception. From the very first sentence, Ted Cruz and his team sought to shape the way the Court saw the case. Medellín's brief began by telling the Court that "the President of the United States has acted to give effect to the Nation's obligation, under duly ratified treaties, to abide by the *Avena* judgment in the cases of the 51 Mexican nationals named in the judgment." While a good summary, it told the Court what happened, not what the case was about.

Texas's brief, by contrast, begins: "This is a separation of powers case." This simple sentence sets the stage for what is at stake and how the Court should view it. It continues powerfully: "It implicates every axis of the structural limitations on government: President vis-à-vis Congress, President vis-à-vis the Supreme Court, international law vis-à-vis domestic law, federal government vis-à-vis the States, and, with a Möbius twist, President vis-à-vis the state judiciary." Cruz hammered his point home, previewing for the Court the numerous consequences of siding with the president and Medellín in this case.

Given the importance of having the United States on your side, the Texas brief goes out of its way to highlight areas where the United States agreed with Texas. It calls Medellín's argument "relatively straightforward." By contrast, it views the United States' argument as "considerably more nuanced." It noted that the United States rejected Medellín's argument and agreed with Texas that *Avena* was not binding.

Cruz's strategy was to divide and conquer. By showing the Court that the United States and Texas largely agreed with respect to Medellín's argument, he was undercutting the apparent support of the Bush administration. He was also demonstrating to the Court that the real battle to be fought was the question of President Bush's authority, not that of the ICJ. This goes back to Cruz's strategy of choosing the ground on which the fight would occur. As Cruz readily acknowledged, the idea that Texas could ignore the World Court was a losing argument. If he could focus the Court's attention purely on the president's overreach, he could win.

Texas's brief does not dispute that the *Avena* judgment created an international obligation on the United States, which may require changes in domestic law to effectuate. But "a laudable goal does not give the President unlimited power to act beyond his constitutional authority." Thus, in order to enforce *Avena*, the president must work with the other branches of government, namely, Congress, to pass some sort of legislation before requiring states to comply.

The brief concluded the opening of its argument the same way it began, by reiterating that this is a case about the separation of powers and federalism. "It infringes on the authority of Congress, it infringes on the constitutional role of the judiciary, and it infringes on the sovereignty of the States."

Texas argued that the United States' arguments did not provide a workable limiting principle. It provided a limiting principle of its own, namely, that the president can enforce *Avena* if he coordinated with either Congress or the states. Because it raised these constitutional questions, the Court should construe the memorandum as a request, not a command, which accords with its plain text. As both Texas and the United States agree, *Avena* is not enforceable by a private party in domestic courts without further action. Finally, the brief argued that Medellín already received the "review and reconsideration" required by the ICJ.

The first argument relied on the idea that even treaties that provide direct benefits to private individuals do not, without more, create private rights of action in domestic courts. Only Congress can transform an international obligation into domestic law. While the president may have powers in foreign affairs, they are limited to enforcing, not creating, law. It is especially important to respect this principle when the president seeks to "infringe[] on the States' authority as sovereigns to order their own judicial departments and criminal-justice systems."

Texas argued that the president's power was at its "lowest ebb" because he was acting in direct contravention of Congress's will. According to Texas, the memorandum contradicted the Senate's understanding of the Vienna Convention. When the Senate consented to the treaty, it did so with the understanding that it created no individual rights, that ICJ judgments could only be enforced through political or diplomatic means, and that complying with the convention would not require changes to domestic law. Thus, the president could not claim to be merely enforcing the will of the Senate that assented to the treaty. Furthermore, the memorandum conflicted with the policy, expressed in the AEDPA, that state court criminal proceedings are to be deferred to.

Texas pointed out that even the United States' brief referred to the memorandum as "unprecedented." In every other case in which plaintiffs sought to enforce the Vienna Convention, the official position of the United States was that it did not create an individual right and was enforceable only via political means. In *Breard*, the United States told the Supreme Court that the federal government's sole power to enforce the convention was persuasion—such as letters from the secretary of state to a governor.

Texas also argued the president's memorandum intruded upon the power of the judiciary. Just a year before in *Sanchez-Llamas*, the Court had ruled the other way on the very questions raised by Medellín. The United States was arguing that the Texas courts should follow the memorandum, rather than the Supreme Court's decision. But, Texas argued, the president does not have the power to overrule the Supreme Court. The Court had considered the existence of *Avena* in *Sanchez-Llamas* and had rejected the idea that the United States was obligated to comply with the ICJ's interpretation of the Vienna Convention.

Texas also argued the memorandum impermissibly intruded on the authority of the states. The federal government cannot intrude on a state's power by "commandeering the machinery of state government to implement federal policy." States have "broad sovereign authority" over their judicial processes, particularly in the criminal justice realm. Nothing in the supremacy clause or the foreign affairs power changed this, and the government may not use a treaty to expand on the powers provided by the Constitution. Similarly, the federal government cannot order a state to change its procedural rules. The presidential memorandum, Texas argued, did both.

This argument was crafted by Daniel Geyser, a new member of the Texas Solicitor General's Office. Geyser admits that his politics did not match those of Ted Cruz, the outspoken conservative Texas solicitor general. But Cruz didn't have any ideological litmus test to work in his office. Geyser described the office as "like the SWAT team that comes in and takes the hard" appeals. Cruz, he said, made sure that the office took only the cases that would benefit from appellate specialists. While Cruz's involvement in briefs depended on his schedule, interest, and the subject matter of the underlying case, he was very involved in *Medellín*. Geyser noted: "You can see his fingerprints pretty clearly in certain aspects of the briefing."

The brief next argued that the United States failed to provide any workable limiting principle for the Court to embrace. Texas told the Court that to side with the United States was to open the door to an unlimited power grab because the government could not provide such a principle. The argument put forward by the US solicitor general would allow the president to use any international obligation as an excuse to set aside any state laws that purportedly violated that obligation.

To prevent the exercise of such an unbridled power, our constitutional order requires interbranch cooperation before setting aside state laws enacted by the democratically elected state legislatures. But here, the United States was insisting that the president, acting alone, through nothing more than a memo to the attorney general, could force open the Texas courthouse doors and sweep aside its neutrally applied doctrine of procedural default. According to Cruz, this went too far.

The brief then provided a way out for the justices. Recognizing that the Court would not issue a decision that prevented the United States entirely from complying with its international obligations, the brief argued that the executive branch could achieve its goals if it worked with either the legislative branch or the states. Texas wisely did not deny the existence of the international obligation. Rather, it offered several alternatives the president could pursue to bring the United States into compliance. Among these were working with Congress to provide a statutory habeas remedy for the *Avena* defendants and those similarly situated; completing a treaty with Mexico that expressly incorporated *Avena* and expressly making it self-executing federal law; or working directly with the states to comply, by issuing an executive order to provide an executive "review and reconsideration" panel for the fifty-one named Mexican nationals. Recommendations from that panel could then be provided to the relevant clemency authorities in the states. Any of these, Texas argued, would be constitutional means to comply with the *Avena* judgment.

While some of Cruz's proposed alternatives would obviously not be of benefit to Texas, that was irrelevant at this stage, and may in fact have helped his argument. By showing the Court a way Medellín could still win, if only the Constitution were followed, he may have made it more palatable for liberal justices, who were inclined to side with Medellín, to rule in favor of Texas in this case. Cruz's goal was merely to demonstrate to the Court that options to enforce *Avena* existed. Whether they were politically feasible was not his, or the Court's, concern.

The brief next argued that nothing in the ICJ's structure or purpose supported Medellín's argument. It was intended and designed to resolve disputes between states, not private parties, and violations were enforceable only through the UN Security Council. Accepting Medellín's argument would strip the political branches of their authority to determine whether and how to comply with an ICJ decision and instead arrogate it to the unelected judicial branch.

Finally, the brief concluded by arguing that Medellín already received the remedy provided for in *Avena*. *Avena*, at its core, provided for a process. It required the United States to ensure that no harm befell defendants because local police failed to provide consular information and notification under Article 36. But the lower courts had already reviewed this question and determined that Medellín suffered no prejudice from the Houston Police Department's mistake. When Medellín first filed his state habeas petition, he raised the denial of rights under Article 36. As an alternative to its reliance on the procedural default doctrine, the lower court concluded Medellín failed to show "that he was harmed by any lack of notification to the Mexican consulate concerning his arrest for capital murder." This is precisely the question the ICJ would have the United States answer in *Avena*. Therefore, the question raised by Medellín was moot.

Medellín's reply brief was filed in September 2007, shortly before the start of the Supreme Court's term. The tone of the brief is stronger than any that Medellín had previously filed. It stated that Texas's view was that "the Framers left the United States with a dysfunctional Constitution." It argued that Texas was seeking to overturn "long-settled understandings about the role of treaties under the Constitution and to ignore dispositive precedents" dating back to the founding on point after point. The brief argued that enforcing the *Avena* decision and the president's determination would not harm Congress, intrude on federal courts, or violate principles of federalism. Furthermore, the memorandum was independently binding. Finally, Texas had not provided Medellín with the relief he sought.

Medellín pointed to a long line of cases in which the Court enforced treaty-based rights, regardless of implementing legislation. The president had the undisputed power to sue a state agency in order to enforce treaty obligations. If he had that power, he certainly had the power to direct compliance in suits brought by others. Furthermore, the government appeared as amicus in cases both in Texas and at the Supreme Court. It would serve no purpose to require the president to file his own independent suit. Finally, the brief argued that the president had the power to enforce *Avena* pursuant to his foreign affairs authority. The Court had long recognized the president's power to settle claims in US courts to avoid international disputes, and nothing in the AEDPA changed this.

The reply then turned to the effect on federal courts. First, it argued that the case was about enforcing a foreign judgment, not the proper interpretation of the Vienna Convention. Under long-established precedent, foreign judgments are given respect, even if the court applying them might have come down differently on the underlying substantive question, unless doing so violates some public policy. The fact that the Supreme Court came to a different conclusion than the ICJ about the meaning of Article 36 in *Sanchez-Llamas* was irrelevant. The president determined that it would be in the best interests of the United States to comply with *Avena*. The only role left for the Court was to apply it.

Next the brief pointed out the long history of submitting to binding arbitration in international tribunals with no ill effects on the separation of powers: "From the earliest days of the Constitution, and even earlier, the United States has made numerous treaties calling for submission of disputes to international tribunals." There were "dozens if not hundreds" of such agreements. Under Texas's logic, all were invalid. This simply could not be the case, and to hold otherwise would upset numerous treaty-based regimes to which the United States was a party.

Medellín's next argument was that ruling in his favor would not offend principles of federalism by creating a new cause of action. Medellín relied on the arguments made by the Texas Court of Criminal Appeals itself. None of the justices on that court held they lacked jurisdiction over his petition. To the contrary, the lower court explicitly recognized that if federal law preempted Texas's procedural default doctrine it would have power to grant relief. The only question was whether the president's memorandum had such preemptive effect. The Texas court had held that it did not; Medellín argued that it did.

Finally, the brief argued that Medellín had not yet received the relief to which he was entitled under *Avena*. It noted that the ICJ had implicitly held that Texas had not provided relief when it determined that "review and reconsideration" was necessary in all fifty-one cases, including Medellín's. Furthermore, the president's determination "makes clear that the obligation of review and reconsideration is prospective." Because the lower court decision lumped the question of Medellín's rights into an analysis of constitutional obligations, an approach "expressly rejected" by the ICJ, "its findings could not possibly have satisfied *Avena*."

Several amici filed briefs on behalf of both parties, just as they had in Medellín's first trip to the Supreme Court. The list of participants was almost identical. Although the solicitor general had switched sides, the switch was not wholehearted. While Medellín argued that he had the right to privately enforce the *Avena* decision even in the absence of the president's declaration, the United States did not go that far. Instead, it argued purely in support of the president's power to require compliance with *Avena*. It explicitly disagreed that Medellín could enforce the judgment absent the president's actions.

The brief of the United States opened by arguing that the president had the authority to require state courts to comply with the *Avena* judgment. The United States noted that the president did not agree with the substance of the ICJ's decision but nevertheless recognized that it created a binding obligation on the United States, which he had decided to enforce. He chose the state courts as the best forums in which to vindicate that obligation.

The brief also argued that the president was uniquely situated to respond to an ICJ decision. Because of the sensitive nature of foreign relations and the speed with which such decisions must sometimes be made, the president was in the best position to decide whether and how to comply with our international obligations.

The United States argued that the president had the independent authority to resolve disputes with foreign nations. Since 1799, when the president settled a dispute with the Netherlands over the schooner *Wilmington Packet*, the president had used this authority. In the century between 1817 and 1917, presidents entered into eighty such agreements. Ten other agreements were entered into between 1952 and 1980. The Supreme Court had consistently recognized this authority, which includes the ability to determine individual rights, even when the president did not secure the agreement of Congress, and even when conflicting state laws had to give way.

The brief argued that the decision to enforce *Avena* fit within this long-recognized authority. In fact, this exercise of power was far more modest. First, there are only limited areas over which the ICJ has jurisdiction, while there is a nearly limitless universe of disputes between nations that the president may agree to resolve. Unlike the ICJ, the president is not restricted to cases covered by specific treaties, where the parties have agreed to appear. He has the inherent authority to settle *any* international dispute between the United States and a foreign country. Second, the Senate, by voting for the treaties at issue in this case, participated in the decision to be bound by the ICJ, whereas the president typically decides on the basis of settlement without any input from the other branches.

By statute, Congress had directed that the president would "direct all functions connected with the United States' participation in the United Nations." This authority allows the president and the executive branch to represent the United States before the ICJ. If the United States were the plaintiff, the president would be responsible for securing a victory and seeking compliance from the other party. The converse must also be true.

Finally, past practice also supported the president. Since the United States agreed to submit disputes to the ICJ, the World Court had issued five decisions, including *Avena*, calling for implementation by the United States. In all those cases the president determined the appropriate response. And in each instance, including this one, Congress acquiesced in the president's action. In no case did Congress object either to the president being the one to take action or to the specific actions taken.

The United States then turned to the decision of the Texas Court of Criminal Appeals and argued that none of the reasons it relied on in its decision were persuasive. Enforcing the ICJ's decision did not, as Texas argued, intrude upon the judiciary. The president merely supplied the rule of decision—*Avena*—he was not preventing the courts from interpreting and applying that rule. The president's memorandum did not mandate any outcome. Courts still retained the power to conduct the "review and reconsideration" and determine for themselves if any harm resulted.

The United States pointed out that the two parties had already agreed to enforce the *Avena* decision by their mutual ratification of the Optional Protocol, which granted the ICJ jurisdiction, and the ratification of the

UN Charter, which made ICJ judgments binding on the parties. A subsequent agreement would be superfluous.

Federalism does not apply in this case, the United States argued, because treaties have already been declared the supreme law of the land in the Constitution. Furthermore, state courts have no place balancing the interests of the parties. That power belonged solely to the president, who gets to determine if compliance outweighs any harm to federal-state relations.

The final argument raised by the Texas court that the United States responded to was that the president's memorandum was not binding because it was a letter to the attorney general rather than a proclamation or executive order. The Constitution does not mandate any particular form for a presidential decree to be binding federal law. In a prior case, the Court had found binding a letter from the State Department to the attorney general. Here, the president personally issued a directive to the attorney general, instructing him to ensure the United States' compliance with *Avena*. Nothing more was required.

The United States then addressed two arguments Texas raised in its opposition to the petition for certiorari. First, Texas argued that the *Avena* judgment was not self-executing; second, it argued that only the UN Security Council can enforce ICJ decisions. Both arguments, the United States averred, were without merit.

The fact that the obligation to comply is not self-executing actually demonstrates the need for the president to act in this case, the brief argued. If it could be privately enforced, the president would have no role. On the contrary, the president has a vital role in determining whether or not to comply with an ICJ decision and the lack of self-execution bolsters this argument.

As for the argument about the Security Council, that just demonstrates that in some cases, countries may choose not to comply with ICJ decisions. In those cases, the UN Charter provides the sole means of seeking recourse. It does not address cases like this one, in which the federal government decides to comply with the ICJ's ruling. In those cases, the domestic law of the nation in question would control, and here the supremacy clause says that treaty obligations preempt conflicting state laws.

Seven other parties filed amicus briefs on behalf of Medellín; one group, EarthRights International, filed a brief in support of neither party, arguing that unilateral executive power to preempt state law, in the absence of a treaty, was not at issue in the case but would raise substantial constitutional questions; and six parties filed amicus briefs on behalf of Texas (one of these was a brief filed by Virginia and twenty-seven other states, as well as Puerto Rico).

This brief, signed by a bipartisan group of state attorneys general, argued that the *Avena* decision was not privately enforceable; that the president's unilateral declaration that private parties could enforce *Avena* violates congressional intent; and that the memorandum violates principles of dual sovereignty.

Much of the content of the states' brief duplicated the arguments made by Texas. The bulk of the brief was devoted to the second argument, regarding congressional intent. The states argued that Congress had quite a robust role to play in foreign affairs.

First, the states told the Court that when the Senate consented to the Vienna Convention, it did so with the understanding that the convention neither created private rights nor disrupted ordinary rules of default. In fact, the executive explicitly told the Senate that prior to securing its concurrence.

Second, the states argued that in enacting the AEDPA, Congress quite recently indicated its intent to protect the final judgments of state courts in criminal cases. Despite a decade of legal wrangling over these issues, Congress had never taken any action to lessen the protections for state court final judgments provided by the AEDPA. The president's actions here, then, which could require disturbing those final judgments, flew in the face of Congress's intent.

The states also argued that past practice by Congress does not justify or signal approval for the president's actions in this case. Despite more than two hundred years of history, neither Medellín nor the United States could point to a single instance in which the president ordered a state court to reopen and readjudicate a final judgment. While the states recognized that "the President has power to take *some* unilateral steps to enforce ICJ decisions, the President does not have the power to take *any and all* unilateral actions."

As for the cases where the president unilaterally settled disputes with other nations, none of them required reopening a final state criminal conviction. Instead, they all dealt with property disputes. While *those* cases extend back to 1799 and Congress had acquiesced in the exercise of that power, it did not justify the president's authority to set aside any and all state laws that may conflict with the foreign policy objectives of the United States, and the Court should not extend its precedents to so conclude.

The states also threw the words of the United States back at it, drawing from briefs filed by the solicitor general in *Breard*, *Sanchez-Llamas*, *Dretke*, and other cases where the United States took the view that the only power available to the federal government was the power of persuasion as opposed to legal compulsion. The United States' position in this case offered a sharp break from the previously consistent argument that the federal government had no authority to order the states to comply with the ICJ.

While perhaps not as powerful an ally as the solicitor general, whenever a group of states speak, the Court is inclined to listen. This is especially true when the group is as large and diverse as the signatories of the Virginia brief in this case. Because it represented the views of more than half the states, the brief would have undoubtedly received considerable attention from the justices. Of particular interest is that three of the signatories, Alaska, North Dakota, and Puerto Rico, did not have the death penalty. Furthermore, of the twenty-five states that imposed the death penalty, only ten executed someone in 2007, the year the brief was filed. Thus, it was a truly diverse list of states and territories that signed on to the brief and could not be waved away as merely advocating in support of capital punishment.

As they headed back to oral arguments, both parties were feeling fairly optimistic. The general consensus among legal academics was that Medellín should win the case. Even with the change in personnel at the Court, the odds were still in his favor. Professor Koh, who again filed an amicus brief on behalf of former diplomats, thought that Chief Justice Roberts was a likely vote for Medellín. Koh had gone to law school with Roberts, graduating a year before him. He also clerked on the Supreme Court the year before Roberts did. And when Roberts was clerking for then Associate Justice Rehnquist, whom he subsequently replaced as chief, he had worked on *Dames & Moore v. Regan*, a case arising from the

Iran hostage crisis, which dealt with the president's power to supplant state court proceedings and replace them with claims before the Iranian Claims Commission. The Court, with Rehnquist writing, upheld the president's authority in that case.

On the other hand, the Court's record in Article 36 cases was quite favorable to Texas. Cruz had prepared extensively for oral argument, participating in moots at Harvard Law School, the University of Texas School of Law, and the National Association of Attorneys General. Texas's team arrived in DC several days before the October 10 argument. Dan Geyser said they prepared one-pagers on each issue, explaining the issue, the best answers Texas had, and the best authorities in support of those answers.

At the time, the tools necessary to prepare were not always readily available. So the advocates from Texas mailed boxes of supplies they would need, including printers. However, according to Kristopher Monson, the team shipped the wrong printer cable. Monson recalls he and a colleague wandering around DC late into the night looking for either the right cable or an open Kinkos, so they could print materials Ted Cruz would need for the morning. As a result, he was "very, very, very tired" on Wednesday, October 10, when he sat down at the counsel's table with Cruz.

At 10:04 a.m., Donald Francis Donovan stepped up to the rostrum to speak at the extra-long argument. Unlike most argument days, on this day the Court had only one argument scheduled. And given the complexity of the issues, the justices ended up needing extra time to question the advocates.

Donovan began by telling the justices that adopting Texas's view would tell the world that "the framers left us with a Constitution in which neither this Court nor the President nor maybe even Congress could ensure that the United States kept the promise that its elective representatives made to its treaty partners." Justice Scalia jumped in, saying that wasn't such an outrageous position, because the president and Senate could not enter into a treaty that required states to take an unconstitutional action. Donovan conceded that was true—there may be constitutional constraints on the treaty power, but they did not arise in this case.

Chief Justice Roberts, one of two potential votes necessary for a winning majority, chimed in, asking who would enforce those limits. He was concerned that there was no role for the Court in interpreting these treaties. What if, the chief justice asked, the ICJ had ruled that the offending officers, who failed to provide Article 36 warnings, should be sentenced to five years in jail—would the Court have to enforce that finding? Justice Kennedy, the other potential swing vote, said he also wanted an answer to the chief's question—what happened if the ICJ went outside its jurisdiction?

Donovan tried to avoid answering the question, but the chief kept pounding at him, redirecting him to the hypothetical. Justice Breyer suggested that if there was something in the ICJ's order that violated the Constitution, the Court would choose the Constitution over the ICJ, and Donovan appeared to concede that was the case. Under more pressure from the chief, Donovan recognized the Court rejected any obligation under the Vienna Convention in *Sanchez-Llamas*. But, he argued, there was a second obligation, under the Optional Protocol, to enforce a binding decision of the ICJ, even if the United States disagreed with the outcome.

Justice Kennedy then asked what happened if the president had determined not to comply with the ICJ. That would run afoul of our international obligations, Donovan replied. "So then the President's determination is not conclusive," Kennedy noted.

Justice Samuel Alito, the newest member of the Court, then jumped in. He clarified that the obligation the United States undertook to comply with ICJ judgments still had to respect its "own domestic constitutional processes." Donovan said this was exactly right.

Justice Ginsburg tried to come to Donovan's rescue, asking if our agreement to submit to the ICJ gave its judgments, not precedential effect, but essentially entitled them to full faith and credit, in the same way a Texas court would not reexamine a decision from a Washington court. Donovan took the lifeline, agreeing that was the exact effect of the ICJ's judgment.

Donovan collapsed his argument down to the notion that the United States is obligated to enforce a judgment that, by its nature, is subject to enforcement in a judicial proceeding. Scalia pounced, arguing that, due to Texas's procedural default rule, this was not such a judgment. Under that rule, Texas courts are prohibited from enforcing this judgment in a judicial proceeding. Was Donovan telling the Court that the ICJ judgment empowers courts to do things contrary to law? Donovan replied that both the presidential memorandum and Article 94 of the UN Charter *were* federal law. Scalia was shocked. He said he could understand that constitutional requirements could preempt state laws, but he was unaware of any federal law that had the ability to empower state courts to take actions forbidden by state law.

Justice Souter then came to Donovan's aid, noting that, in his understanding, there was no question that Texas courts had jurisdiction to hear Medellín's claim. They were just barred by a procedural, not substantive, rule. In this case, wasn't it correct that the only preemption was of this procedural bar? Donovan agreed that was the case.

At this point, Donovan attempted to preserve the rest of his time for rebuttal, but the chief justice offered him an additional five minutes to continue answering questions, while still preserving that time. The chief then used that additional time to ask Donovan about the Court's role. Donovan told the chief that the federal law at issue was the United States' agreement to comply with a judgment it voluntarily submitted to the ICJ.

Justice Kennedy asked whether the Court had the authority to interpret the *Avena* judgment to the extent it found portions of the judgment ambiguous. He also made an ominous admission: "I have a problem, incidentally, because I think Medellín did receive all the hearing that he's entitled to under the judgment anyway." This statement was a blow to Medellín's team. There were only so many ways to cobble together a majority of justices for his side, and one of the two swing votes, if not *the* swing vote, just indicated that he felt Medellín was not entitled to relief. Assuming he would get the votes of the four liberals, Medellín would have to win the chief's vote to win the day.

Donovan did a good job not being shaken by this revelation in the middle of his argument. The Court then moved on to the question of the president's authority.

Chief Justice Roberts offered a hypothetical in which the president determined not to enforce *Avena* but the Court determined that the treaty required enforcement. In that scenario, which determination controls? Donovan told him that, to the extent the *Avena* judgment constituted federal law, the Court had the ultimate authority to determine whether or not it should be complied with. Roberts then asked why the Court would not have the authority to determine if *Avena* should be complied with without regard to the president's determination.

Donovan argued that the Court had the authority to apply the judgment under the supremacy clause. The president's determination merely provided another independent basis for enforcement using his Article II powers. And while the Court had the authority to interpret the president's determination, in this case it was crystal clear. The chief then thanked Mr. Donovan and called upon Solicitor General Paul Clement to speak on behalf of the United States.

Clement stood up and began with the ritual opening, "Mr. Chief Justice and may it please the Court." He got no further before Justice Scalia jumped in noting that he did not agree with Donovan's last statement. Clement acknowledged that was true. The president's determination was the sole reason the *Avena* judgment could be enforced. Absent that, the solicitor general would be arguing on behalf of Texas.

Clement argued that Article 94 of the UN Charter made it clear that countries had the option of not complying with the ICJ's judgment, and in cases where they did not, it was a matter for the Security Council. Justice Ginsburg noted that the decision not to comply would take place in the United States, and that since that had not happened, Article 94 would never be triggered. Clement agreed. That was the reason the United States was supporting Medellín.

The chief justice asked what would happen if the president decided to abide by the ICJ's decision, but to do so in a different manner. He proposed that courts would ask whether a defendant had had his claims of prejudice adjudicated, and in cases where he had, no further action would be taken, but in cases where it had not, "review and reconsideration" would occur. Clement answered that, in those latter cases, *Avena* would supply the rule of decision.

He also argued there was precedent. In 1977, Congress had passed the Foreign Sovereign Immunities Act, which determined by statute when a foreign nation could be sued in US courts. Prior to 1977, the president made a unilateral determination about whether the United States would treat a particular sovereign as immune in a particular case, and the state and federal courts had been bound by that determination. There, the president provided the rule of decision. This was no different.

Chief Justice Roberts asked, could the president take actions inconsistent with the Supreme Court's interpretation of federal law? In *Sanchez-Llamas*, the Court had already determined that the ICJ's interpretation of the Vienna Convention was incorrect. Clement answered that the president could not. But there was an important distinction here. In *Sanchez-Llamas*, the administration agreed with the Court's interpretation of the Vienna Convention. Here, the question addressed the proper interpretation of the Optional Protocol and the UN Charter. Clement agreed that *Avena* runs directly counter to *Sanchez-Llamas*. *Sanchez-Llamas* was the proper interpretation for anyone but the fifty-one nationals named in *Avena*.

Justice Stevens asked Clement if the issue was just a question of choice of laws—under this doctrine, it did not matter whether the judgment was correct; the only judicial role was to determine if the ICJ had jurisdiction. If it did, then the Court should enforce the judgment, even if it believed the ICJ was wrong on the merits. Clement said that was correct.

Justice Kennedy then repeated the hypothetical posed to Donovan: Suppose the president had determined not to comply with *Avena*? "Then I'd be on that side of the podium, Your Honor," Clement replied, indicating Texas's side.

Clement's time expired, but the chief justice allowed Justice Souter to ask another question. In an attempt to fully understand Clement's argument, Souter offered one more variation on the hypothetical. Assume the president determined that the United States would not comply with *Avena*, but the Court determined that the *Avena* judgment was binding on the United States. Would the Court's authority to make that decision be displaced by the president's determination to the contrary? "Of course not, Justice Souter," Clement replied. It would be no different than the Court accepting Medellín's first argument, that the *Avena* decision was binding in and of itself. In that case, the United States would of course comply.

Justice Scalia asked about Texas's argument that the memorandum had no effect whatsoever, because it is a letter to the attorney general, not a directive to the states, and it relies on the notion of comity, which suggests it is not a requirement of international law. What was Clement's response?

Clement argued Scalia was actually asking two questions. The first was a question of formality, and in historical practice, a great deal of formality had never been required. In a variety of cases, going back hundreds of years, the executive expressed its will via an exchange of diplomatic notes, or a letter from an undersecretary of state to the attorney general, or a letter from the secretary of state to a state judge. While Clement received some pushback from the chief justice and Kennedy, he strongly advocated that these precedents showed no need for a formal executive order or presidential proclamation.

Addressing the second question raised by Justice Scalia, about the reference to comity, Clement argued that when courts looked at comity, it provided an answer about what to do in the absence of guidance from the political branches. Here, the president provided that answer. In the president's opinion, it would be in the interests of comity to apply the judgment.

The chief justice then recognized Ted Cruz and noted that he would be providing Cruz with an additional ten minutes of argument time. Interestingly, Cruz began his argument not by attacking Medellín but by going after the United States. "The entirety of the United States' argument," he began, "is predicated on the idea that the President's two-paragraph memorandum is in and of itself binding Federal law."

Justices Souter and Breyer asked about Medellín's first theory, that the decision was binding federal law by its own terms under the supremacy clause. Justice Breyer even elicited a laugh from the audience when he suggested that the supremacy clause bound all states, and he presumed that included Texas. Cruz acknowledged that Texas law must give way to federal law and treaties, but the president's memorandum did not qualify. He further clarified that the *Avena* judgment was not a judgment as understood in United States law for six reasons.

Sitting in the audience, Dan Geyser's initial impression was, "Oh, God, I hope he can remember all six." Because when you promise a justice a certain number of arguments, you have to be able to follow through. Cruz actually did one better. After a colloquy with Justices Breyer, Ginsburg, and Scalia about the Optional Protocol and Article 94 of the UN Charter that lasted several minutes, Justice Stevens asked Cruz for his six reasons. And he delivered.

According to Cruz, the *Avena* decision was not a judgment entitled to presumptive treatment for the following reasons: (1) the Optional Protocol was not self-executing; (2) if it were binding, that would violate Article III of the US Constitution; (3) under *Sanchez-Llamas*, ICJ decisions were not binding on US courts; (4) the United States and Mexico were parties to the judgment and were not parties to this case; (5) the Supreme Court in *Breard* had determined that ICJ orders (in that case provisional measures) did not trump US law; and (6) treating *Avena* as binding would remove the president's ability to decide not to comply.

Justice Kennedy again showed his hand, stating that in his view, Cruz's argument seemed consistent and that for two hundred years, the United States had entered treaties, many of them very important, that were not self-executing in the sense that the states were not compelled to comply with them, even if their failure to do so put the United States in breach of its international obligations. He believed that the Vienna Convention was self-executing in the sense that no legislation was required to create obligations under Article 36, but not in the sense that the State "has to accept whatever procedural framework the foreign national demands."

Cruz agreed and went further. In both *Breard* and *Sanchez-Llamas*, the Court assumed the Vienna Convention created individual rights and still held they could be procedurally defaulted. Medellín defaulted on his claims here. The only question was whether the *Avena* judgment, and the president's memorandum, formed some sort of independent source of federal law beyond the treaty.

Justice Ginsburg then weighed in, asking Cruz why, if the United States agreed to have the ICJ adjudicate the meaning of the treaty when it signed on to the Optional Protocol, that did not come with an understanding that the United States would be bound by that determination. She noted that most ICJ judgments were complied with. Cruz acknowledged that was true as a political and diplomatic matter. But, "of the fifty nations that signed on to the Optional Protocol, zero—not a single nation—treats ICJ judgments as binding in their domestic courts." He pointed out that even in Mexico such a claim would not be recognized as a defense to a criminal prosecution.

Justice Scalia chimed in to say he saw it as a constitutional problem to allow a foreign tribunal to interpret federal law. "I'm rather jealous of that power," he noted wryly, drawing laughter from the audience. In his view, this problem was avoided with a non-self-executing treaty because it only became law after Congress and the president took action, in accordance with the Constitution, not based on a letter from the president to the attorney general. Cruz called that observation "absolutely correct."

Justice Ginsburg was concerned that Cruz's interpretation would prevent the United States from entering into a treaty that promised due respect to the decisions of each country's courts. In *Sanchez-Llamas*, an opinion she joined, the Supreme Court was required to interpret the Vienna Convention. But in this case, the United States was faced with a binding judgment from the ICJ; thus, for that case only, shouldn't it provide the rule of decision?

Cruz responded that for forty years it had been the consistent position of the United States that the Optional Protocol was not self-executing, and thus ICJ decisions were not to be treated as judgments by US courts. Decisions of the ICJ are complied with around the world as a matter of goodwill, and the president had a host of means to provide for compliance with the *Avena* decision.

Cruz went on to describe the president's assertion of power as "very curious" because it is not directed at federal courts but solely at state courts. Cruz said he was unaware of any similar attempt to exercise such power in the two-hundred-year history of the United States. "So what's absent in your view is Congress," Ginsburg clarified. "Absolutely," Cruz responded.

The chief justice recognized Mr. Donovan to return to the podium for his five-minute rebuttal. Donovan opened by arguing that there was no issue about whether the Optional Protocol was self-executing. The issue to be addressed was the following: What is the scope of the enforceability of an ICJ judgment? He recognized there were obvious constraints. One, pointed out by the chief justice, was if there are affirmative constraints in the Constitution itself preventing enforcement. Another was if the order was directed at a constitutional branch, such as an obligation to enforce an active statute. That, Donovan conceded, would not be enforceable in court. Third, there was a political constraint. Congress could pass a statute saying the United States is not going to comply with the ICJ's judgment. Here, however, the ICJ identified an individually enforceable right, and for two centuries the Court had said that in those circumstances, the courts would uphold those rights.

Furthermore, there is a long line of cases in which the Supreme Court recognized that when an issue is submitted to international arbitration, the Court will enforce any matter decided by the panel and that doing so does not intrude on the Court's Article III authority. The Court had even sent a question of federal antitrust law to a panel in Tokyo and stated that the outcome of that panel would be decisive.

Donovan concluded by stressing that the *Avena* judgment called for a prospective application. The Texas courts, according to Donovan, did not conclude Medellín had received "review and reconsideration." Medellín was entitled to have the Article 36 violation on its own reviewed for any prejudicial effect, entirely apart from the question of any constitutional rights he may have.

Walking out of oral arguments, the team from Texas was feeling really good. There were a variety of perspectives on how the advocates performed. Dan Geyser said that he thought they had done very well. He also thought Solicitor General Paul Clement had done well. A court watcher who attended the argument that day was somewhat less generous, saying that Clement wasn't as strong as he needed to be. According to this observer, Clement didn't really seem to believe what he was saying. This same observer thought that Ted Cruz got away with giving a "press conference answer," not actually answering the questions asked, but sounding like he was, so he got to say what he wanted to. In Geyser's estimation, Cruz was captivating: "He was really a master at organizing his thoughts, keeping it all in his head, speaking in paragraphs. It just comes across as very eloquent, using very interesting turns of phrase."

Both sides would have a long wait to find out which viewpoint was correct. The justices gathered that Friday in their private conference room to discuss the case, along with the others heard that week, and to assign the opinion. By tradition, the seniormost member of the majority gets to assign the opinion to any member voting in the majority. If the chief justice is in the majority, the decision is his. Sometimes, the decision is strategic, to hold on to a wavering fifth vote. Other times, assignments are made in the interests of balance. Sometimes, a justice who has a particular affinity for the issue will be given the assignment. In cases dealing with the proper role of the judiciary, Chief Justice Roberts often assigns the opinion to himself, so long as he is in the majority. Such was the case here.

Although the justices knew the outcome on October 12, the parties, and the world, would have to wait five and a half months, until Tuesday, March 25, 2008. No one except the justices and those working inside the building know exactly when a decision will be issued, except for the last day of the term in June, when the Court dispenses all remaining opinions. Unlike the ICJ, which tells the parties precisely when it will be ruling, none of the advocates gets so much as a heads-up. They just have to check in with the press that follows the Court and reports on its decisions.

The justices announce their decisions in reverse order of seniority, with junior justices presenting opinions from the bench before more senior members. On March 25, the chief justice announced that he had the opinion in 06-984, *José Medellín v. State of Texas*. It was a 6–3 decision in favor of Texas.

The justices provided three opinions. Chief Justice Roberts wrote for a majority of five, including Justices Scalia, Kennedy, Thomas, and Alito. Justice Stevens wrote a separate opinion in which he concurred in the outcome of the case but offered different reasons for his decision. Finally, Justice Breyer authored a dissent that was joined by Justices Souter and Ginsburg.

As is often the case, the chief justice got right to the heart of the matter, noting that the Court had concluded that neither the *Avena* judgment itself nor the president's memorandum "constitutes directly enforceable federal law that pre-empts state limitations on the filing of successive habeas petitions." Therefore, the Court affirmed the decision of the Texas Court of Criminal Appeals dismissing Medellín's case. Medellín had lost.

The Court's opinion noted that Medellín was arrested at approximately 4:00 a.m. on June 29, 1993, and, after being Mirandized, authored a confession between 5:54 and 7:23 a.m. the same day. In a footnote, the Court noted that even under *Avena*, the ICJ had determined that the United States' obligation to inform the Mexican consulate of the arrest of one of its citizens would not be violated for seventy-two hours from the time of arrest. Here, Medellín confessed within three hours, so there could be no violation of his right to have the consulate notified "without delay" even as that phrase had been interpreted by the ICJ.

The opinion then turned to the two arguments raised by Medellín and the United States. First, it addressed Medellín's claim that, under the supremacy clause, the *Avena* decision was binding federal law and enforceable on its own. The Court noted that there was no dispute that the *Avena* decision constituted a binding international obligation on the United States. The only question was whether that decision was enforceable in the courts of the United States without any further action, or whether Texas was correct that Congress needed to pass a law to implement it.

Turning to the question of whether the *Avena* judgment was self-executing, the Court concluded that neither the Optional Protocol to the Vienna Convention, nor the UN Charter, nor the Statute of the ICJ created binding federal law without implementing legislation. Tellingly, and as the majority would bring up multiple times, Medellín did not rely on the Vienna Convention itself. And because there was no argument that such legislation had been passed, the Court was forced to conclude that *Avena* was not directly enforceable federal law.

The Court held that there was a difference between allowing the ICJ to hear the case and agreeing to being bound by any decision it made. According to the chief justice's opinion, the "most natural" reading of the Optional Protocol was a "bare grant of jurisdiction." The obligation to comply with ICJ judgments comes from a different treaty—the UN Charter.

Article 94(1) of the charter states that a State will "undertake to comply" with decisions rendered by the International Court of Justice in any case where it is a party. Here, the chief looked to the argument of the solicitor general that this language does not create an immediate right to enforce ICJ decisions in domestic courts. Instead, it reflects a commitment to take future action on the part of States, through their political branches. The Court agreed this was the best reading of Article 94.

It looked to Article 94(2) to support this reading. That provision provides the sole remedy for violations of Article 94(1)—reference to the Security Council for a diplomatic resolution. The UN Charter's enforcement mechanism is nonjudicial, which provided further evidence that ICJ judgments were not intended to be directly enforceable in domestic courts. The ratification history demonstrated that the president and Senate believed the United States would always have the freedom to disregard particular ICJ judgments.

The ICJ statute provides no support for the idea that its decisions are domestically enforceable. First, the ICJ can hear disputes only between States, not between individuals. Second, its decisions are binding only on the parties that appear before it in that particular case. The fact that Mexico may have been moved by the plight of Medellín and his fellow nationals did nothing to change the fact that the dispute was between the United States and Mexico, and the decision was consequently binding only on those parties and in respect to each other.

Furthermore, the executive had been consistent in its view that the relevant treaties did not create binding federal law, and it was "well settled" that these views deserved due deference. Even respecting the decision of the ICJ as to the meaning of a treaty over which it has jurisdiction, it is not clear that *Avena* should be directly enforceable in domestic courts. The ICJ directed the United States "by means of its own choosing" to enforce the judgment.

The Court also looked to post-ratification conduct to demonstrate that its reading of the treaty was the proper one. The Court noted that, as of the time of its decision, there were 47 nations that were signatories to the Optional Protocol and 171 parties to the Vienna Convention. Yet neither Medellín nor his amici had pointed to a single nation that treated ICJ judgments as binding in its domestic courts.

Finally, the Court noted that the consequences of Medellín's proposed rule were untenable. Because, according to Medellín, ICJ decisions are both automatically enforceable and not to be second-guessed, they could overrule both federal and state law with no domestic input. Even the dissent, the majority noted, did not go so far as to embrace the automatic execution of every ICJ judgment. But there is no power in the judiciary to decide which decisions deserve enforcement and which are too "politically sensitive" to merit such treatment.

The Court was quick to concede that treaties can provide a binding effect to the decisions of international tribunals. The Court merely noted that the treaties Medellín relied on did not have this effect. Additionally, it is the province and duty of the Supreme Court to determine whether the treaties purporting to have that effect actually do.

The Court did agree with Medellín that, "as a general matter, 'an agreement to abide by the result' of an international adjudication—or what he really means, an agreement to give the result of such adjudication domestic legal effect—can be a treaty obligation like any other, so long as the agreement is consistent with the Constitution." But the treaties he relied on did not meet this threshold. The Court's holding did not render treaties that do not meet this standard useless. Rather, they can create binding international obligations, which form the basis of diplomatic negotiations. Or Congress can choose to give them domestic effect via implementing legislation.

As to Medellín's argument that the *Avena* judgment overrides the contrary state law of Texas and is directly enforceable in state and federal courts, the Court disagreed. While it created an international legal obligation, it simply did not require any action by domestic courts and could not, consistent with the Constitution, overcome a state law to the contrary.

The Court then turned to the argument pressed by Medellín and the United States, that the president's memorandum had a transformative effect and, in essence, implemented the *Avena* judgment.

The Court began by noting that it did not disagree with the United States that the president was "uniquely qualified" to resolve the sensitive foreign policy issues raised by the *Avena* decision and to do so quickly. The Court recognized that these concerns were "plainly compelling." But however compelling these interests may be, they did not allow the Court to set aside first principles. The Court noted that any action taken by the president in pursuit of these interests "'must stem from either an act of Congress or from the Constitution itself.'"

While the Court recognized that the president has a host of political and diplomatic means at his disposal to ensure compliance with our international obligations, the unilateral authority to implement a non-self-executing treaty is not among them. The authority to "transform[] an international obligation arising from a non-self-executing treaty into domestic law falls to Congress." This conclusion arose from the Constitution, which divides the treaty-making power between the executive and legislative branches.

While only the Senate is required to consent to a treaty, if the language so consented to does not provide for the domestic implementation of treaty obligations, the normal lawmaking process must be followed. The president has the power to enforce the laws. But only Congress can make them. By definition, a non-self-executing treaty is one that is adopted with the understanding that it has no domestic effect without further action on the part of Congress. Therefore, the president cannot argue that Congress implicitly authorized the president to implement the treaty.

The Court recognized that the president may act to ensure the United States complies with its international obligations. But his actions must comply with the Constitution. That means he may not rely on a non-self-executing treaty to provide the rule of decision, binding on domestic courts, which preempts contrary state law.

The majority then turned to the second argument made by the United States, that the president has an independent "foreign affairs" authority to enforce the *Avena* decision. Here, the Court was referring to the series of cases, including *Dames & Moore*, in which Congress acquiesced in the president's actions settling civil claims between the United States and foreign nations via executive agreements. A long, unbroken line of cases had upheld such actions despite the failure of Congress to approve. But the United States acknowledged that the presidential action here was unprecedented. The United States could not point to a single presidential action directed to state courts, let alone one that ordered them to set aside laws at the heart of their criminal justice systems. Thus, no long-standing practice could support the exercise of the president's power here.

Justice Stevens penned a short concurring opinion. He began by noting that he agreed with much of the dissent. Specifically, he agreed that the text and history of the supremacy clause did not support a presumption against self-execution of treaties. Nonetheless, he agreed that the treaties at issue did not authorize the Supreme Court to enforce the *Avena* decision.

Justice Stevens relied on the specific language of Article 94 of the UN Charter. While acknowledging it was "not the model of either a self-executing or a non-self-executing commitment," he found it telling that Congress had passed specific legislation to ensure enforcement of other international judgments, even though those judgments were rendered pursuant to treaties with much more mandatory-sounding language than the UN Charter.

On the other hand, the charter lacks the sort of unambiguous language that would foreclose self-execution of the treaty. The Senate did not issue a declaration denoting the UN Charter was non-self-executing, despite doing so with other treaties. But without the aid of a presumption one way or the other, Justice Stevens felt the best reading of "undertakes to comply" is one that calls for future action by the political branches. Like the dissent, he believed that Congress would not assent to the automatic enforcement of all ICJ judgments. But he found in that reality another reason to treat Article 94's ambiguity as counseling in favor of leaving the question of enforcing ICJ decisions up to the political branches.

Like the majority, he noted that no one disputed that the *Avena* judgment formed a binding international obligation on the United States. He commended the president for attempting to comply. But he agreed that the president's memorandum did not transform *Avena* into binding federal law. However, he noted, under the supremacy clause, the binding nature of the international obligation falls on states as well as the national government. "Having already put the Nation in breach of one treaty, it is now up to Texas to prevent the breach of another."

He argued that the cost for Texas to comply with *Avena* would be minimal. He thought this was particularly so given the small likelihood that a violation of the Vienna Convention would have actually prejudiced Medellín. And he noted that Oklahoma had accepted the cost, further demonstrating how insubstantial it was. On the other side of the scale, the costs of failing to abide by *Avena* were high. Both the president and the Court acknowledged that such failure would jeopardize the "compelling interests" of the United States in ensuring reciprocal respect of the Vienna Convention rights of US citizens abroad. Because the Court's opinion did not prevent Texas from upholding the honor of the nation, he joined the outcome of the majority's decision, though not its reasoning.

Justice Breyer, writing for himself, Justice Souter, and Justice Ginsburg, dissented. They believed that José Medellín had successfully demonstrated that the *Avena* judgment was directly enforceable in US courts at both the state and the federal level without any further action by the government. Because they reached this conclusion, they felt no need to answer whether the president's memorandum was new federal law, though they did think the majority's answer to the question was problematic.

In the dissenters' view, by ratifying the Optional Protocol, the United States agreed to voluntarily submit disputes over the meaning of the Vienna Convention to the binding jurisdiction of the ICJ for purposes of "compulsory settlement." By ratifying the UN Charter, the United States agreed that it would abide by ICJ decisions in which it was a party. President Bush determined it was in the best interests of the United States to comply, and Congress did nothing to second-guess that judgment. Thus, in their minds, the *Avena* decision was directly enforceable by Medellín in domestic courts.

The dissent felt that the majority "place[d] too much weight upon treaty language that says little about the matter" of whether ICJ judgments rendered pursuant to the Optional Protocol are automatically part of domestic law. It looked to some of the earliest cases decided by the Court dealing with treaties, in the late 1790s, when the ratification of the Constitution was fresh in the minds of the justices. These cases traced the history of treaty enforcement under British rule and the Articles of Confederation and compared it to the time after 1787. In 1796 the Court concluded that if a treaty was binding upon the United States, then under the supremacy clause it was to be executed without further action by Congress.

In a later decision, the Court clarified that under the supremacy clause, treaties were to be treated the same as statutes passed by Congress and signed by the president and operated without any need for additional legislation. The only exception was in cases where the treaty explicitly contemplated action by the legislature.

The dissent also pointed to *Comegys v. Vasse* (1828), a case Medellín relied upon, which answered the same question. In that case, the Supreme Court held that a treaty may compel the United States to comply with a decision by an international tribunal interpreting that treaty "despite the absence of any congressional enactment specifically requiring such compliance." According to Breyer, this long history demonstrated that self-executing treaty provisions—which can and must be enforced in domestic courts without further action by Congress or the executive—were commonplace and not peculiar creatures of domestic law.

While the dissent acknowledged that the case law did not provide any clear guidance to determine whether treaty language is self-executing, it noted that nowhere is the majority's "clear statement" rule to be found.

To the contrary, the Court had recognized as self-executing provisions of treaties that displaced state law on a frequent basis without any such clear statement in the text. The dissent pointed out that the majority failed to cite to a single example of a treaty that contained language that would meet its test. This is to be expected, Breyer noted, because the answer is contained in a nation's domestic laws, which can differ significantly.

Instead of some formal, language-based test, the dissent pointed out that throughout two hundred years of history, the Court had approached the question of self-execution using "practical, context-specific criteria" to make its determination. Text and drafting history matter: they help determine if the treaty is directed to the political branches for further action, or whether it is directed to the judicial branch for direct enforcement.

Also of import in the Court's prior cases was the subject matter of the treaty provision at issue. Did it concern itself with the adjudication of private legal rights? Did it confer such rights? Did it set forth clear standards that judges can easily enforce? All things being equal, the dissent argued, provisions that list specific and easily enforceable rights are more likely to be "addressed" to the judiciary. In such cases, they would be self-executing.

The dissent then applied its test to the question before the Court and concluded that the *Avena* judgment was self-executing and directly enforceable in domestic courts without the need for any further action. The dissent provided several considerations to demonstrate this point.

First, the plain language of the treaties at issue "strongly supports direct judicial enforceability." Enforcing a binding judgment is a "quintessential judicial activity." To decide otherwise is to place the United States' compliance with its international obligations in the hands of one state, which is an outcome the supremacy clause was explicitly crafted to avoid.

Second, the decision in this case involved the interpretation of a treaty provision that all parties agree *is* self-executing and judicially enforceable. Texas did not argue its courts were incapable of providing relief for such violations if they are raised at an appropriate time. Its argument was that Medellín waited too long to complain. The treaty discusses an individual's "rights" to be informed, and this is an easily manageable standard. The decision Medellín seeks to enforce calls for a judicial hearing. In every possible way, this is addressed to the judicial department.

Third, simple logic suggested that a treaty that provides for "final" and "binding" judgments regarding the interpretation of a self-executing treaty provision should itself be self-executing. How does it make sense to make a self-executing promise, to agree to accept as binding the ICJ's determination of the meaning of that self-executing promise, but then argue that putting that determination into practice required some further action by Congress? *Sanchez-Llamas* provided no succor because that case did not deal with individuals whose rights were subjected to the ICJ's consideration. The United States voluntarily accepted the possibility that its interpretation of Article 36 would lose. Once it had done so, it must live with the consequences.

Fourth, the United States is party to at least seventy treaties that provide for mandatory arbitration before the ICJ, and those treaties use language similar to the Optional Protocol. If this decision was not enforceable without congressional action, it is hard to see why other nations would expect us to respect any decisions made under those treaties. Congress was unlikely to pass a law granting blanket enforcement by the judicial branch. Nor did it have the time or inclination for a judgment-by-judgment enforcement scheme. The Court's approach risked putting the United States in continual breach of its international commitments.

Fifth, factors specific to *Avena* made it particularly well suited to judicial enforcement. The ICJ noted that the judicial process was particularly apt to provide the "review and reconsideration" it called for. Judicial standards were readily available to judge whether Medellín and his fellows were prejudiced by the denial of Article 36 information. In short, judges dealt with these sorts of questions on a regular basis, while legislatures were not well equipped to consider individual cases.

Sixth, directly upholding the international obligations of the United States in this case would not create conflict with other branches, did not require the Court to engage in nonjudicial activity, and did not require the creation of a new cause of action. The only question before the Court was whether Texas may rely on one particular defense, the procedural default doctrine, in the adjudication of Medellín's claims. Holding that it may not did not create a new private right or implicate nonjudicial authority.

Seventh, the political branches had not expressed concern with the direct judicial enforcement of *Avena*. On the contrary, the president explicitly supported it. Justice Breyer, on behalf of his colleagues, concluded this section of the argument: "The majority reaches a different conclusion because it looks for the wrong thing (explicit textual expression about self-execution) using the wrong standard (clarity) in the wrong place (the treaty language). Hunting for what the test cannot contain, it takes a wrong turn."

The dissent recognized that determining *Avena* was self-executing was not the end of the inquiry. The Court must also choose the means of executing it. The appropriate means was to remand the case to the Texas Court of Criminal Appeals. First, this was the normal course for a case upon reversal by the Supreme Court. Second, this was the course chosen by the president. This would allow the Texas courts to provide the "review and reconsideration" ordered by *Avena*.

The dissent then briefly addressed the president's memorandum. Unlike the majority, the dissent viewed the president as exercising his foreign affairs authority consistent with the treaty obligations of the United States. The dissent believed the majority went too far when it held that the president, when acting in this capacity, can *never* set aside a conflicting state law. At the same time, the dissent did recognize that the Constitution "must impose significant restrictions" on the president's authority:

> Given the Court's comparative lack of expertise in foreign affairs; given the importance of the Nation's foreign relations; given the difficulty of finding the proper constitutional balance among state and federal, executive and legislative, powers in such matters; and given the likely future importance of this Court's efforts to do so, I would very much hesitate before concluding that the Constitution implicitly sets forth broad prohibitions (or permissions) in this area.

The dissent felt there was no need to address the complex question of the outer limits of the president's foreign affairs powers and thus elected not to do so. But the dissenters wanted to make clear that their silence did not signal their agreement with the majority's treatment of the question.

The opinion concluded by noting its concern that the majority's actions in this case would have sweeping implications for the foreign policy of the United States. Denying the president's power to enforce the ICJ's decision could lead to a showdown in the UN Security Council, forcing the United States to exercise its veto powers. It would undoubtedly worsen our relationship with Mexico. And it threatened to risk noncompliance with Article 36 when American citizens were detained abroad. Finally, it risked diminishing the international reputation of the United States as a country that respected the rule of law.

The decision came as a shock to many legal commentators, who had viewed a win by Texas as unlikely. To some in the legal community, the fact that Justice Kennedy both joined the majority opinion and failed to write his own concurrence was surprising, as Justice Kennedy had authored *Roper v. Simmons*, where he relied on international law to restrict the application of the death penalty to those who were juveniles when they committed their crimes. In fact, two of Medellín's codefendants were spared the death chamber because of Kennedy's opinion in *Roper.* John Bellinger had predicted to Secretary Rice that the administration's position would prevail: "I thought we would have the more liberal justices, I thought we would have Justice Stevens. . . . I thought we would have Justice Kennedy because he's Mr. International, and I thought . . . the Chief would agree with us." While Bellinger recognized Chief Justice Roberts was unlikely to believe in the result found by the ICJ, he expected him to defer to the views of the president when it came to the interests of the United States.

Several people felt that the replacement of Justice O'Connor by Justice Alito made a difference. Both Sandra Babcock and Harold Hongju Koh said that her presence would have made the case more contested, certainly. Koh said, "O'Connor was a person who had strong views and tended to be quite consistent." In some ways, Babcock said, the fact that President Bush issued his memorandum may have hurt José Medellín more than it helped.

With a 6–3 victory in hand, the State of Texas was now legally cleared, fifteen years after the murders of Jennifer Ertman and Elizabeth Peña, to put José Medellín to death.

CHAPTER 8

The Aftermath

Several things happened following the Supreme Court's decision in *Medellín v. Texas*. The federal government did not take the loss sitting down. John Bellinger, the new legal adviser at the State Department, went to his boss, Secretary Condoleezza Rice, in her office on the seventh floor of the State Department and urged her to take more action. "We still have an international obligation," he told her. "Just because the Supreme Court has told us that the president can't order Texas to do this, the country as a whole still has an obligation and Texas still needs to comply." Rice looked at Bellinger and arched an eyebrow. "John, haven't we done enough?" He again stressed the continuing obligation the United States had, and Rice said she would be willing to write a letter to Governor Rick Perry of Texas, so long as Attorney General Michael Mukasey would join her in signing it. The attorney general agreed, and so Bellinger helped staff at Justice draft a letter. On June 17, 2008, the letter was sent to Governor Perry, reminding him of the international obligation incumbent upon the United States and asking to discuss with him methods of ensuring compliance.

A month later, on July 18, Perry responded. He maintained that, as an individual state, Texas was not bound by the *Avena* decision. While he understood the concerns the federal government had about complying with our international obligations, he felt that that was a concern best handled by the federal executive branch and Congress. Nevertheless, he believed that any time Article 36 claims were raised in federal habeas proceedings by an *Avena* defendant who had not already raised them, the State of Texas urged "review and reconsideration." However, when it came to José Medellín, Perry would not budge.

In addition to these moves by the executive branch, the legislative branch was also taking action. On July 14, 2008, Congressman Howard Berman and Congresswoman Zoe Lofgren, both of California, introduced the Avena Case Implementation Act of 2008. This short bill allowed any noncitizen whose Article 36 rights were violated by domestic law enforcement officers to file a civil action to obtain appropriate relief. The act allowed for all relief necessary to remedy the harm done by the Article 36 violation, including vacating any convictions or sentences. The act was unlimited in its application. It applied to violations of Article 36 whether they occurred before or after the implementation of the act. Despite its name, the act was not limited to the fifty-one nationals named by Mexico in *Avena*. Any foreign national, of any nationality, was entitled to relief under the act. Had it passed quickly, Medellín would have been entitled to a new hearing. Despite attracting additional cosponsors from Massachusetts and Michigan, the act was referred to the House Judiciary Committee, where it never emerged. The committee failed to schedule a hearing, and the act quietly died.

The federal government was not alone in urging action to hold off on Medellín's execution. Texas state senator Rodney Ellis, a Democrat from Houston, wrote two letters, one to Judge Caprice Cosper and one to Governor Perry, urging them not to schedule or carry out the execution of José Medellín until at least January 2009, when the Texas legislature was scheduled to reconvene. In his letter to Judge Cosper, sent May 5, 2008, Ellis told her he felt it was incumbent upon Texas to comply with the international obligations of the United States, in order to ensure that Texans traveling abroad would be similarly protected. He indicated his intention to introduce legislation providing for the relief ordered by *Avena*. This would not be Senator Ellis's first bill related to the Vienna Convention. In 2005, he had introduced a bill that would have required magistrate judges to inform any known or suspected foreign national of their Article 36 rights, and in the case of Mexican or Canadian foreign nationals, to inform the consulate as well. The bill also required that all law enforcement personnel undergo specific training on properly handling the arrest and detention of a foreign national within two years of hire. The bill was referred to the Committee on Criminal Justice and never emerged. Despite Ellis's urging, the court set Medellín's execution date for August 5, 2008.

Ellis's letter to Governor Perry was sent on July 18, the same day Perry responded to Rice and Mukasey. Referencing the Avena Case Implementation Act, Ellis urged Perry to grant Medellín a reprieve to allow time for Congress and the Texas legislature to take appropriate action. Again, he stressed the importance of the international obligation undertaken by the United States and the potential for backlash against citizens of Texas traveling or working abroad. He sent a copy of this latter letter to the Texas Board of Pardons and Paroles.

Mexico also took action following the Supreme Court's decision. On June 5, 2008, it returned to the International Court of Justice, filing what it called a "Request for Interpretation of the Judgment of 31 March 2004 in the Case Concerning Avena and Other Mexican Nationals (Mexico v. United States)." As it had in 2003, Mexico sought provisional measures from the ICJ, ordering the United States to halt the pending execution of five Mexican nationals named in the *Avena* judgment. The first name on its list was José Medellín's.

The ICJ heard oral argument on the question just two weeks later. John Bellinger represented the United States, while Ambassador Gómez Robledo reprised his role as Mexico's main advocate. Twelve judges heard the argument, and the court issued its order on July 16, 2008. By a vote of 7 to 5, the ICJ refused to dismiss Mexico's claims and ordered the United States to take all measures necessary to prevent the execution of the named Mexican nationals, including Medellín, until such time as the court could issue its final decision.

Mexico also reached out to Governor Perry. On July 28, 2008, Patricia Espinosa Cantellano, Mexican secretary of foreign affairs, sent a three-page letter to Perry, asking him to grant a reprieve for José Medellín. She made three arguments. First, she referenced the ICJ's *Avena* decision. Second, she mentioned the proposed Avena Case Implementation Act and noted that there was not enough time before Medellín's execution to allow passage of that act. Third, she reminded Perry about the ICJ's latest provisional measures order.

Letters to Perry and the Texas Board of Pardons and Paroles also flowed in from several other nations, urging them to suspend the execution of José Medellín. Ambassadors from Brazil, Uruguay, Argentina, Bolivia, Ecuador, El Salvador, Guatemala, Honduras, Peru, Paraguay, Chile, and the Council of Europe all sent letters on Medellín's behalf.

Perry turned a blind eye to all of these requests and indicated a willingness to continue to move forward with Medellín's execution. The Texas Board of Pardons and Paroles voted unanimously against granting

Medellín a reprieve, though one member of the Texas Court of Criminal Appeals, Tom Price, had urged Perry to do so. Perry said the facts were part of "the most gruesome death penalty case I have reviewed while in office" as he denied a requested thirty-day stay of execution. Perry also maintained that complying with international obligations was a role for the United States, not Texas.

So on July 31, 2008, Donald Donovan and Sandra Babcock made a last-ditch plea to the US Supreme Court, asking it to stay Medellín's execution, pending congressional action on the Avena Case Implementation Act. On August 5, 2008, the date Medellín was scheduled to be executed, the Court issued a 5–4 per curiam decision denying his petition and request for a stay. It noted that in the four years since *Avena* and in the four months since its decision in *Medellín v. Texas*, Congress had taken no action other than the mere introduction of a bill. Given the lack of movement, it was too speculative to interfere with Texas's criminal justice system. Therefore, Medellín's request for a stay was denied.

The three *Medellín v. Texas* dissenters were joined this time by Justice Stevens. He argued that the Court should call for the views of the solicitor general, given Texas's refusal to comply with its obligations under *Avena* and the Vienna Convention. Justice Souter stood by his dissent in the earlier case and would have stayed the execution long enough to get the views of the solicitor general. Justice Ginsburg also wanted to hear the solicitor general's views, especially in light of the statement of the United States at the ICJ that it would continue to work to give the *Avena* judgment full effect.

Justice Breyer wrote the lengthiest dissent. He identified six factors he believed counseled in favor of delaying Medellín's execution. First, the ICJ had indicated provisional measures, ordering the United States to take all steps necessary to prevent Medellín's death. Second, Congress had introduced legislation to remedy the flaw the Court had identified in its earlier decision. Third, Congress may have been unaware of its need to pass legislation until the Court's earlier decision; the timing of the upcoming election likely required more than a few weeks to pass the Avena Case Implementation Act. Fourth, allowing Medellín's execution would irremediably violate the international law obligations of the United States. Fifth, the president had indicated the need to carry out our treaty-based obligations in this case. And sixth, the Court itself seemed to have deeply inconsistent views about what the case was about, that would merit a stay and a full hearing.

Since enough justices had indicated a willingness to hear these cases, it was "particularly disappointing" that no member of the majority would provide a courtesy fifth vote to issue a stay to allow those issues to be heard. It is a sad fact of Supreme Court practice that it takes only four justices to agree to hear a case, but it takes five votes to take most other actions. Thus, while the dissenters had the votes to grant Medellín's petition, they lacked the necessary majority needed to stay his execution until that petition could be heard. But aside from the short opinion the Court issued, there is no indication why no justice in the majority was willing to provide that fifth vote.

That evening, Randy Ertman, the father of Jennifer Ertman, climbed the steps of the redbrick building that housed the Huntsville Unit, where Medellín was scheduled to die. These cases had led to a change in Texas policy, which had previously prohibited family members from witnessing executions. Ertman had watched as the other members of the Black and White gang were put to death. Except for those who were spared by the Supreme Court's decision in *Roper v. Simmons*, Medellín was the last.

At 9:48 p.m., with needles in his arms, Medellín uttered his last words. To Ertman and the other family members present, he said, "I am sorry my actions caused pain. I hope this brings closure to what you seek." To his family, he said, "Don't ever hate them for what they do. Never harbor hate. I love you." He then turned and said, "Alright, Warden." Nine minutes later, he was dead. Medellín was thirty-three years, five months, and one day old. He had spent nearly half his life on Texas's death row. Had he committed his offense just four months earlier, he would have been spared the needle under the Supreme Court's decision in *Roper v. Simmons*.

That was not the end of matters, however. The ICJ was still deciding Mexico's petition for interpretation of the *Avena* decision. It announced that it would issue its decision on January 19, 2009, Martin Luther King Day and John Bellinger's last full day as the legal adviser at the Department of State. "We were notified about a week beforehand, that it was going to come down on Martin Luther King Day," Bellinger said. "I wasn't going to get paid to work on yet another federal holiday." He considered not going. "My first instinct was, why should I fly to The Hague one more time in a coach class seat overnight?" He expected to win on the legal issue, but because Texas had carried out Medellín's execution in the face of the provisional measures, he knew there was going to be some anger from the court.

But he thought about it and realized he had worked on this case his entire time as legal adviser, and even before; it was coming out on his last full day, so he really ought to be there. But there was one other logistical issue. His flight home would be on another federal holiday—Inauguration Day. And technically, he would no longer be a federal employee. He was concerned about receiving a bill from the federal government for his airfare back to the United States. He reached out to Greg Craig, the counsel to incoming President Obama, and got a promise that he could extend his employment long enough to get home.

So, Bellinger flew to The Hague to hear the final judgment of the ICJ in this matter. His prediction bore out. The court ruled that there was no dispute between Mexico and the United States over the meaning of the *Avena* judgment. Instead, it stated Mexico's request "concerns the general question of the effects of a judgment of the Court in the legal order" of the United States, and not the meaning or scope of the *Avena* judgment itself. The court reiterated that its judgment left it to the United States to choose the means of implementing the decision. Mexico's objection to how the United States implemented (or failed to implement) *Avena* was outside the court's jurisdiction. Therefore, by a vote of 11 to 1, the ICJ ruled in favor of the United States.

However, Bellinger was also correct about the ICJ's reaction to Medellín's execution. The court unanimously found that the United States breached its international obligations when it allowed the execution of José Medellín in the face of a provisional measures order.

Due to the expiration of the 110th Congress on January 3, 2009, the Avena Case Implementation Act never became federal law. But this was not the last time that Congress would attempt to grant *Avena*-like rights. On June 14, 2011, Senator Patrick Leahy from Vermont introduced the "Consular Notification Compliance Act of 2011." While this bill did not directly mention the *Avena* judgment, it created a new right in federal court to raise a violation of Article 36 of the Vienna Convention or any similar bilateral treaty, but only if an individual was convicted and sentenced to death following an Article 36 violation prior to the passage of the act.

The act was an amendment to the Antiterrorism and Effective Death Penalty Act and would create a new basis for filing a habeas application, but mandated that it must be brought up in a prisoner's first such petition. It required the defendant to make "a substantial showing of actual prejudice to the criminal conviction or sentence of the individual as a result of a violation of Article 36(1)" or similar bilateral agreement.

The Senate Judiciary Committee held hearings on the act. John Bellinger testified about *Avena* and the importance of the United States keeping its commitments. He said he strongly supported the act because of the need for reciprocal enforcement from other countries. While he could not guarantee that other countries had failed to abide by their commitments as a result of the United States' actions, he noted it made it harder for the United States to complain when violations did occur.

Harold Hongju Koh, Bellinger's successor at the legal adviser's office, worked with Leahy on the act. He said there were initial indications that Senator John Cornyn would support the bill. At the time, there was a case pending before the Supreme Court, *Leal Garcia v. Texas*. Leal Garcia was another of the named *Avena* defendants, and, like Medellín, he was seeking a stay so that Congress could vote on the Leahy bill. As in *Medellín*, the Court refused to grant the stay. And that, according to Koh, removed the pressure from Cornyn and others. As a result, like the Avena Case Implementation Act of 2008, the bill never left committee.

To this day, Congress has yet to take the steps required by the Supreme Court in *Medellín v. Texas* to provide some form of judicial relief to those who are denied their rights under Article 36, unless they raise those issues at trial. But it keeps trying. The annual budget put forth by the State Department always includes a legislative fix for *Medellín v. Texas*, but every year, it is removed during the budget process. Unfortunately, as the ICJ noted, the failure to inform detainees of their rights under the Vienna Convention directly results in failing to raise an Article 36 violation until it is too late. Thus, all too often, these claims end up the victim of procedural default or similar rules. As a response, appellate attorneys supporting foreign nationals who have defaulted their claims have begun raising the issue as an example of ineffective assistance of trial counsel in violation of the Sixth Amendment, rather than raising the violation of the treaty itself.

Senator Ellis, in Texas, did not give up either. In 2009, he again introduced a bill that would have required magistrate judges to inform all known or suspected foreign nationals of their Article 36 rights and required training for law enforcement. In addition, this version of his bill provided a right of any foreign national sentenced to death following a violation of Article 36 to file a motion seeking "any appropriate relief required to remedy the harm done by the violation, including a vitiation of the death penalty." Unfortunately, like his prior effort, this one did not make it to the floor of the Texas Senate. Ellis said he introduced the legislation because the legal system "can't serve justice if it doesn't respect the rights of every individual. The right to [contact] a foreign consulate is not just a courtesy, these are part of the due process rights of an individual." He noted the need for Texas in particular to comply with Article 36 and *Avena* due to the close business, political, and cultural ties between it and Mexico. Finally, he noted the broader international implications for Americans traveling abroad. What incentive did other nations have to respect the rights of Americans if we did not respect the rights of their citizens here?

Ellis also recognized the risk he was taking to his political career, but he was pursuing higher values. As he explained, "I was well aware that he was not a sympathetic figure. But this is about ensuring due process. It is the process itself that should judge Mr. Medellín—officials should not have the discretion to modify the process or withhold rights from individuals based on their own perceptions of an individual's guilt." He recognized that "review and reconsideration" were unlikely to change the outcome in Medellín's case. He stated:

I never denied that what Mr. Medellín confessed to doing was absolutely heinous. But our policy with regard to the criminal legal system cannot be driven by a few exceptional, high-profile crimes. It has been for too long. And this impacts the civil rights and liberties of too many others. In this case, I was thinking of Americans abroad—missionaries, teachers, students—they deserve to have their rights upheld, and that depends on applying the rules equally across the board.

Texas's insistence on carrying on with executions is particularly jarring in the case of criminal defendants covered by *Avena* and those similarly situated for two reasons. First, as Justice Stevens pointed out in his concurrence, the cost of providing the extra process called for by the ICJ is minimal, from Texas's perspective, but could ensure that foreign nationals on Texas's death row are not among the wrongfully convicted. Second, and more important, the failure of criminal defendants to exercise their rights under Article 36 can be traced directly to Texas's failure to abide by its obligations under the Vienna Convention.

As more time has passed since the ICJ's ruling in *Avena* and the Supreme Court's subsequent ruling in *Medellín v. Texas*, interest in the issue appears to have waned. In 2014, the Republican Party retook control of the Senate, ending much hope for further action, as the party tends to be more favorable toward state control of criminal matters, more favorable toward the death penalty, and less enamored of international law. The Trump administration continued this trend, withdrawing from a number of international agreements to which the United States was a party. While the Biden administration has taken some steps to reverse course, it has not rejoined the Optional Protocol, nor has it taken steps to vindicate the rights of *Avena* defendants. The only thing preventing a solution to the trap identified by Medellín's case is a lack of political will. Unless Congress acts to provide a remedy, either directly preempting state procedural default rules or providing a federal habeas remedy, more and more foreign nationals, like José Medellín, will be denied their rights and the United States will continue to ignore its international obligations. Because it is the very lack of notification that leads to the default of the claim, only the ability to overcome procedural default can provide a remedy.

Perhaps recognizing the Court's role in facilitating this Catch-22, the judiciary took preliminary steps to prevent a recurrence of Medellín's case, at least in federal court. Under Section 2072 of Title 28 of the *United States Code*, the Supreme Court has the authority to promulgate rules of procedure and practice for all cases in district courts. Changes to these rules follow recommendations from the Judicial Conference of the United States and the US Supreme Court and consideration by Congress. The Judicial Conference sets up advisory committees to propose rules and receive comments on those proposals. It then determines which rules to forward to the Supreme Court for its approval. If the Court approves the proposal, it goes into effect unless Congress enacts legislation to reject, modify, or delay implementation of the proposed change. The whole process takes two to three years.

On December 1, 2014, Federal Rule of Criminal Procedure 5(d) was amended to create a new subsection (1)(f). This rule applies to all felony cases brought before the federal district courts and requires the judge overseeing an arraignment to inform the defendant of certain rights. The new rule, 5(d)(1)(f), now requires a federal district judge to inform a criminal defendant in a felony proceeding that if he or she is not a US citizen, they may request an attorney or federal law enforcement official to notify a consular officer from their country of origin of their arrest, thus ensuring that a criminal defendant is aware of their rights under Article 36 of the Vienna Convention. However, the Federal Rules are not binding on state courts, where the vast majority of criminal prosecutions, particularly capital cases, occur.

The committee's notes to the amendment indicate that the rule was enacted not to relieve arresting officers of their responsibilities to inform detained foreign nationals of their Article 36 rights, but rather as a backstop to assure that US treaty obligations are fulfilled and to create a judicial record of that action. Judges are required to provide this notice without trying to ascertain the nationality of the defendant. The notes also make clear that this rule is not intended to create any additional rights or remedies not available under Article 36 itself, a question that, it notes, was still open at the time the rule was drafted.

While Rule 5(d)(1)(f) is a step in the right direction, it leaves much to be desired. The rule does not come into play until a criminal defendant is arraigned, which occurs hours or days after arrest and interrogation. As Mexico exhaustively explained to the ICJ, the need for legal representation is often the most vital at the earliest stages following arrest. By the time a federal judge informs a criminal defendant of his or her rights to contact the consulate, incriminating statements may already have been made to law enforcement officers.

Perhaps the biggest gap in the rule's coverage is that it applies solely in federal court. The vast majority of prosecutions of foreign nationals, and the lion's share of death penalty decisions, occur at the state and local level. While the Federal Rules of Criminal Procedure are certainly a model for states, there is no requirement that they be adopted whole-sale. Indeed, since 1965, only five states have codified a requirement that foreign nationals be informed of their Vienna Convention rights: Florida (1965), California (1999), North Carolina (2003), Oregon (2003), and Illinois (2016). However, even many of these statutes are limited in nature. For example, the North Carolina statute applies only to those held in the custody of a mental health facility. In 2000, Florida amended its statute to expressly prohibit criminal defendants from relying on the failure to notify them of their Article 36 rights as a defense. Some states, while recognizing the importance of Article 36, do not even go so far as to codify a requirement to inform detainees of their rights. In 2013, Nevada provided by statute that the attorney general may set up training on Article 36 compliance, but this permissive statute does not require law enforcement to attend.

For the average foreign national detained in the United States, compliance with Article 36 still depends on state and local police and sheriffs. The Commission on Accreditation for Law Enforcement Agencies (CALEA) issued standard 1.1.4, dealing with consular notification. Law enforcement agencies that wish to be accredited are trained on Article 36. However, as of 2019, this was considered a tier 2 standard, which is not taught as part of the basic accreditation course and is instead reserved for police departments that seek advanced accreditation. This is a voluntary choice made at the individual department level. As of January 2021, CALEA had accredited 743 law enforcement agencies, with another 113 participating in a self-assessment. The Houston Police Department was not among them. As a result, the honor of the United States in the international community and also the lives of foreign nationals are largely in the hands of local law enforcement.

CHAPTER 9

The United States, the Death Penalty, and International Law

The failure of the United States to comply with the *Avena* judgment has had long-lasting impacts. With the United States already set apart from much of the Western world on the basis of its use of capital punishment, the Supreme Court's decision has further eroded our standing with these nations. When Harold Hongju Koh served as legal adviser to the State Department, he was regularly harangued by our allies about the United States' use of the death penalty. Ambassador Santiago Oñate, who worked on *Avena* and is currently serving as the permanent observer of Mexico to the Council of Europe, stated that the decision in *Medellín v. Texas* has negatively impacted the view of the United States among the diplomatic community. "It is further proof that the US does not abide by international law whenever they consider it against their own interests," he said.

The case also continues to cause friction between the United States and Mexico. Ambassador Juan Manuel Gómez Robledo, who led the *Avena* case for Mexico and currently serves as the Mexican ambassador to France, indicated that while important progress has been made and that some states provided the "review and reconsideration" mandated by *Avena*, the Mexican government continues to "reiterate our position [on the case] at every occasion and in all instances." In 2013, Mexico circulated a letter to members of the UN Security Council, arguing that the United States had failed to comply with the judgment as required by the UN Charter. More recently, in December 2018, the UN General Assembly adopted a resolution calling on the United States to immediately comply with the *Avena* judgment. This followed action from other international bodies, including the Inter-American Commission on Human Rights and the United Nations Human Rights Office of the High

Commissioner, which each issued statements condemning the United States for executing José Medellín, in contravention of the decision of the International Court of Justice (ICJ) in *Avena*.

Rulings by foreign courts have also come in the wake of *Avena*, which undercut arguments made by the United States before both the ICJ and the US Supreme Court. The United States and Texas had argued that no country gives domestic effect to ICJ judgments and expressly pointed out that an Article 36 violation would not provide any form of judicial relief in Mexico. But that is no longer the case. In 2005, the Federal Constitutional Court of Germany held that German courts were bound to follow the ICJ's decisions in *LaGrand* and *Avena*. Mexico followed suit in 2013, when its Supreme Court recognized that violations of Article 36 implicate due process and must be considered in determining whether a foreign national received a fair trial. The court held that it was "unquestionable that the right of foreign nationals to consular notification, contact and assistance is a fundamental right in force in our country." As a result of the Article 36 violation, the court ordered the release of a French national.

But it is not just parties to suits in the ICJ that have applied the decisions in their courts. In two cases in 2005 and 2009, the Supreme Federal Court of Brazil relied upon the ICJ's decisions when it held that "there is a human right to request consular assistance." In the latter case, the court referred to the rights protected by Article 36 as "indispensable." And in two cases in 2017, the High Court of Malawi found that Article 36 violations required resentencing two foreign nationals who had been condemned to death. Explicitly relying on *Avena*, the court commuted one sentence to thirty years, and in light of mitigating evidence and the fact the defendant had served twenty years, the court ordered the immediate release of the defendant in the second case.

Finally, while not a court case, in 2020 Pakistan passed an ordinance codifying the right to "review and reconsideration" in cases in which Article 36 has been violated. Titled the "International Court of Justice Review and Re-consideration Ordinance, 2020," it permits foreign nationals convicted by a military court to file a petition raising Article 36 claims with the High Court and gives the provision "overriding effect" over any other law that might hold the contrary.

Pakistan's action was in direct response to a case it lost in the ICJ,

India v. Pakistan, known as the *Jadhav Case*, issued in 2019. Pakistan arrested Jadhav and accused him of espionage. He was tried by a military court and sentenced to death. Pakistan failed to observe Jadhav's rights under Article 36, and India brought suit before the ICJ. Relying on *Avena*, the court issued judgment in favor of India. As to remedy, it issued its strongest statement yet, explicitly tying consular access to the receipt of a fair trial. While recognizing that, like the United States, Pakistan had the right to choose the means of enforcing the judgment, the ICJ noted that "freedom in the choice is not without qualification." Relying on Mexico's second petition requesting clarification of the *Avena* judgment, the court ordered Pakistan to take all appropriate measures to provide effective "review and reconsideration," "including, if necessary, by enacting appropriate legislation."

It is hard to read the court's order in *Jadhav* as anything less than a direct response to the United States' failure to provide relief and reconsideration under *Avena*. The Supreme Court's decision in *Medellín* relied on the failure of Congress to enact implementing legislation. At the next opportunity the ICJ had, it ordered the losing party to enact exactly such legislation. While the United States is no longer susceptible to suit before the ICJ, it is still a party to the Vienna Convention. And while ICJ cases formally bind only the parties before it, the court strives for a uniform interpretation of the treaty, and its judgments weigh in on the appropriate meaning of its terms.

———

In the years following the execution of José Medellín, eleven more foreign nationals have been put to death, in three states. Once again, Texas led the way with seven, while Virginia and Florida each put two foreign nationals to death. Nine of the eleven alleged that their rights under the Vienna Convention were violated. Five of those eleven were Mexican. All five of them alleged an Article 36 violation. Another five foreign nationals—four of them Mexican—died in custody, although their deaths were not the result of executions. All five raised Vienna Convention violations. This is a relative slowdown. In the twelve years before *Medellín v. Texas*, nineteen foreign nationals were put to death by the United States. Fourteen of them alleged their Article 36 rights had been violated.

As of September 2020, a total of 124 foreign nationals from thirty-four nations resided on death rows in fourteen states and the federal prison system. California leads the way here, with 60 foreign nationals on death row. Yet, due to a moratorium on executions, California has carried out only one execution of a foreign national since 1976, and that was in 1999. Mexican nationals make up the lion's share of foreign nationals on death row, representing 50 of the 124 foreign nationals. Cuba and Vietnam come next with 8 nationals each. Canada only has 2 nationals currently on death row anywhere in the United States. Forty-one of the Mexican nationals allege that their Article 36 rights were violated. Of those Mexican foreign nationals on currently on death row, only 13 have been sentenced since 2008.

This decrease in the use of the death penalty for foreign nationals mirrors a broader trend in the twenty-first century. According to the Death Penalty Information Center, the population on death row in the United States has declined every year since 2001. In part, this is attributable to the fact that several states have abolished the death penalty since the Supreme Court decided *Medellín v. Texas*. Since 2008, eight states (New Mexico, Illinois, Connecticut, Maryland, Delaware, Washington, New Hampshire, and Colorado) have removed death as an option. The governors of another three states (Oregon, Pennsylvania, and California) have imposed a moratorium on implementing the death penalty, which explains why California has such a large population of foreign nationals still on death row, including five Mexican nationals sentenced to die since 2008. A total of eleven Mexican nationals who were originally sentenced to death have had those sentences reversed since 2009 for a variety of reasons.

While some had hoped that *Medellín v. Texas* would be a blow against the death penalty, it turned out not to be the case. Despite the signals sent by the Supreme Court in cases like *Atkins v. Virginia* and *Roper v. Simmons*, international condemnation of the death penalty would not be enough to save José Medellín and those similarly situated. This seems to be the case even if, as noted earlier, other nations have started to give effect to the ICJ's decisions in their domestic courts. The departure of Justice O'Connor was a real blow to the effort. As former White House Counsel Harriet Miers noted at the time *Medellín v. Dretke* was decided, Justice O'Connor had a real interest in international law, an interest Justice Samuel Alito has shown no inclination toward. Mark Warren, of the Human Rights Research Center, stated that if you read Justice O'Connor's dissent in *Medellín v. Dretke*, it was clear that she understood the arguments being made by Medellín's team: "I think she understood it better than just about anybody on that side of the fence." Likewise, the departure of Justice Anthony Kennedy and his replacement by his former clerk Brett Kavanaugh does not bode well for the future impact of international law in US courts, although, as Warren pointed out, Justice Kennedy did not write a single word in any of the cases dealing with the Vienna Convention when they were before the Court.

At the same time, it's not clear that international opponents of the death penalty viewed *Medellín v. Texas* as part of the broader strategy to further the abolition of the death penalty. Mark Warren didn't view it that way. "If you compare the *Medellín* case to a case like *Atkins v. Virginia*, there's a world of difference there from an abolitionist perspective," he said. *Medellín* was never going to be a categorical blow against the death penalty. At best, Warren noted, even a complete win by Medellín's team would only result in a procedural remedy. "In no sense was that exempting foreign nationals from the death penalty. And in no sense that I can think of was anybody actually arguing that that should be so." Even the amicus briefs submitted by international human rights groups did not argue that foreign nationals should be exempted from the death penalty as a class.

This points up another issue with the Supreme Court's decision in *Medellín v. Texas*. Absent congressional action, which itself would be subject to challenge, the United States is incapable of honoring its international obligations, so long as the states are free to disregard the strictures of international law. As Medellín's counsel argued, the supremacy clause of the Constitution was authored in direct response to states violating national treaty obligations under the Articles of Confederation. But under the rationale of *Medellín*, states are not beholden to enforce the Vienna Convention, or any treaty deemed "non-self-executing," unless Congress provides some means of vindication. But even had Congress acted to pass either of the bills specifically designed to address the *Avena* decision, it still would not be enough to honor the United States' international obligations.

The ICJ's demand for "review and reconsideration" was a remedy for violations that had already occurred. Even had Texas acquiesced and provided José Medellín and the other defendants a hearing on whether the denial of Article 36 had harmed their defense, and even if Texas or federal courts reversed every conviction and death sentence as Mexico asked, the violation of international law would still have occurred. Only compliance in the first instance can prevent the United States from breaching its international obligations. And despite the best efforts of the State Department, compliance still remains spotty at best. This can likely be traced to the attitudes of those at the top, such as Governor Rick Perry, who remained steadfast that complying with the Vienna Convention was a responsibility of the United States and was no concern of Texas. So long as that remains the attitude of those in charge of ensuring compliance with Article 36, violations will continue to occur, often to the detriment of foreign nationals who are woefully unfamiliar with our legal system.

1963

March 4–April 22 The Vienna Convention on Consular Relations is negotiated.

March 4–April 22 The Optional Protocol concerning the Compulsory Settlement of Disputes is negotiated.

April 24 Vienna Convention on Consular Relations opened for signature.

April 24 The United States signs the Vienna Convention on Consular Relations and the Optional Protocol concerning the Compulsory Settlement of Disputes.

October 7 Mexico signs the Vienna Convention on Consular Relations.

1965

June 16 Mexico ratifies the Vienna Convention on Consular Relations.

1967

March 19 The Vienna Convention on Consular Relations and the Optional Protocol concerning the Compulsory Settlement of Disputes enter into force.

1969

November 24 The United States ratifies the Vienna Convention on Consular Relations and the Optional Protocol concerning the Compulsory Settlement of Disputes.

1972

June 29 The US Supreme Court decides *Furman v. Georgia*, holding that the death penalty, as practiced in all states, violated the Eighth Amendment.

1974

January 1 Texas reinstitutes the death penalty, which had been struck down by the US Supreme Court.

1976

July 2 The US Supreme Court decides *Gregg v. Georgia*, and four companion cases, upholding newly implemented death penalty procedures in Georgia, Florida, Texas, Louisiana, and North Carolina.

1979

November 4 During the Iranian Revolution, Iranian forces storm the US embassy in Tehran and take fifty-two diplomats and American citizens hostage.

November 29 The United States sues Iran before the International Court of Justice, alleging a violation of the Vienna Convention on Consular Relations. It relies on the Optional Protocol concerning the Compulsory Settlement of Disputes. This is the first case brought requesting an interpretation of Article 36 of the convention.

1980

March 22–24   The International Court of Justice hears arguments in *United States v. Iran.*

May 24   The International Court of Justice issues its decision in *United States v. Iran,* holding that Iran violated numerous international obligations owed to the United States under various treaties, including Article 36 of the Vienna Convention on Consular Relations.

1982

January 7   Two German citizens, Walter and Karl LaGrand, are arrested for murder in Arizona. They are not notified of their rights under Article 36 of the Vienna Convention on Consular Relations.

1984

José Medellín comes to the United States from Nuevo Laredo, Mexico.

December 14   The LaGrand brothers are sentenced to death in Arizona.

1992

February 17   A Paraguayan citizen, Angel Breard, commits an attempted rape and murder in Virginia. Six months later he would be arrested. He was not informed of his rights under Article 36 of the Vienna Convention on Consular Relations.

December 2   Sandra Babcock first raises an Article 36 claim in a petition for habeas corpus in *Faulder v. Johnson, Director Texas Department of Criminal Justice.*

1993

June 24   José Medellín, along with fellow members of the Black and White gang, rape and murder Jennifer Ertman and Elizabeth Peña.

June 29   José Medellín is arrested and confesses to the murders. Despite telling the arresting officer that he was born in Mexico, he is not provided notification of his rights under Article 36 of the Vienna Convention on Consular Relations.

August 22   Angel Breard sentenced to death in Virginia.

1994

September 12   José Medellín's trial begins in Houston, Texas.

September 16   After only thirteen minutes of jury deliberation, José Medellín is convicted of capital murder.

October 11   José Medellín is sentenced to death.

1995
January 17   George W. Bush becomes governor of Texas.

1997
April 29   José Medellín sends a letter to the Mexican consulate, inform-
                    ing it of his conviction and sentence. It is the first time the gov-
                    ernment of Mexico is made aware that he has been detained.

December 9   Mexico files a case at the Inter-American Court of Human
                    Rights, alleging that the continual violation of Article 36 of the
                    Vienna Convention on Consular Relations by the United States
                    violates the human rights of Mexican nationals on death row.

1998
March 26   José Medellín files a habeas corpus petition raising the violation
                    of Article 36.

April 3   Paraguay files suit against the United States at the International
                    Court of Justice, arguing that the United States violated Article
                    36 of the Vienna Convention on Consular Relations when it
                    arrested, tried, and sentenced Angel Breard without inform-
                    ing him of his rights. Paraguay relies on the Optional Protocol
                    concerning the Compulsory Settlement of Disputes to invoke
                    the ICJ's jurisdiction. Paraguay asks the ICJ to issue provi-
                    sional measures, ordering the United States to prevent Breard's
                    execution.

April 9   The International Court of Justice issues a provisional mea-
                    sures order, requesting that the United States not execute Angel
                    Breard until after the court has ruled on the merits.

April 14   The Supreme Court issues a per curiam opinion in *Breard v.
                    Greene*. The case came to the Court as a motion for stay and
                    petition for certiorari on the eve of Breard's scheduled execu-
                    tion. The Court issued its decision without the benefit of brief-
                    ing and oral argument. It rejected Breard's claim, holding that
                    Breard procedurally defaulted any claims under the Vienna
                    Convention on Consular Relations.

April 14   Angel Breard is executed by the State of Virginia.

October 9   Paraguay files its memorial at the International Court of Jus-
                    tice, laying out the facts and arguments relating to its claim that
                    the United States violated Article 36.

November 2   Paraguay sends a letter to the International Court of Justice
                    withdrawing its case against the United States. The court dis-
                    misses the case without issuing a decision.

1999
February 24   Karl LaGrand is executed by the State of Arizona.

March 2	Germany files suit in the International Court of Justice against the United States, arguing that the United States violated the rights of Germany when it failed to provide the LaGrand brothers with the information required by Article 36 of the Vienna Convention on Consular Relations. It relies on the Optional Protocol concerning the Compulsory Settlement of Disputes to invoke the court's jurisdiction. It requests a provisional measures order in respect of Walter LaGrand.
March 3	The International Court of Justice issues a provisional measures order requesting that the United States take all steps to prevent the execution of Walter LaGrand
March 3	Walter LaGrand is executed by the State of Arizona.
October 1	The Inter-American Court of Human Rights issues Opinion OC 16-99, addressing Mexico's claims. It holds that Article 36 of the Vienna Convention on Consular Relations concerns the human rights of detained foreign nationals and that failing to provide notification of Article 36 rights violates due process as protected by the International Covenant on Civil and Political Rights. It further holds that imposing the death penalty when Article 36 rights have been denied violates the right not to be "arbitrarily" deprived of one's life.
November 13–17	The International Court of Justice hears arguments in *Germany v. United States*.

2000

September	The Mexican Capital Legal Assistance Program is established by the Mexican Foreign Ministry. Sandra Babcock is hired as the first director.
December 21	Rick Perry becomes governor of Texas.

2001

January 20	George W. Bush becomes president of the United States.
June 27	The International Court of Justice issues its judgment in *LaGrand*. It holds that the United States violated the rights of Germany and the LaGrand brothers when it failed to inform them of their rights under Article 36. It declared that the appropriate remedy in future cases was "review and reconsideration" of the convictions and sentences, in a manner of the United States' choosing, which takes into account the Article 36 violation.
October 3	The Texas Court of Criminal Appeals rejects an application for habeas corpus filed by José Medellín in which he raised the

Article 36 violation. The court held that he procedurally defaulted the claim by not raising it at his trial and that the Vienna Convention on Consular Relations did not create any individually enforceable rights.

2002

March 15   Mexico accedes to the Optional Protocol concerning the Compulsory Settlement of Disputes.

June 20   The US Supreme Court decides *Atkins v. Virginia*, holding that under the Eighth Amendment, the death penalty may not be imposed on defendants who suffer from mental disabilities. The decision, authored by Justice Anthony Kennedy, draws on practices from foreign nations and international law.

2003

January 9   Ted Cruz appointed solicitor general of Texas.

January 9   Mexico files suit against the United States in the International Court of Justice, alleging that the United States failed to provide Article 36 notifications to fifty-five Mexican nationals on death rows in several states. It invoked the court's jurisdiction under the Optional Protocol concerning the Compulsory Settlement of Disputes.

January 11   Governor George H. Ryan of Illinois commutes the death sentences of all 167 prisoners on Illinois's death row to life in prison.

June 26   The Southern District of Texas issues its opinion in *Medellín v. Cockrell*, denying Medellín's petition for habeas corpus. Relying on *Breard v. Greene*, the district court held that Medellín procedurally defaulted his Vienna Convention claim, that the Vienna Convention did not confer individual rights on Medellín, and that he could not show that the violation of Article 36 prejudiced his defense.

December 15–19   The International Court of Justice hears arguments in *Mexico v. United States*.

2004

March 31   The International Court of Justice issues its decision in *Avena and Other Mexican Nationals (Mexico v. United States)*. The court holds that the United States violated the Article 36 rights of over fifty Mexican nationals, including José Medellín. It orders the United States, by means of its own choosing, to provide "review and reconsideration" of their convictions and sentences. It holds that the procedural default rule, as applied, violates Article 36 and may not serve as a reason for denying review.

May 14	Oklahoma governor Brad Henry commutes the death sentence of Osvaldo Torres, one of the *Avena* defendants, to life without the possibility of parole based on the *Avena* decision.
May 20	The Fifth Circuit Court of Appeals issues its decision denying José Medellín a certificate of appealability, as required by the Antiterrorism and Effective Death Penalty Act. This appeal arose from the denial of Medellín's habeas petition in *Medellín v. Cockrell*. The case is now styled *Medellín v. Dretke*.
August 18	The US Supreme Court grants the petition for certiorari in *Medellín v. Dretke*.
2005	
January 26	Condoleezza Rice is confirmed as secretary of state.
February 18	Texas state senator Rodney Ellis files SB 603, which would require magistrate judges to inform all known and suspected foreign nationals of their Article 36 rights. The bill also mandates training regarding the arrest and detention of foreign nationals for all law enforcement officers in Texas.
February 28	President George W. Bush issues a memorandum to the attorney general stating that the United States will comply with the *Avena* judgment by having state courts provide the "review and reconsideration" called for by the International Court of Justice.
March 1	The US Supreme Court issues its decision in *Roper v. Simmons* holding that the Eighth Amendment prohibits imposing the death penalty on those who were under eighteen at the time they committed their crimes. Justice Anthony Kennedy, writing for the Court, relies upon international practice in determining that executing such individuals is cruel and unusual. As a result of the Court's decision, two of José Medellín's codefendants are resentenced to forty-year terms.
March 7	Secretary of State Condoleezza Rice sends a letter to United Nations Secretary-General Kofi Annan informing him that the United States is withdrawing from the Optional Protocol concerning the Compulsory Settlement of Disputes. The International Court of Justice will no longer have jurisdiction over claims that the United States violated the Vienna Convention on Consular Relations.
March 28	The Supreme Court hears oral argument in *Medellín v. Dretke*.
May 23	The Supreme Court issues its decision in *Medellín v. Dretke*. It dismisses the case as improvidently granted and allows the state courts of Texas an opportunity to comply with President Bush's

declaration. Four justices, led by Justice Sandra Day O'Connor, dissent, arguing the Court should decide the important questions raised.

July 1 — Justice Sandra Day O'Connor announces her retirement.

September 3 — Chief Justice William H. Rehnquist dies.

September 14 — The Texas Court of Criminal Appeals hears argument in *Ex parte Medellín*, José Medellín's subsequent petition for habeas corpus seeking "review and reconsideration" of his conviction and sentence based on the International Court of Justice's *Avena* decision and President Bush's declaration.

September 29 — John Roberts is confirmed as chief justice of the United States, replacing William Rehnquist.

2006

January 31 — Samuel Alito is confirmed as associate justice of the Supreme Court, replacing Sandra Day O'Connor.

June 28 — The US Supreme Court issues its decision in *Sanchez-Llamas v. Oregon*. In this case, two foreign nationals, not covered by the *Avena* decision, argued that statements made following an Article 36 violation should be suppressed. The Supreme Court held that suppression was not a required remedy for Article 36 violations and that state procedural default rules could operate to preclude an Article 36 claim.

August — Sandra Babcock steps down as the director of the Mexican Capital Legal Assistance Program.

November 15 — The Texas Court of Criminal Appeals issues its decision in *Ex parte Medellín*. The court held that neither the *Avena* decision nor the president's declaration constitutes binding federal law that overcomes Texas's prohibition on successive habeas petitions.

November 22 — On behalf of José Medellín, Sandra Babcock files a petition with the Inter-American Commission on Human Rights claiming violations of several articles of the American Declaration of the Rights and Duties of Man caused by the failure to be notified of his Article 36 rights at the time of his arrest.

December 12 — Sandra Babcock files additional petitions on behalf of two other *Avena* defendants, Ruben Ramirez Cardenas and Humberto Leal Garcia, with the Inter-American Commission on Human Rights

2007

January 16 — José Medellín files a petition for certiorari with the US Supreme Court, appealing the Texas Court of Criminal Appeals' decision denying his habeas petition. The case is styled *Medellín v. Texas.*

April 30	The Supreme Court grants the petition for certiorari in *Medellín v. Texas.*
October 9	The Supreme Court hears oral arguments in *Medellín v. Texas.*

2008

March 24	The Supreme Court issues its 6–3 decision in *Medellín v. Texas.* It holds that neither the *Avena* decision nor the president's declaration constitutes binding federal law that overcomes Texas's bar on successive habeas petitions. International Court of Justice decisions do not constitute binding obligations unless Congress enacts implementing legislation or the treaty is "self-executing." Here, none of the treaties at issue are self-executing, and Congress has not acted to implement the *Avena* decision. The president lacks the power to displace state procedural default rules on his own, and such rules may preclude "review and reconsideration" of Article 36 violations.
June 5	Mexico requests an interpretation of the *Avena* decision from the International Court of Justice and asks for provisional measures on behalf of José Medellín.
June 17	Attorney General Michael Mukasey and Secretary of State Condoleezza Rice send a joint letter to Texas governor Rick Perry urging him to comply with the *Avena* decision.
July 14	California congresspeople Howard Berman and Zoe Lofgren introduce the Avena Case Implementation Act of 2008 in response to the Supreme Court's ruling in *Medellín v. Texas.*
July 16	The International Court of Justice issues a provisional measures order, instructing the United States to take all steps necessary to prevent the execution of José Medellín.
July 18	Governor Perry responds to Attorney General Mukasey and Secretary Rice, declining to take any action and arguing that international obligations bind the United States, not Texas.
July 31	José Medellín files a motion for stay and cert petition at the US Supreme Court, arguing for more time to allow Congress to pass the Avena Case Implementation Act.
August 5	The Supreme Court denies Medellín's stay request and cert petition, stating that the mere introduction of a bill is not enough to justify action by the Court.
August 5	José Medellín is executed for his participation in the rape and murder of Jennifer Ertman and Elizabeth Peña.

November 10	Texas state senator Rodney Ellis files SB 125. In addition to the requirements of SB 603, which he introduced in 2005, SB 125 provided foreign nationals sentenced to death following an Article 36 violation a right to file a motion in state court seeking relief for any harm caused by that violation.
2009	
August 7	The Inter-American Commission on Human Rights issues its decision on José Medellín's petition. The commission concludes that the United States is responsible for several violations of the American Declaration on the Rights and Duties of Man, as well as for failing to prevent Medellín's execution while his petition was pending. The commission recommends vacating the death sentences of Ramirez Cardenas and Leal Garcia. It also recommends the United States provide reparations to José Medellín's family.
2011	
June 14	Vermont senator Patrick Leahy introduces the Consular Notification Compliance Act in the Senate.
July 7	The Supreme Court issues a per curiam opinion in *Leal Garcia v. Texas*, rejecting a request for a stay by Humberto Leal Garcia, an *Avena* defendant. Both Leal Garcia and the United States urged the stay to allow Congress time to act to implement the Consular Notification Compliance Act. The Court holds that Leal Garcia's claims are foreclosed by *Medellín v. Texas* and that the possibility of congressional action is not enough to justify implementing a stay, since Congress has had many years since both *Avena* and *Medellín* to act and had not done so.
2019	
July 17	The International Court of Justice issues a judgment in *Jadhav Case (India v. Pakistan)*, holding that Pakistan violated Article 36 of the Vienna Convention when it failed to notify an accused foreign espionage agent of his rights to contact his consulate. It orders effective "review and reconsideration" as the remedy. It stresses that to be effective, the remedy must give full weight to the effect of the violation. It specifically orders Pakistan to enact legislation if necessary to provide the appropriate "review and reconsideration."

LIST OF CASES

American Insurance Association v. Garamendi, 539 U.S. 396 (2003)

Atkins v. Virginia, 536 U.S. 304 (2002)

Breard v. Greene, 523 U.S. 371 (1998)

Case Concerning Avena and Other Mexican Nationals (Mexico v. United States), 2004 I.C.J. 12 (March 31)

Coker v. Georgia, 433 U.S. 584 (1977)

Comegys v. Vasse, 26 U.S. (1 Pet.) 193 (1828)

Dames & Moore v. Regan, 453 U.S. 654 (1981)

Ex parte Medellín, 223 S.W.3d 315 (2006)

Faulder v. Johnson, Director Texas Department of Criminal Justice, 178 F.3d 741 (1999)

Furman v. Georgia, 408 U.S. 238 (1972)

Gregg v. Georgia, 428 U.S. 153 (1976)

Jadhav Case (India v. Pakistan) 2019 I.C.J. 418 (July 17)

LaGrand Case (Germany v. United States) 2001 I.C.J. 466 (June 27)

Lawrence v. Texas, 539 U.S. 558 (2003)

Leal Garcia v. Texas, 564 U.S. 940 (2011)

Medellín v. Cockrell, No. H-01-4078 (2003)

Medellín v. Dretke, 544 U.S. 660 (2005)

Medellín v. Dretke, 371 F.3d 270 (5th Cir. 2004)

Medellín v. Texas, 552 U.S. 491 (2008)

Miranda v. Arizona, 384 U.S. 436 (1966)

The Paquete Habana, 175 U.S. 677 (1900)

Request for Interpretation of the Judgment of 31 March 2004 in the Case Concerning Avena and Other Mexican Nationals (Mexico v. United States) 2008 I.C.J. 139 (July 16)

Roper v. Simmons, 543 U.S. 551 (2005)

Sanchez-Llamas v. Oregon, 548 U.S. 331 (2006)

United States Diplomatic and Consular Staff in Tehran (United States v. Iran), 1981 I.C.J. 3 (May 24)

United States v. Curtiss-Wright Export Corporation, 299 U.S. 304 (1936)

United States v. Pink, 315 U.S. 203 (1942)

BIBLIOGRAPHIC ESSAY

Information contained in this work comes from both primary and secondary sources. Thanks to the recency of the decisions in *Medellín v. Texas, Medellín v. Dretke*, and *Mexico v. United States*, firsthand accounts were provided by several members of the teams representing Medellín, Mexico, the United States, the State of Texas, and amici. On-the-record interviews were conducted with Professor Sandra Babcock, John Bellinger, Rodney Ellis, Daniel Geyser, Ambassador Juan Manuel Gómez Robledo, Professor Harold Hongju Koh, Judge Kristopher Monson, Ambassador Santiago Oñate, and Mark Warren. Others who represented various parties agreed to speak on background because they were not authorized to speak on the record. In each case, they provided invaluable insight to the inner workings of the decisions made by the various parties, as well as providing details not contained in the record.

Information on the murder of Jennifer Ertman and Elizabeth Peña, along with that on the subsequent actions of José Medellín and the other members of the Black and White gang, came from several sources. For details regarding the perpetrators and a timeline of June 24, 1993, see Corey Mitchell, *Pure Murder* (New York: Pinnacle, 2008). Other information was obtained from reviewing newspaper coverage of the murders and subsequent trial. See Sam Howe Verhovek, "Houston Knows Murder, but This . . . ," *New York Times*, July 9, 1993; Associated Press, "2 Texas Dads Confront 3 of Daughters' Killers," *Deseret News*, October 13, 1994; John Makeig, "Slain Girls' Kin Describe Fear, Anguish," *Houston Chronicle*, February 9, 1994. The transcript of the trial in *State v. José Ernesto Medellín*, along with copies of exhibits, such as Medellín's confession and a copy of his arrest report, was obtained from the Texas State Archives in Court of Criminal Appeals No. 71,997. For information on Harris County District Attorney John B. Holmes Jr., see Allan Turner, "Former DA Ran Powerful Death Penalty Machine," *Houston Chronicle*, July 25, 2007.

Information on the death penalty, including its history, statistics, and current status, was obtained from numerous nonprofit and scholarly sources. The information collected by the Death Penalty Information Center was invaluable in this regard. Scholarly studies of the differential application of the death penalty, by location, race of the offender, race of the victim, and time period, have been published in numerous law reviews and social science journals. See Stephen R. Bright, "Discrimination, Death, and Denial: The Tolerance of Racial Discrimination in Infliction of the Death Penalty," *Santa Clara Law Review* 35 (1994–1995): 433–483; Michael Fraser, "Crime for Crime: Racism and the Death Penalty in the American South," *Social Sciences Journal* 10, no. 1 (2010): 20–24; Kenneth Williams, "The Deregulation of the Death Penalty," *Santa Clara Law Review* 40 (2000): 677–728; Scott

Phillips, "Legal Disparities in the Capital of Capital Punishment," *Journal of Criminal Law and Criminality* 99 (2008–2009): 717–756; Scott Phillips, "Racial Disparities in the Capital of Capital Punishment," *Houston Law Review* 45 (2008): 807–840; Scott Phillips, "Continued Racial Disparities in the Capital of Capital Punishment: The Rosenthal Era," *Houston Law Review* 50 (2012): 131–155; Robert J. Smith, "The Geography of the Death Penalty and Its Ramifications," *Boston University Law Review* 92 (2012): 227–289; David McCord, "What's Messing with Texas Death Sentences?," *Texas Tech Law Review* 43 (2011): 601–613; Adam M. Gershowitz, "Statewide Capital Punishment: The Case for Eliminating Counties' Role in the Death Penalty," *Vanderbilt Law Review* 63 (2010): 307–359.

Mark Warren of the Human Rights Research Center maintains a website (http://users.xplornet.com/~mwarren) with information about foreign nationals on death row, various state and federal measures related to consular notification, and information on foreign court judgments regarding compliance with Article 36. Another invaluable resource was John Quigley's *Foreigners on America's Death Rows* (New York: Cambridge University Press, 2018).

The US State Department publishes a handbook on consular notification and access, as well as a pocket card for law enforcement. See US Department of State, *Consular Notification and Access*, 5th ed., September 2018. The Congressional Research Service has published reports on US compliance with Article 36 requirements. See Michael John Garcia, "Vienna Convention on Consular Relations: Overview of U.S. Implementation and International Court of Justice (ICJ) Interpretation of Consular Notification Requirements," Congressional Research Service, RL32390, May 17, 2004. Other information about US compliance with Article 36 can be found in the memorial of Mexico. See Memorial of Mexico, *Mexico v. United States*, June 20, 2003, pp. 38–40. Information about Annette Sorensen and her lawsuit against the City of New York can be found in the Death Penalty Information Center's article "Consular Rights, Foreign Nationals and the Death Penalty," https://deathpenaltyinfo.org/death-row/foreign-nationals/consular-rights-foreign-nationals-and-the-death-penalty.

Examinations of the use of the death penalty on foreign nationals and its effect on international relations can be found at the Death Penalty Information Center, as well as in various law journals. See Mark Warren, "Death, Dissent, and Diplomacy: The U.S. Death Penalty as an Obstacle to Foreign Relations," *William and Mary Bill of Rights Journal* 13 (2004): 309–337; John Quigley, "Execution of Foreign Nationals in the United States: Pressure from Foreign Governments against the Death Penalty," *ILSA Journal of International and Comparative Law* 4 (1998): 589–598; James Michael Olivero, "The Imposition of the Death Penalty on Mexican Nationals in the United States and the Cultural, Legal and Political Context," *Laws* 2 (2013): 33–50.

Filings in *Mexico v. United States* were graciously provided by Donald Francis

Donovan and are also available from the International Court of Justice's website (https://www.icj-cij.org). The judgments of the ICJ, along with transcripts of the oral proceedings, are also available on the court's website. The ICJ website also hosts the written filings, oral transcripts, and judgments in *United States v. Mexico (Request for Interpretation of the Judgment of 31 March 2004 in the Case Concerning Avena and Other Mexican Nationals)*, *Paraguay v. United States*, *Germany v. United States*, and *India v. Pakistan*.

Information on the Mexican Capital Legal Assistance Program and the various efforts made by Mexico on behalf of its citizens was presented to the ICJ and the US Supreme Court. See Memorial of Mexico, *Mexico v. United States*, June 20, 2003, pp. 11–37; Brief of the United States of Mexico as Amicus Curiae, *Medellín v. Texas*, No. 06-984, June 27, 2007, pp. 13–17. See also Michael Fleishman, "Reciprocity Unmasked: The Role of the Mexican Government in Defense of Its Foreign Nationals in United States Death Penalty Cases," *Arizona Journal of International and Comparative Law* 20 (2003): 359–407.

Numerous studies have identified the impact of amicus briefs on the Supreme Court's decision to hear a case, as well as their impact on decision-making. See Gregory Caldiera and John R. Wright, "Amici Curiae before the Supreme Court: Who Participates, When, and How Much?," *Journal of Politics* 52 (1990): 782–806; Gregory Caldiera and John R. Wright, "Organized Interests and Agenda Setting in the U.S. Supreme Court," *American Political Science Review* 82 (1988): 1109–1127; Katie Zuber, Udi Sommer, and Johnathan Parent, "Setting the Agenda of the United States Supreme Court? Organized Interests and the Decision to File an Amicus Brief at Cert," *Justice System Journal* 36 (2015): 119–137.

For information about the US solicitor general's success in arguing international law cases, see Alan Tauber, *International Law in the Supreme Court of the United States: An Empirical Analysis*, ProQuest Dissertations Publishing, 2010.

Information about Ted Cruz was drawn from a number of newspaper accounts discussing his life and career, including several interviews and statements about his role in *Medellín v. Texas*. For long-form reporting on Cruz's life and career, see Erica Grieder, "The Man in the Arena," *Texas Monthly*, February 2014; Erica Grieder, "The Field Guide to Ted Cruz: Ten Tips for Figuring Out the 'Wacko Bird,'" *Texas Monthly*, January 29, 2016; Erica Grieder, "The Most Hated Man in the Senate," *Foreign Policy*, April 1, 2013; Andrew Romano, "Ted Cruz Always Had a Master Plan. Now It Could Win Him the White House," *Yahoo News*, November 24, 2015; Jason Zengerle, "Ted Cruz: The Distinguished Wacko Bird from Texas," *GQ*, September 22, 2013; Jeffrey Toobin, "The Absolutist," *New Yorker*, June 30, 2014; Sarah Smith, "The Best Reporting on Ted Cruz through the Years," *Pro Publica*, April 12, 2016; and Michael Kruse, "How Ted Cruz Became Ted Cruz," *Politico Magazine*, January 5, 2016.

Many articles have focused specifically on Cruz's advocacy before the Supreme

Court. See Aman Batheja, "In Nine Trips to Supreme Court, Ted Cruz Saw Mixed Results," *Texas Tribune*, January 24, 2016; Aman Batheja, "Senate Candidate and Supreme Court Have a History," *New York Times*, July 22, 2012; Adam Liptak and Matt Flegenheimer, "After a Rocky Start, Ted Cruz Had Success before Supreme Court," *New York Times*, February 16, 2016.

Other articles focused on Cruz's use of the Texas solicitor general's office to advance conservative causes. See "Meet Solicitor General Cruz: Extreme and Far-Right Wing," *American Bridge PAC*, January 5, 2016; "Ted Cruz Promoted Himself and Conservative Causes as Texas' Solicitor General," *Post News Report*, March 5, 2016. For newspaper coverage of the arguments in the *Medellín* cases, see Mark Sherman, "Supreme Court Weighs Bush Role in Texas Death Penalty for Mexican," Associated Press, October 11, 2007; Mark Sherman, "High Court Case Pits Bush against Texas over Death Penalty," Associated Press, October 8, 2007; Bill Mears, "Death Row Case Pits Bush Administration against Texas," CNN, October 10, 2007; "Bush Backs Mexico, Rapist-Murderer," www.wnd.com, October 8, 2007.

For other articles about Ted Cruz, see Emily Stephenson, "How Ted Cruz Win in Supreme Court Hurt U.S.-Mexico Relations," *Reuters*, April 6, 2016; Jen Kuznicki, "The Real Reason G. W. Bush Hates Ted Cruz," *Conservative Review*, November 9, 2015; Kent Scheidegger, "An NYT Hatchet Job on Ted Cruz and the *Medellín* Case," www.crimeandconsequences.com, March 5, 2016; Ian Millhiser, "Ted Cruz: Vote for Me Because I Helped Execute an 'Illegal Alien,'" *Think Progress*, March 22, 2012; David Weigel, "Ted Talks," *Slate*, February 25, 2013; Luke Johnson, "Ted Cruz Talks Up Limiting Executive Power," *Huffington Post*, October 30, 2013; James Barrett, "Ted Cruz Was Asked If He'd Accept a Supreme Court Nomination. Here's His Response," *Daily Wire*, May 17, 2006; Michelle Malkin, "Hey, World Court: Bug Off!," www.unz.com, July 16, 2008.

Finally, Ted Cruz has written about the *Medellín* cases as well as his own history on many occasions. See Ted Cruz, "*Medellín v. Texas*: A Case of More Than Murder," *Houston Chronicle*, March 30, 2008; Ted Cruz, "The Supreme Court Can Use a Soap-Opera Case to Stop Federal Overreach," *Washington Post*, November 4, 2013; "About Senator Cruz," www.cruz.senate.gov.

Information on the internal deliberations in the White House and President Bush's decisions to issue his declaration as well as withdraw from the Optional Protocol concerning the Compulsory Settlement of Disputes comes from two sources. First, an interview with John Bellinger, legal adviser to the State Department, provided insight into the decision-making process. Additionally, records provided by the George W. Bush Presidential Library provided information about the views of the Bush administration.

Briefs by counsel and amici in *Medellín v. Texas* and *Medellín v. Dretke* are available from the US Supreme Court or one of its many depositories of briefs across the United States. The copies relied upon in writing this book were accessed at the library of the University of Washington School of Law. Decisions in *Medellín v. Dretke* and *Medellín v. Texas* are available in the U.S. Reports at 544 U.S. 660 (2005) and 552 U.S. 491 (2008). Transcripts of oral argument in both cases are available at the Supreme Court's website.

The decisions in *Ex parte Medellín* are reported in the Southwest Reporter and are available at 206 S.W.3d 584 (Ct. Crim. App. Tx. June 22, 2005), 223 S.W.3d 315 (Ct. Crim. App. Tx. Nov. 15, 2006), and 280 S.W.3d 854 (Ct. Crim. App. Tx. July 31, 2008). Medellín's request for a stay of execution and petition for certiorari can be found at the Supreme Court, Docket No. 08A98 and 08A99.

The Avena Case Implementation Act was introduced in the 110th Congress as H.R. 6481. The Consular Notification Compliance Act of 2011 was introduced in the 112th Congress as S. 1194. Both are available on Congress's website.

The Inter-American Court of Human Rights issued a decision finding that failing to provide Article 36 rights violated the due process protections in the International Covenant on Civil and Political Rights. See OC-16/99, October 1, 1999. The Inter-American Commission on Human Rights issued a decision finding that the United States violated the rights of José Ernesto Medellín and two other foreign nationals when it sentenced them to death without informing them of their rights under Article 36. See Report No. 90/09, Case 12.644, Admissibility and Merits, Medellín, Ramirez Cardenas and Leal Garcia, August 7, 2009.

INDEX

Valdez Maltos, Gerardo, 39–40

Vienna Convention on Consular Relations (VCCR), 8, 40, 46, 47, 53, 54, 59, 64, 69, 70, 71, 73, 74, 75, 77, 80, 88, 92, 95, 96, 100, 105, 107, 126, 136, 153, 159, 161; AEDPA and, 110; complying with, 27, 33, 56, 78, 97, 166, 174; consular notification and, 28, 38, 43; enforcement of, 128; history of, 6–7, 29–30, 82, 113; human rights and, 34, 71; ICJ and, 27, 33, 44, 45, 67–68, 90–91, 98, 129, 142, 145; individual rights and, 34, 117; interpretation of, 10, 60–61, 78–79, 132, 145; meaning of, 9–10; Medellín and, 44, 78, 89, 148, 152; negotiation of, 175; obligations under, 45, 58, 61, 176; Optional Protocol of, 30; procedural default rule and, 89, 125; protections under, 152; protocols for, 9; purpose of, 62; ratification of, 125; "review and reconsideration" and, 72; rights conferred by, 18, 34, 44, 84, 168; *Sanchez-Llamas* and, 139; self-execution and, 144; violation of, 31, 32, 35, 39, 44, 92, 98, 102, 113, 152, 163–164, 171, 175–176. *See also* Article 36

Villareal, Raul, 12–13, 16, 21, 23; trial of, 24, 26

Vinson, Mark, 25

Warren, Mark, 55, 172, 173

Washington Legal Foundation, 92, 96

Weigend, Thomas, 62

World Court, 45, 51, 88, 127, 134

writ of certiorari, 79, 81, 113, 115, 116, 124, 135, 177

Zoller, Elisabeth, 58–59, 63